No Small Hope

No Small Hope

Towards the Universal Provision of Basic Goods

KENNETH A. REINERT

OXFORD
UNIVERSITY PRESS

OXFORD

UNIVERSITY PRESS

Oxford University Press is a department of the University of Oxford. It furthers
the University's objective of excellence in research, scholarship, and education
by publishing worldwide. Oxford is a registered trade mark of Oxford University
Press in the UK and certain other countries.

Published in the United States of America by Oxford University Press
198 Madison Avenue, New York, NY 10016, United States of America.

© Oxford University Press 2018

Library of Congress Cataloging-in-Publication Data
Names: Reinert, Kenneth A., author.
Title: No small hope : towards the universal provision of basic goods /
Kenneth A. Reinert.
Description: New York, NY : Oxford University Press, [2018]
Identifiers: LCCN 2017053691 | ISBN 9780190499440 (hardcover : alk. paper) |
ISBN 9780190499464 (epub)
Subjects: LCSH: Basic needs. | Human security. | Economic development. |
Economic policy.
Classification: LCC HC79.B38 R45 2018 | DDC 361—dc23
LC record available at https://lccn.loc.gov/2017053691

1 3 5 7 9 8 6 4 2

Printed by Sheridan Books, Inc., United States of America

To Gelaye, Oda, and Ayantu who are truly basic goods

CONTENTS

PREFACE

This book is a call to the various policy communities and to world citizens to consider rethinking *what matters* most. Among some of these individuals, national security interests are considered to be paramount, but the world seems to become ever less secure. To others (my fellow economists), economic growth is the sine qua non, but absolute numbers of poor people remain stubbornly persistent, and there is increasing evidence that improvements in health and education are not always predicated on growth. However to others, technology is the key to unlock human potential, yet more than two billion individuals do not have access to 19th century technology in the form of sanitation. More recent, we also have the new perspective of human development and capabilities, but we remain unable to provide the necessary prerequisites at anywhere near universal levels.

In this book, I argue for an alternative approach, something less glorious and succinct, but still a useful focus for the 21st century, a century during which our planet is likely to play host to an additional four billion persons (equivalent to the entire world population in 1975). The suggested focus involves *the attempt to put a minimal set of basic goods and services into the hands of everyone*, in short the *universal provision of basic goods*. These basic goods and services are: nutritious food, clean water, sanitation, health services, education services, housing, electricity, and human security services. In the chapters that follow, I examine this focus from a number of different and complementary perspectives: economics, ethics and human rights, technology, and policy. I try to defend the universal provision of basic goods and services as an essential global policy focus for this century, understanding its difficulty, that it is *no small hope*.

Why basic goods and services provision? Because this focus is compelling from both ethical and practical perspectives. And because basic goods provision can mediate between one set of concerns with growth and another set of concerns with human development and capabilities. The *basic goods approach* also better informs us about and prepares us for current and future crises in the form of conflict, refugee flows, climate change, and pandemics. The approach pulls us away from simplistic prescriptions (an overemphasis on economic growth) and idealistic visions (it is all about human potential). Finally, basic goods provision may be something on which many different types of people locked in allegedly intractable cultural and religious conflicts could agree to value in the form of a minimalist system of ethics.

The book covers a lot of ground: economics, ethics, human rights, science, and technology to name a few. Although I can claim some amount of expertise in economics, I cannot do so in the other relevant fields. So apologies are due for where I have fallen short. Nevertheless, I think it is essential that basic goods provision be considered from these multiple perspectives in as integrated a manner possible, and I have tried to do so to the best of my ability.

This book draws on previously published work in the *Review of Social Economy* (69:1, 2011), the *Global Water Forum* (2014), and *World Medical and Health Policy* (7:3, 2015). I am indebted to these outlets for valuing my initial work, as well as to those who commented on it. I also am indebted to a number of anonymous referees who commented directly on drafts of this book and to Scott Parris and David Pervin at Oxford University Press for their support of my vision. I would also like to thank Gelaye Debebe, Mufeeza Iqbal, Christopher Jeffords, Elsa Khwaja, Chris Kuzdas, Lanse Minkler, J. P. Singh, Bonnie Stabile, Phil Thomas, and Paul Wyrwoll for helpful conversations.

I hope that the arguments presented here are at least somewhat persuasive. If not, I hope they provoke a discussion as to exactly *why* they fail to persuade and *which alternative approach* would better inform us as we travel through the 21st century and attempt to achieve the universal provision of basic goods. It is my hope that the book helps in this effort.

Kenneth A. Reinert
2018

ACRONYMS

AMR	anti-microbial resistance
APF	achievement possibility frontier (of SERF index)
ATT	arms trade treaty
BDGs	basic development goals
BoP	bottom/base of pyramid
CBO	community-based organization
CCSS	Caja Costarricense de Seguro Social (Costa Rica)
CCTs	conditional cash transfers
CEDAW	Convention on the Elimination of all Forms of Discrimination Against Women
CESCR	United Nations Committee on Economic, Social and Cultural Rights
CGIAR	Consultative Group for International Agricultural Research
CLTS	community-led total sanitation
COPD	chronic obstructive pulmonary disease
DDR	disarming, demobilizing, and reintegrating
DG	distributed generation (of electricity)
DHR	Declaration of Human Rights
D-Lab	Development Through Dialogue, Design, and Dissemination
DOTS	directly observed treatment short-course
FAO	Food and Agriculture Organization
FDI	foreign direct investment
GDP	gross domestic product
GW	gigawatt
HCFP	Health Care Fund for the Poor (Vietnam)
HDI	human development index
HGSF	home-grown school feeding
HMF	housing microfinance
ICESCR	International Covenant on Economic, Social, and Cultural Rights

IEA	International Energy Agency
IPCC	Intergovernmental Panel on Climate Change
MDGs	Millennium Development Goals
MSF	multistage flash (desalination)
MW	megawatt
NGO	nongovernmental organization
OECD	Organization for Economic Cooperation and Development
OSS	on-site sanitation systems
PAUL	portable aqua lifesaving unit
PHC	primary healthcare
PISA	Program for International Student Assessment
PoC	protection of civilians
PTA	Parent Teacher Association
RES-DES	renewable energy sources desalination
RO	reverse osmosis (desalination)
RORE	rate of return to education
R2P	Responsibility to Protect
SARS	severe acute respiratory syndrome
SBM	school-based management
SCI	system of crop intensification
SDGs	Sustainable Development Goals
SERF	Index of Social and Economic Rights
SELF	Solar Electric Light Fund
SHI	Social Health Insurance (Vietnam)
SRI	system of rice intensification
SSI	Sustainable Sugarcane Initiative
STI	system of teff intensification
SWI	system of wheat intensification
TB	tuberculosis
UDHR	Universal Declaration of Human Rights
UNDP	United Nations Development Program's
UNDPA	United Nations Department of Political Affairs
UNESCO	United Nations Education, Scientific and Cultural Organization
UNHCR	United Nations High Commissioner for Refugees
UNICEF	United Nations Children's Fund
VHI	Voluntary Health Insurance (Vietnam)
VIP	ventilated improved pit latrine
WASH	water, sanitation, and hygiene
WHO	World Health Organization
XDR	extremely drug resistant

No Small Hope

1

What Matters

Global policy formation is an unavoidably-normative enterprise. It requires a concept of *what matters*, and there are many competing alternatives: stopping the spread of weapons of mass destruction; supporting the free international movement of goods, services, foreign direct investment, and financial capital; promoting growth; advocating the expansion of human capabilities; combating global warming; supporting the spread of democracy and nation building; and promoting global health. The list is long, and who is to say which is best?

In this book, I argue for an alternative approach, namely a focus on *attempting to put a minimal set of basic goods and services into the hands of everyone*. In short, this is a call for the *universal provision of basic goods and services*. These basic goods and services are: nutritious food, clean water, sanitation, health services, education services, housing, electricity, and human security services. I argue that this focus is appropriate both for practical and for ethical reasons, but that success in this provision will not be easy and is therefore *no small hope*.

Within the narrow realm of economics, the conception of what matters has changed slowly but steadily over time. Employing a rather broad brush, we can trace a movement from mercantilism and its value placed on *precious metals* to Adam Smith[1] and his emphasis on the *consumption of goods and services*. In a later historical period, there was a second movement from Smith and consumption to an emphasis on *growth*. Recently, there has been a third movement from growth to *human capabilities* and *human development*. Thankfully, the emphasis on precious metals is all but gone. Currently, there is a creative and sometimes acrimonious tension between advocates of growth and advocates of human capabilities and human development. The basic goods approach developed in this book is meant to make this tension less acrimonious and more productive.

The basic goods approach developed in this book returns to Smith's focus on the consumption of goods and services. In a claim to what matters, however, it narrows Smith's focus from all goods and services to a *particular subset* of basic goods and services that meet central and objective human *needs*. In doing so, it tries to build a bridge between the growth view and the capabilities/human development view. It argues that what really matters about growth is the possibility that growth will lead to an increase in the broad-based provision of basic goods and services, an outcome that is not always guaranteed. It also argues that the hoped-for expansion of human capabilities and development is predicated on this expanded provision of basic goods. Without basic goods and services, the capabilities and human development paradigm remains merely aspirational. Basic goods and services are therefore a critical link between growth and human development.

The emphasis on basic goods and services provision does have some precedent in economic thinking. Although the book begins with Smith's emphasis on consumption, it also draws on an insight from Cambridge University economist Alfred Marshall. As part of his emphasis on the consumption of goods and services, Smith had a notion of "necessaries." But Marshall went a step further and made a distinction between "necessaries" or "things required to meet wants which must be satisfied" and "comforts or luxuries" or "things that meet wants of a less urgent character."[2] In this way, Marshall recognized a distinction between *needs* and *wants*, a distinction that the basic goods approach uses to emphasize particular types of goods and services as more important than others. Marshall's follower, Arthur Pigou, continued in this vein and identified a minimum standard of needs satisfaction that we draw on in this book.[3]

Basic goods consist of both goods and services that address *needs* rather than merely wants. Since Marshall, modern economics has evolved largely without the needs concept, replacing it with *preferences*.[4] Nevertheless, as discussed in the Appendix, basic needs have made reappearances here and there over the ensuing decades. In the late 1970s and early 1980s, development policy (if not economics itself) was briefly focused on the *basic needs approach*.[5] This approach emphasized six types of needs in the form of food and nutrition, basic educational services, basic health services, sanitation, water supply, and housing. The basic needs approach was not as well worked out as it could have been. It was sometimes stated as an expansive, subjective concept and sometimes as a relatively narrow objective concept; it was never closely related to the economics of consumer behavior. Nevertheless, the types of provision it emphasized have proven to be of continued importance, and along with Smith and Marshall, it is another touchstone of the basic goods approach.

If one looks closely, basic needs are explicitly recognized here and there in economics. In one source, for example, basic needs have been characterized in a number of useful ways.[6] Basic needs are *universal* in the sense that they are common to all consumers. They are *hierarchical* because they take precedence over nonbasic goods consumption. Even more important, they are *irreducible* in that there is a minimum threshold of basic goods consumption below which life becomes precarious. This irreducible quality is what makes basic needs an ethical issue. Basic needs are also *measurable*. In particular, basic needs consumption tends to be more *stable* than consumption of nonbasic goods. Basic needs consumption is also *satiable* as evidenced in the fact that, once they are satisfied, expenditures on them tend to approach a measurable maximum.

The basic goods approach recognizes that such economic properties set needs apart from wants as suggested by Marshall and allow us to identify basic goods among the much larger set of goods and services that make up household consumption. This is not to say that there is no cultural element to the way that needs are fulfilled, but simply that we can use evidence from household expenditure patterns to identify what groups of goods and services address basic needs. The cultural element suggests that we proceed with some humility in addressing basic goods provision but does not obviate the importance of the provision itself.

More generally, the fact that basic needs and basic goods are not theoretically necessary in modern economic theory does not imply that they are empirically and ethically unimportant. Indeed, they prove to be particularly important in development ethics and as a catalyst between growth and human development. They are an important part of what matters, and this book will explain why.

Growth

Beginning after the Second World War and with the birth of the World Bank and International Monetary Fund, economists and development policy analysts began to emphasize *growth* as the key to development. Indeed development was largely conceptualized *as growth itself*. The World Bank and International Monetary Fund developed just after the founding of modern macroeconomics and the identification and measurement of basic macroeconomic variables. Consequently, these institutions internalized the emerging macroeconomic concepts. Perhaps the most fundamental of all macroeconomic variables is gross domestic product (GDP), the value of domestic output. At the same time, theorizing about the growth of domestic output resulted in the Solow growth model, a central component of modern economics.[7] All of these factors pushed GDP and GDP per capita to the forefront of what matters.[8]

To put the growth emphasis in historical context, it is important to remember what came before it. To go back some centuries, a very influential claim was made by a body of thought and practice known as *mercantilism*. The central concern in mercantilism was the military strength of kingdoms. The power of the crown was to be supported by the accumulation of precious metals (gold and silver) in royal treasuries to pay armies. There were two means to gain access to these precious metals: mining and trade surpluses. Gold and silver could be taken directly out of the ground, such as by the Spanish empire in the 16th century in Latin America. They also could be accumulated by maintaining trade surpluses through which a net inflow of gold or silver would result. As a consequence of mercantilist thinking, there ensued centuries of exploitative extraction and trade in the name of various crowns and the consequent underdevelopment of their colonies.[9]

Notable for our purposes here is the fact that, under the mercantilist regime, consumption was completely subordinated to royal interests. As previously mentioned, mercantilist thought was overturned by Adam Smith who emphasized the role of consumption of goods and services *by all households*. This was a radical departure from the past that still (fortunately) affects us today.[10] Indeed, the shift from the precious-metals-in-support-of-war perspective to the broad-based-consumption perspective made possible an unprecedented focus on an early notion of human betterment.[11]

How does growth fit into this brief intellectual history? The fact that GDP per capita is what funds consumption is the link between modern notions of growth and the revolution in thought brought about by Adam Smith. For example, this link was emphasized by contemporary economist William Easterly, who commented that "We experts don't care about rising gross domestic product for its own sake. We care because it betters the lot of the poor and reduces the proportion of people who are poor. We care because richer people can eat more and buy more medicines for their babies."[12] This quote, however, reveals that it is not growth per se that matters in and of itself but rather *what can be done with it*, namely the increase in consumption of basic goods such as food and medicine. But growth can fund other things as well. Along with food and medicine, there are champagne and weaponry. What this book emphasizes is that the way that growth translates into different types of consumption (basic vs. nonbasic) is worth more attention than it normally receives.

Capabilities and Human Development

A challenge to the growth paradigm emerged in the form of what became known as the *capabilities approach* to development and its subsequent absorption into *the human development* paradigm. The origin of this new thinking was the work of Nobel Laureate Amartya Sen.[13] Sen noted that, in some cases, life expectancies can be quite unrelated to levels of GDP per capita and to growth itself. He emphasized that the growth paradigm views human beings as means to the growth ends, whereas they should be viewed as ends in and of themselves. His version of human beings as ends conceptualized well-being in terms of *capabilities* in the realm of "doings and beings" or, in somewhat awkward terminology, *functionings*.[14] In stark contrast to Smith, however, Sen conceptually distanced well-being from consumption of goods and services.

Sen's original thinking was further and somewhat differently developed by the political philosopher Martha Nussbaum.[15] It also was codified by Pakistani economist Mahbub ul Haq as part of the United Nations Development Program's (UNDP) Human Development Index (HDI). The relationship between growth and human development from the UNDP's perspective was captured in the 1995 *Human Development Report* that stated, "Economic growth is essential for human development. But to fully exploit the opportunities for improved well-being that growth offers, it must be properly managed, for there is no automatic link between economic growth and human progress."[16] This is the very link this book attempts to highlight.

The capabilities approach has done much to expand our conception of development beyond GDP per capita to include health, education, and certain aspects of empowerment.[17] In this, it has done a great service. However, the approach is quite adamant in its separation of well-being from Smith's emphasis on the consumption of goods and services. Indeed, Sen, Nussbaum, and others have repeatedly associated an emphasis on the consumption of goods and services with Karl Marx's notion of "commodity fetishism." Consequently, basic goods and services provision have been downplayed in the capabilities approach. Given that even fundamental human capabilities (e.g., to avoid premature mortality) are contingent on such basic goods, the reluctance to emphasize their provision is perplexing.

Basic Goods

As we have seen, Adam Smith drew attention away from the mercantilist obsession with precious metals to the consumption of actual goods and services, and Alfred Marshall allowed for the categorization of these goods and services as either basic (meeting needs) or nonbasic (addressing wants). The growth perspective reveals that growth can provide the resources with which to achieve basic and nonbasic consumption. The capabilities approach gives a sense of what we are ultimately trying to achieve when we consider humans as ends rather than means, but downplays the role of basic goods consumption in this process.

This book puts basic goods and services at the center of what matters and does so for a number of reasons. First, as previously stated, basic goods are a key link between growth and human capabilities and human development. What really matters about growth is the possibility that it will lead to an increase in the broad-based provision of basic goods and services, and any expansion of human capabilities and development is predicated on this provision. Second, basic goods and services are currently underprovided on vast scales. Consider the following examples:

- *Food*: Approximately 800 million people suffer from chronic hunger in the sense that they are not well-nourished enough for an active life.[18]

- *Water*: More than 700 million people do not have access to an improved drinking-water source.[19]
- *Sanitation*: Approximately 2.4 billion individuals do not have access to clean and safe toilets, and nearly one billion individuals practice open defecation.[20]
- *Health services*: Approximately six million infants and children die each year, largely due to preventable causes.[21]
- *Education services*: Approximately 250 million of the 650 primary school-age children (nearly 40 percent) have not mastered basic literacy and numeracy, and there are more than 750 million illiterate adults.[22]
- *Housing*: A much quoted but *unverifiable* statistic is that at least one billion people lack access to adequate housing, with approximately 100 million of these being homeless.[23]
- *Electricity*: Approximately 1.1 billion people live without access to electricity.[24]
- *Human security services*: Half a million people die each year as a result of armed violence.[25]

Third, a few interconnected trends will make basic goods provision more challenging than some optimists suggest. These include increased global population from the current seven billion to perhaps eleven billion over the century, climate change (global warming), increased conflict in certain parts of the world, and an increased number of refugees.[26] For these reasons, we need to be prepared for optimistic scenarios to prove to be overly optimistic. Finally, some basic goods and services are important for *growth itself*. Although early notions of growth emphasized only the accumulation of physical capital, more recent investigations have revealed the importance of human capital (the end result of basic goods provision). Thus, growth and basic goods provision are mutually reinforcing.

Ethics and Rights

The provision of basic goods can be usefully conceived to be part of evolving systems of *development ethics*. The field of development ethics attempts to provide appropriate structures for normative issues that arise in development studies and development policy.[27] Development ethics provide arguments in favor of a number of approaches to outcomes assessment, allowing analysts to determine whether a development situation has improved or worsened. Most of development ethics, however, is identified with the capabilities approach. As it has evolved, particularly in the extraordinary hands of Martha Nussbaum, the capabilities approach to development ethics has expanded into a generalized, normative theory of human (and even nonhuman) politics. Nussbaum and her followers call for the constitutional and judicial enshrinement of her version of the capabilities approach in all the countries of the world to ensure the protection of human (and animal) dignity and to pursue a conception of justice. This is an expansive and ambitious project and one that is largely rejected in this book.

The basic goods approach is an alternative conception of development ethics that is more narrowly defined. It falls within what can be called the "minimalist" approach to ethical issues.[28] It is an attempt to establish a *moral minimum* within the realm of the consumption of goods and services. As such, it is indeed an exercise in "commodity fetishism." Nevertheless, for a number of reasons, it is a useful focus. First, it draws attention to the necessary material preconditions for capabilities expansion and human development. To use the terminology of political philosopher Henry Shue, it focuses on foundations rather than spires.[29] Second, the basic goods approach focuses on determinants rather than outcomes. As has been emphasized in a number of contexts, policy deliberations need to connect directly to determinants rather than outcomes to be effective rather than simply aspirational.[30] Third, the approach provides a set of policy-actionable priorities, indeed imperatives, on which any more elaborate conception of human flourishing would depend.

With regard to rights, the basic goods approach is more closely aligned than the capabilities approach with how human rights have developed within the United Nations system. The United Nations Universal Declaration of Human Rights, the International Covenant on Economic, Social and Cultural Rights, the Alma-Ata Declaration on Primary Health Care, and United Nations General Assembly[31] resolutions have outlined basic human rights largely in terms of most of the basic goods and services considered in this book. Therefore, the approach proposed here is closely conformable with evolving notions of human rights even if there are some disagreements (e.g., the right to health services vs. the right to health itself). This conformity is an advantage of the basic goods approach.

Technology

To the extent that the universal provision of basic goods is a challenge, some analysts claim a powerful solution: technology. Some of these technology optimists suggest that the 21st century will actually be an era of plentitude rather than continued scarcity.[32] Although technology will be an important component of this book, the conclusions drawn will be much less optimistic. One reason for this lack of optimism is the observation that, for a variety of reasons, technologies do not always diffuse as fast as advertised. The book will view technology as a *potentially restricted flow* rather than as a *freely available stock*. The technology flow restriction, for example, helps to explain why 2.4 billion individuals do not have access to clean and safe toilets despite the fact that this technology originated in the late 18th century. Other reasons for the less optimistic approach include population growth, climate change, refugee flows, and conflict. Technology is critical for basic goods provision, but its potential contribution needs to be realistically assessed on a case-by-case basis.

No Small Hope

This book will address challenges to the provision of each of the basic goods and services identified. In each case, the challenges will be a mix of demand- and supply-side factors. As just noted, technology will be active on the supply side but will not be a panacea. In some cases, imperfect information will be a barrier on the demand side. Provision can take place through private means, in particular through "bottom of the pyramid" and "frugal innovation" activities. In many instances, though, government activities also will be important. In some notable cases (food and water), environmental conditions will be paramount. In other cases (human security services), conflict will be a key factor. In no case will a magic bullet appear. Rather, progress will be a long trudge from one "small win" to another.

The agenda of providing adequate nutrition, clean water, sanitation, health services, education services, housing, electricity, and security services to the large number of individuals who will otherwise be without them is both immensely important and daunting. It may not be the only thing that matters on the global policy agenda, but it matters greatly. It is the *no small hope* that this book tries to draw attention to. Attention itself is important given humankind's tendency to ignore real problems and focus instead on other temping issues (sports, celebrities, and socio-religious hatreds to name a few). Maintaining sustained attention is half the battle, and hopefully this book will help in this effort.

Notes

1. Smith (1937, originally 1776)
2. Marshall (1949).
3. Pigou (1932).
4. In a review of the subject, Georgescu-Roegen (1954) noted that "Preferences . . . are all we need for a rational theory of demand" (p. 509). See, however, Seeley (1992) for an example where needs have been explicitly recognized in a theory of consumer demand.
5. See International Labor Office (1976), Lisk (1977); Streeten (1979, 1984); and Streeten and Burki (1978).
6. Baxter and Moosa (1996). See also further consideration in the Appendix.
7. See Solow (1956).
8. On the evolution of the GDP concept, see Coyle (2014).

9. Spiegel (1983) depicted mercantilism as "economic warfare for national gain" (p. 93). On the role of trade in mercantilist thought, Mun (1924, orig. 1664) famously stated: "The ordinary means . . . to encrease our wealth and treasure is by Forraign Trade, wherein we must ever observe this rule; to sell more to strangers than we consume of theirs in value" (p. 171). David Hume (1752) also demonstrated in his famous price-specie flow mechanism that the increase in stocks of precious metals would contribute to an increase in the price level or a reduction in the export competitiveness of the country pursuing mercantilist policies.

10. It was Heilbroner (1953) who recognized this most directly. Heilbroner wrote, "He is concerned with promoting the wealth of the entire nation. And wealth, to Adam Smith, consists of the goods which *all* the people of society consume; note *all*—this is a democratic, and hence radical, philosophy of wealth. . . . We are in the modern world where the flow of goods and services consumed by everyone constitutes the ultimate aim and end of economic life" (p. 45).

11. There was also an additional shift of thought to be found in the *Wealth of Nations* (Smith, 1937, orig. 1776), subtle and incomplete but nevertheless important. Whereas mercantilist philosophy cast human being as mere *means to an end* (royal power), Smith's approach moved humans toward being *ends in themselves*. Smith's conception of human beings as ends in and of themselves, in addition to his democratic vision of consumption, made him a truly radical thinker.

12. Easterly (2001), p. 3. Likewise, Rodrik (2007) stated that "Economic growth is the most powerful instrument for reducing poverty. . . . (N)othing has worked better than economic growth in enabling societies to improve the life chances of their members, including those at the very bottom" (p. 2).

13. See in particular Sen (1987, 1989).

14. Capabilities are seen as an *outer envelope* of achievable outcomes available to an individual. Functionings are the *actual outcomes* chosen by the individual within or on this outer envelope. For example, I may have a capability to achieve a certain level of health but chose not to be so healthy for various psychological reasons. Or I may have the capability to produce a certain creative work but chose not do so because my creative interests incline elsewhere. Strictly speaking, capabilities are not observable. Only functionings are observable.

15. See Nussbaum (2000, 2011).

16. UNDP (1995), pp. 122–123.

17. See Goldin and Reinert (2010).

18. Food and Agriculture Organization ([FAO] 2014).

19. World Health Organization (WHO) and UNICEF (2014).

20. WHO and UNICEF (2014, 2015).

21. United Nations Inter-Agency Groups for Child Mortality Estimation (2013, 2015).

22. United Nations Education, Scientific and Cultural Organization (2014) and World Bank, World Development Indicators.

23. This is the least defined of the statistics reported here. It comes from a 2005 estimate of the United Nations Special Rapporteur on Adequate Housing. Given population growth since 2005, and a record number of sixty-six million refugees in 2016 (United Nations High Commissioner for Refugees [UNHCR] 2014, 2015, 2016, 2017), these figures seem to be minimums.

24. UNDP (2009) and Sustainable Energy for All (2015).

25. Geneva Declaration on Armed Violence and Development (2011, 2015).

26. On the last of these trends, the number of refugees in the world reached fifty million in 2013, the highest figure since World War II and then increased to sixty-six million in 2016. See UNHCR (2014, 2015, 2016, 2017). This increase reflects persistent conflict and, in some cases, climate change.

27. See, for example, Crocker (2008).

28. Works that can be considered to be part of the minimalist approach to ethics include Bok (2002); Cohen (2004); Ignatieff (2001); Shue (1996); and Walzer (1994). The most relevant of these is Shue (1996) who emphasized basic security rights and basic subsistence rights and their correlative duties.

29. Shue (1996).
30. This point is made repeatedly in World Bank (2011a), for example.
31. See United Nations General Assembly (1948, 1966b, 2010); World Health Organization (1978).
32. See, for example, Diamandis and Kotler (2012) and Ridley (2010).

PART I

PERSPECTIVES

2

Growth and Capabilities

In Chapter 1, I mentioned the creative and occasionally acrimonious tension between the growth perspective and the capabilities/human development approach as alternative answers to *what matters* in global policy. The purpose of this chapter is to set out these two points of view to evaluate them and search for some common ground in the realm of basic goods provision. The chapter argues three things. First, what really matters about growth is the possibility that it will lead to a sustained increase in the broad-based provision of basic goods and services. In other words, Adam Smith's insight about democratic consumption mentioned in Chapter 1 is still important, and particularly so where it addresses basic needs. Second, because capabilities have important material preconditions, the expansion of human capabilities and the promotion of human development are predicated on the broad-based provision of basic goods and services. Without basic goods provision, the capabilities approach remains only a collection of aspirations. Third, the broad-based provision of basic goods and services can potentially contribute to hoped-for growth processes, making possible a virtuous circle among growth, basic goods provision, and human development. These virtuous circles are essential features of successful development trajectories.

Growth

Since the end of World War II, GDP per capita has been the most fundamental and widespread conception of development. For example, as early as 1950, a noted international economics textbook stated that "the problem of economic development is that of raising the level of national income through increased per capita output so that each individual will be able to consume more."[1] Despite this long-held, central position in development thinking, the way we conceive of growth taking place has changed in important ways over time. The growth process now appears to be somewhat more complicated and less predictable than previously thought. What also has changed is the *degree* to which growth is considered to be necessary for certain desirable outcomes in the realm of human development. Although growth is still important, some real human progress can be made even where growth is relatively modest.

Suppose for the moment, however, that growth in GDP per capita really is *what matters*. If this is the case, then we want to know as much as we can about what causes growth. In the economics profession, a veritable factory of researchers has dedicated itself to this task. At first, it was all about what economists call *capital deepening* or increasing the amounts of physical capital per worker. Noted political scientist Frances Fukuyama summed up this period of thought very well: "Under the influence of . . . growth models, it was common to think about less-developed countries as if they were simply developed countries minus the resources and could be set on a path to self-sustaining growth through the infusion of sufficient investment capital."[2] The goal of development policy became to increase the amount of physical capital in areas such as infrastructure and manufacturing, and the World Bank was there to help in this process.

Empirical evidence suggests that capital deepening is indeed important to growth processes, but that the link between capital deepening and growth is not uniform across countries or time periods. Some countries are able to make better use of increasing amounts of physical capital per worker either because their institutional environment is better or because the investments themselves are more appropriate to that environment. Institutional environments determine the extent to which individuals and firms can make the most of increases in physical capital. And there is a difference between white-elephant investments to assuage the vanity of authoritarian leaders and productive investments that reflect the entrepreneurial interests of firms and the resources and skills of citizens. So the extent to which capital deepening matters is less than uniform.

Along with physical capital, there is also *human capital*, the education, knowledge, skills, and creativity of workers. Growth theory and growth studies began to recognize the importance of this factor as well. However, the empirical relevance of human capital proved to be a bit contentious for a while. For example, in his widely read book *The Elusive Quest for Growth*, economist William Easterly stated that, due to a lack of empirical evidence on the contribution of education to growth, "education is worth little more than hula-hoops to a society."[3] More recent empirical work, however, has suggested that education is indeed worth more than hula-hoops (is statistically significant) provided that it is measured correctly.[4] So if we do think that GDP per capita is what matters, we still need to be concerned with the provision of educational services, as well as with the *quality* of these services. Further, although it is not often emphasized in growth studies, *health* also enters into the picture as part of human capital, and therefore quality health services matter as well.[5]

The next shift in thinking about growth was an emphasis on *openness*. By this, economists mean openness to international trade (particularly exports) and to foreign direct investment (particularly inflows of foreign direct investment;

FDI). The idea was that exports and FDI would contribute to the technological advancement of the exporting country and therefore to growth. This view was pushed enthusiastically by the World Bank in the 1980s and 1990s based on the experience of East Asia. It proved to be very controversial in part because it was an incomplete interpretation of the East Asian development experience.[6] Recent evidence has suggested that openness is important, but not as much as initially alleged.[7] As in the case of capital deepening, the relationship between openness and growth can vary greatly between one country and another.

Then economists turned to *institutions* or, more precisely, *good institutions* as an explanation of growth. Focus shifted to the rule of law, property rights, contract enforcement, regulatory systems, and social insurance systems as potential contributors to growth, with many empirical studies conducted within this perspective.[8] In many ways, this was a process of modern economists reacquainting themselves with Adam Smith's observations on the subject.[9] As it turned out, institutions do matter for growth, and they seem to matter more than openness.[10] It is unfortunate that we do not really know how to *build* institutions. Despite a good deal of talk about improving governance and institutional performance, as well as conditioning foreign aid to such improvements, it is not clear that it has always helped. One problem is that institutions do not transfer well from one place to another.[11] Therefore, we inevitably need to confront the issue of how to develop them *in place*, and it is unlikely that there is a single, relevant approach to this. Local experimentation appears to be necessary.

Capital deepening, human capital, openness, and institutions all matter for growth. However, there is no simple explanatory factor for growth processes.[12] One thing that is known, however, is that the amount of growth can vary significantly from one country to another. To take just one example, Figure 2.1

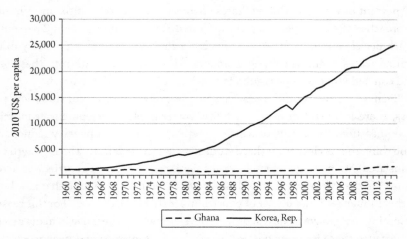

Figure 2.1 Gross domestic product per capita in Ghana and South Korea, 1960 to 2015 (2010 US$). Source: World Bank, World Development Indicators.

plots inflation-adjusted GDP per capita for Ghana and South Korea from 1960 to 2015. Although a great deal of growth has taken place in South Korea, relatively little growth has occurred in Ghana. From the growth perspective, making Ghana more like South Korea is what matters. How exactly to do this, however, remains somewhat a mystery. Indeed, it is clear that what works for growth can differ significantly from one country to another.[13]

The Role of Growth

To what extent and how does growth matter? There is some disagreement on these questions. One reason for the disagreement is that it appears to be possible to make sustained progress in some desired outcomes, particularly in health outcomes, at lower levels of GDP per capita than previously thought. For example, Charles Kenny of the Center for Global Development concluded that "even without *any* increase at all in GDP per capita, significant improvements in quality of life can be—and frequently have been—accomplished."[14] This is mostly due to improvements in health systems that deliver basic health technologies through basic health services. On the other hand, it is also possible for countries to grow with little progress in desired development outcomes.[15]

To see this at work, consider the United States, Costa Rica, and Vietnam. The 2015 life expectancy for the United States was 78.7 years. In Costa Rica it was 79.6, higher than that of the United States, and in Vietnam it was 75.8, not too far below that of the United States. More important, these positive health outcomes were achieved with only 20 percent of the U.S. GDP per capita in Costa Rica and 4 percent of the U.S. GDP per capita in Vietnam (both adjusted for cost of living). But there is more. Costa Rica achieved its higher life expectancy spending 10 percent of what the United States spends per capita on health, and Vietnam approached the life expectancy of the United States spending about 2 percent as much per capita. Further, there is evidence that gains in life expectancy in the United States might be coming to an end.[16] It is difficult to confront these facts and conclude that GDP per capita is as crucial as sometimes claimed.

Even when we confine ourselves to the growth-income-consumption process, there is a great deal of variability. For example, development economists have measured the extent to which growth translates into poverty reduction.[17] One thing that is clear from these studies is that the extent to which growth gets translated into poverty reduction varies significantly among countries and across time.[18] So the link between growth and poverty reduction is not mechanistic but is rather influenced by a number of policies and institutional factors. For this reason, assuming that *growth alone* will provide development can be naïve in many cases.[19]

Because these issues generate a great deal of controversy, I need to be clear about what is being said here. I am not saying that growth is irrelevant or unimportant. Growth *is* relevant and *can be* important. Growth can generate additional incomes for the poor, and it can support consumption of basic goods, including in health.[20] Growth does thereby have a positive impact on life expectancy.[21] But basic goods and services provision in nearly all forms, in addition to addressing needs, can also support growth processes. A poorly educated and sick workforce is not good for growth. The trick is to make these two processes mutually reinforcing.

Capabilities and Human Development

Beginning in the late 1980s a challenge to the growth perspective was introduced by economist, philosopher, and Nobel Laureate Amartya Sen. He was soon joined by leading political philosopher Martha Nussbaum. Together, these individuals pioneered what became known and the capabilities approach to development and the associated idea of *human development*. These efforts helped to spawn the new field of development ethics, led to a new development index (the Human Development Index) as part of the United Nations Development Program's annual *Human Development Report*, and coalesced around a new professional organization (the Human Development and Capability Association). In the process, the capabilities/human development approach questioned the accepted relationship between growth and development.

Amartya Sen emphasized that humans are not just *means* in growth processes but also *ends* in and of themselves.[22] He pointed out that, in some countries at least, the relationship between growth and valued human outcomes such as life expectancy are less than direct. This is the same observation we made in the example of the United States, Costa Rica, and Vietnam. He placed emphasis on the twin human capabilities "to be" and "to do," both in multiple forms and at basic and advanced levels. For example, the ability to escape premature death is a basic capability, and the ability to run for political office is an advanced capability. According to the capabilities approach, what matters in development processes is the expansion of such human capabilities. As Sen stated, "to broaden the limited lives into which the majority of human beings are willy-nilly imprisoned by force of circumstances is the major challenge of human development in the contemporary world."[23]

Although Amartya Sen was notably reluctant to specify a full list of central capabilities, Martha Nussbaum did just that. She put forward a list of ten central capabilities that form the heart of her version of the capabilities project. It is worth reproducing these in full to give a clear sense of the spirit of her approach:[24]

1. *Life*. Being able to live to the end of a human life of normal length; not dying prematurely, or before one's life is so reduced as to be not worth living.

2. *Bodily health*. Being able to have good health, including reproductive health; to be adequately nourished; to have adequate shelter.

3. *Bodily integrity*. Being able to move freely from place to place; to be secure against violent assault, including sexual assault and domestic violence; having opportunities for sexual satisfaction and for choice in matters of reproduction.

4. *Senses, imagination, and thought*. Being able to use the senses, to imagine, think, and reason—and to do these things in a "truly human" way, a way informed and cultivated by an adequate education, including, but by no means limited to, literacy and basic mathematical and scientific training. Being able to use imagination and thought in connection with experiencing and producing works and events of one's own choice, religious, literary, musical, and so forth. Being able to use one's mind in ways protected by guarantees of freedom of expression with respect to both political and artistic speech, and freedom of religious exercise. Being able to have pleasurable experiences and to avoid non-beneficial pain.

5. *Emotions*. Being able to have attachments to things and people outside of ourselves; to love those who love and care for us, to grieve at their absence; in general, to love, to grieve, to experience longing, gratitude, and justified anger. Not having one's emotional development blighted by fear and anxiety.

6. *Practical reason*. Being able to form a conception of the good and to engage in critical reflection about the planning of one's life.

7. *Affiliation*. (A) Being able to live with and toward others, to recognize and show concern for other human beings, to engage in various forms of social interaction; to be able to imagine the situation of another. (B) Having the social bases of self-respect and non-humiliation; being able to be treated as a dignified human being whose worth is equal to that of others. This entails nondiscrimination on the basis of race, sex, sexual orientation, ethnicity, caste, religion, national origin.

8. *Other species*. Being able to live with concern for and in relation to animals, plants, and the world of nature.

9. *Play*. Being able to laugh, to play, to enjoy recreational activities.

10. *Control over one's environment*. (A) *Political*. Being able to participate effectively in political choices that govern one's life; having the right of political participation, protections of free speech and association. (B) *Material*. Being able to hold property (both land and movable goods), and having property rights on an equal basis with others; having the freedom from unwarranted search and seizure. In work, being able to work as a human being, exercising practical reason and entering into meaningful relationships of mutual recognition with other workers.

Nussbaum's stated intention is for her list to be incorporated into the *constitutional institutions* of all the countries of the world, albeit through persuasion rather than imposition.[25] The framework is also to be extended to animals.[26] In her view, human dignity and social justice requires that all persons be above a threshold for *each* of the ten capabilities. If a threshold is not met in *any* of the ten capabilities, an injustice has been committed and redress is in order. And trade-offs among the ten capabilities (what Nussbaum calls "tragic choice") are to be avoided.

The Human Development Index

Sen began to work with the late Pakistani economist Mahbub ul Haq who had taken over as head of the United Nations Development Program (UNDP) in the late 1980s. Together, they devised an index that would address some of Sen's concerns with GDP per capita, and this resulted in the UNDP's HDI. This index became part of the UNDP's annual *Human Development Report*, and together they were responsible for a thematic shift in development discussions in which the most important component of development processes became people themselves. As the first *Human Development Report* stated, "People are the real wealth of a nation. The basic objective of development is to create an enabling environment for people to enjoy long, healthy and creative lives."[27]

The HDI ranges from zero to one and measures development as reflecting three components: per capita income, health, and education. More specifically, the HDI consists of equal, one-third components of per capita income, life expectancy, and education. The per capita income component is adjusted across countries to account for differences in the cost of living. Life expectancy is taken as an overall measure of health. Education is measured with one-half weights given to mean years of schooling and expected years of schooling. Based on these measures, HDI rankings have become a focal point for development progress around the world.[28]

The HDI has done a great service in expanding our gaze beyond GDP per capita to health and education outcomes. However, there is a significant inconsistency inherent in the HDI. In theory, it is an implementation of the capabilities approach. But it actually mixes together two very different approaches. Income per capita is a growth concept and is emphatically *not a capability*. Indeed, it is exactly what the capability approach says does *not* matter in and of itself. It only matters instrumentally to the extent that it supports capability development. So what does *not* matter in and of itself is weighted together with what *does* matter in and of itself (according to the capabilities approach), resulting in a bit of a muddle.

There is a second inconsistency with the HDI as well. A basic component of the capabilities approach is *methodological individualism*.[29] This is the practice of treating each and every person as an end rather than as just a means. In the famous words of Dr. Seuss's Horton the Elephant, "a person is a person no matter how small." One implication of methodological individualism is to make sure not to hide individuals within averages and percentages because each individual counts. Instead, the focus is on absolute numbers of individuals, a practice this book embraces wholeheartedly. But the HDI rejects this practice, eschewing absolute numbers of people in favor of an average of averages. It is therefore a violation of methodological individualism.

So although the HDI has gained a great deal of attention in the development policy community and has helpfully expanded our view beyond GDP or income per capita, it is an inconsistent measure, particularly from the point of view of the capabilities approach itself.

The Rejection of Goods and Services

It is difficult to argue that people are not the real ends in development processes, even if they are also means. It is also difficult not to argue that at least some set of human capabilities need to be at the center of development thinking and development policy. For example, if development processes do not support the expansion of capabilities to avoid premature mortality, to be literate, and to be numerate, how can these processes be considered successful? But the capabilities approach has also rather ardently rejected Adam Smith's emphasis on the democratic consumption of goods and services, including basic goods and services. This poses a problem because these basic goods and services are an important part of what makes capabilities expansion possible. The objections to the provision of basic goods and services as critically important can be categorized into the *opulence* argument, the *commodity fetishism* argument, and the *individuation* argument, and we need to consider each in turn.

An initial example of the opulence argument can be found in Amartya Sen's book *The Standard of Living*. Here, Sen briefly considered what he called "vitally important commodities." He stated that "As a direction to go, concentration on the possession of vital commodities seems fair enough."[30] But then he went on to say, "Opulence in the form of commodity possession is undoubtedly important in enhancing the standard of living, but is the standard of living best seen as opulence *itself*? . . . (I)t is reasonable to argue that while well-being is related to being well off, they are not the same and may possibly diverge a good deal." The problem here is that "commodity possession" and well-being can only diverge so far because, without "vitally important commodities," capability expansion is impossible.

Sen did say that "When discussing socially widespread deprivation (e.g.. famines), focusing on entitlement failures . . . may provide an adequate starting point of analysis." And indeed Sen did just that. In his own well-known work on famines, he emphasized the role of "entitlements" to the basic good food.[31] The question is why we would only take this approach in the case of food. As I have shown, widespread deprivations exist across the *full set* of basic goods and services. What Sen termed "the possession of vital commodities" is not just a place to start, but a place to linger as long as those deprivations persist.

Next consider the commodity fetishism argument, which is rather widespread in the capabilities approach. In an early contribution to the approach, Sen described the basic goods approach as "imprisoned in the mould of commodity-centered evaluation" and as an approach that can be "accused of adopting a form of 'commodity fetishism.'"[32] Martha Nussbaum took a similar approach. Even while allowing for the undisputable fact that promoting capabilities requires "material preconditions," Nussbaum cautioned against "fetishizing possessions."[33] Other researchers in the capabilities approach also have used the commodity fetish argument.[34]

It is strange that a concern with providing clean water, sanitation, basic health services, basic education services, and other necessities of life should be dismissed as a "fetish." Note also that invoking both "opulence" and "commodity fetishism" is largely a rhetorical device. The term *opulence* refers to a significant amount of wealth and consequently does not apply to subsistence levels of provision. The term *fetishism* implies belief in magical powers and is therefore completely off the mark. Being largely rhetorical, both the opulence and commodity fetishism arguments fall short. Capabilities expansion is predicated on basic goods provision.

Finally, consider the individuation argument. This is set out by both Sen and Nussbaum in terms of important individual differences in needs. They both do this in terms of individuals "A" and "B." Sen argued,[35]

> Consider two persons A and B. Both are quite poor, but B is poorer. A has a higher income and succeeds in particular in buying more food and consuming more of it. But A also has a higher metabolic rate and some parasitic disease, so that despite his higher food consumption, he is in fact more undernourished and debilitated than B is.

Nussbaum (2000) made a more general argument:[36]

> To treat A and B as equally well-off because they command the same amount of resources is . . . to neglect A's separate and distinct life, to pretend that A's circumstances are interchangeable with B's, which may not be the case.

This individuation argument has some validity. Needs differ among individuals in important ways. However, the relevant policies are generally not made at the individual level. There are necessary limits to accounting for individual metabolic rates in policy development formation, and the case of parasitic disease needs to be addressed through the provision of basic health services. We are dealing here with public policy and not physician–patient relationships. For this reason, it is not clear that, in practice, the individuation argument is valid.

Try as it may not to do so, in the end, the capabilities approach cannot avoid basic goods and services. By necessity, it is present in the work of capability researchers on hunger and famine. But if one reads the capabilities literature carefully, the importance of housing, healthcare, sanitation, education, credit, and clean water are all referred to in the context of capabilities, usually in the form of the "material preconditions" for capability achievement but even occasionally (and incorrectly) *as capabilities themselves*.[37] One can also find multiple references to minimal thresholds of basic goods and services provision. This simply reflects the fact that we inevitably return to the universal provision of the basic goods and services that make human flourishing (conceived of in terms of capabilities or otherwise) possible.[38]

Let us take just one example of this inevitable role of basic goods and services in human development. Consider the World Bank's 2012 *World Development Report* on the important subject of gender equality and development.[39] At the final chapter of this report and the final set of policy recommendations, many of the recommendations are in terms of basic goods and services provision, namely the following:

- Increasing access to education among severely disadvantaged populations.
- Improving public health: clean water, sanitation, waste removal, and disease vector control.
- Increasing access to specialized maternal services.
- Strengthening support for the prevention and treatment of HIV/AIDS.
- Increased access to child care and early childhood development programs.

This is not accidental. It is indeed difficult to think about improving gender outcomes in development without returning to basic needs and basic goods. And this is a *more effective approach*. As this same *World Development Report* emphasized, it is more effective to target *determinants* rather than *outcomes*.[40] Why? Because there is no other way of effecting outcomes other than through their determinants.

A practical example of the outcomes versus determinants issue is encountered in the form of the United Nations' Sustainable Development Goals (SDGs). The SGDs had been preceded by the Millennium Development Goals (MGDs) that were in effect from 2000 to 2015 and consisted of sixty targeted indicators. Under the SDGs, the number of targeted indicators was expanded to an astonishing 169, a hodgepodge of measures based on income, capabilities achievement (functionings), basic goods provision, specific policies, expenditures, and physical outcomes (e.g., emissions). Both the MDGs and the SDGS have been plagued by trying to legislate and enforce too many outcomes too far removed from the relevant and actual policies (the determinants). A simpler, alternative approach is available that focuses exclusively on determinants. Chapter 12 presents a set of ten basic development goals (BDGs) as an alternative to the SGDs.

Other Issues with the Capabilities Approach

As previously mentioned, the capabilities approach is resistant to allowing for tradeoffs among valued human development outcomes, what it calls "tragic choice." A counterargument is that tradeoffs should be embraced as a means of addressing the most pressing needs first. Can a person achieve the capability to play when engulfed in a malarial fever? Can a person achieve dignity in affiliation without safe access to a latrine? Can a person exercise practical reason without clean water to avoid diarrheal infection? Can a person produce literary works if there are no trained teachers in the classrooms? And the most tragic choices actually occur when a person is forced to choose among the most basic of goods and services due to lack of access. Do they take their child to a doctor or pay the rent? Do they buy their child a required school uniform or buy food? These are the real tragic choices that hundreds of millions of people face on a day-to-day basis.[41]

If we are really so concerned about human flourishing, why not commit to the universal provision of the most basic goods and services to allow individuals to actually flourish. Why quibble over constitutional guarantees of the capability to "use the senses in a truly human way" (whatever that might mean)? If we are really so concerned about dignity, why not ensure universal access to safe latrines (or better forms of sanitation services) and put aside for the moment capabilities of "being able to experience longing and gratitude." No doubt the more than 2.4 billion individuals who do not have access to clean and safe toilets (including the one billion individuals condemned to defecate in the open) would be very grateful for improved sanitation services.[42]

By overemphasizing ultimate outcomes and underemphasizing determinants, the capability approach has been less than helpful.[43] Despite being described as "thin," the capabilities approach has morphed into a rather maximalist agenda in which the capacity to play and relate to animals has been put on the same level as importance as actually staying alive, with potential tradeoffs being rejected. The goal of enshrining this maximalist agenda in national constitutional law around the world seems a bridge too far. Better to first focus on a more minimalist agenda of meeting existing, subsistence-rights-based commitments to the universal provision of essential basic goods and services.[44]

Ongoing Debates

In 2011, the tension between the growth perspective and the capabilities/ human development approach came to a head in the basic-goods-deprived context of India. This was in the form of what became known as the Bhagwati–Sen debate. Economist Jagdish Bhagwati advocated a greater emphasis on growth to help India's poor in the form of what sometimes is called the Gujarat model after the Indian state where this approach had been pursued. Amartya Sen advocated a greater emphasis on capabilities (health and education achievements) in the form of what is sometimes called the Kerala model after another Indian state known for positive human development outcomes. The debate resurfaced in 2013 when the participants wrote competing books on the subject.[45] It is unfortunate that the tone of the debate quickly became personal and bitter.[46] Matters that one would hope would be settled among some of the world's most prominent economists appeared to be anything but.

It would not be productive to review this entire debate here, but it is instructive to touch on some specific aspects of it. In response to Bhagwati's claim that Sen had downplayed the importance of growth, Sen responded as follows: "Economic growth is very important as a means for bettering people's lives, but . . . it has to be combined with devoting resources to remove illiteracy, ill health, undernutrition and other deprivations."[47] In other words, the provision of basic goods and services (commodity fetishism) is actually important in Sen's view, and not just in the case of food and famines. If this is the case, why has the capabilities/ human development approach (and Sen himself) been so reticent to say so?

Similar reticence is also present on the growth side of the debate. Although Bhagwati spent a lot of time talking about the correct role of redistribution in growth processes (he favors cash transfers), he gave much less attention to some important types of basic goods deprivation. Nearly 500 million Indian citizens practice open defecation with all manner of negative health effects, and approximately 260 million of India's adults are illiterate. It is difficult to imagine that these characteristics of the Indian economy do not hold back its growth prospects.[48] The aim of this book is to try to find a way to overcome these lapses and to find a productive middle ground between these opposing views of these two prominent economists.

Summary

How do basic goods fit into the competing ideas of the growth paradigm and the capabilities/human development approach? To get a sense of this, it is instructive to visit the final chapter of MIT economists Abhijit Banerjee and Esther Duflo's well-received book *Poor Economics*. This chapter has the delightful title of "In Place of a Sweeping Conclusion," and it stated the following:[49]

Economists (and other experts) seem to have very little useful to say about why some countries grow and others do not. Basket cases, such as Bangladesh or Cambodia, turn into small miracles. Poster children, such as Côte d'Ivoire, fall into the "bottom billion." In retrospect, it is always possible to construct a rationale for what happened in each place. But the truth is, we are largely incapable of predicting where growth will happen, and we don't understand very well why things suddenly fire up.

Given that economic growth requires manpower and brainpower, it seem plausible, however, that whenever that spark occurs, it is more likely to catch fire if women and men are properly educated, well fed, and healthy, and if citizens feel secure and confident enough to invest in their children, and to let them leave home to get the new jobs in the city.

It is also probably true that until that happens, something needs to be done to make that wait for the spark more bearable. If misery and frustration are allowed to have their way, and anger and violence take over, it is not clear that the spark will ever arrive.

These few short paragraphs nicely sum up the doubt that exists among some prominent development economists with regard to our ability to turn on growth as a matter of policy, and the potential role of basic goods in both directly addressing misery and making growth more likely. Whether from the point of view of growth or capabilities, the minimalist agenda of basic goods provision plays an important supporting role. To be more specific, what really matters about growth is the possibility that it will lead to a sustained increase in the broad-based provision of basic goods and services. And the expansion of human capabilities and development is actually predicated on the broad-based provision of basic goods and services. Without basic goods provision, the capabilities approach remains only a collection of aspirations. Finally, the broad-based provision of basic goods and services can potentially contribute to hoped-for growth processes, making possible a virtuous circle among growth, basic goods provision and capabilities.[50]

Notes

1. Ellsworth (1950), p. 796.
2. Fukuyama (2005), p. 6.
3. Easterly (2001), p. 82.
4. See Cohen and Soto (2007), for example. For the specific case of Latin America, see Hanuschek and Woessmann (2012).
5. See Pio (1994). For empirical evidence on the contribution of health to growth, see Weil (2007) and Barro (2013).
6. For a fuller account, see Stiglitz (1996) and Davis (2004).

7. The World Bank's enthusiasm for openness began in the East Asian context with World Bank (1993). For some recent evidence, see Rodrik, Subramanian, and Trebbi (2004) and Wacziarg and Welch (2008). For a comprehensive look at openness and development, see Goldin and Reinert (2012).

8. For an excellent summary, see Rodrik (2007).

9. Smith (1937, orig. 1776) famously stated, "Commerce and manufactures can eldom flourish long in any state which does not enjoy a regular administration of justice, in which the people do ot feel themselves secure in the possession of their property, (and) in which the faith of contracts is not supported by law. . . . Commerce and manufactures, in short, can seldom flourish in any state in which there is not a certain degree of confidence in the justice of government" (Book V, Chapter 3, p. 862).

10. For one well-known study, see Rodrik, Subramanian, and Trebbi 2004).

11. See Fukuyama (2009).

12. This point was forcibly made by Adelman (2001). North, Wallis, and Weingast (2009) also stated, "The persistent patterns across societies suggest that modern social development involves simultaneous improvement in human capital, physical capital, technology, and institutions. Because changes in these elements happen roughly at the same time, quantitative social scientist have been persistently frustrated in their attempts to identify causal forces at work in the midst of a sea of contemporaneous correlation" (p. 12).

13. This is the point forcibly made by Rodrik (2007), among others.

14. Kenny (2011), p. 109. This point was made in more general terms a long time ago by Preston (1975).

15. See Easterly (2003) for the case of Pakistan and the phenomenon of "growth without development." In the arena of health, see the Ghanaian case in Frimpong, Okoye, and Pongou (2016) who concluded that "appropriate polices are needed to ensure that economic growth leads to an improvement in child well-being" (p. 41).

16. See Olshansky et al. (2014).

17. This is measured in terms of what is known as the "growth elasticity of poverty reduction."

18. For evidence of this, see Bourguignon (2003) and Ram (2013).

19. See Cord (2007). She stated, "Because poverty reduction's sensitivity to growth can vary significantly across countries and growth spells, more favorable outcomes are observed where policies have been implemented to enhance the capacity of poor people to participate in and contribute to growth" (p. 19).

20. For the case of Vietnam where growth has supported an increase in demand for health services, see Ekman et al. (2008).

21. In simple regression models of low- and middle-income countries (those of greatest concern in this book), GDP per capita (or log of GDP per capita) explains less than half the variance in life expectancy. Again, I am not arguing that GDP per capita does not contribute positively to life expectancy, just that there is a significant role for policy, including basic goods provision. This is the same point that was made decades ago by Preston (1975).

22. For this and other of Sen's early ideas mentioned here, see Sen (1987, 1989). This point of view was also present in the work of the philosopher Immanual Kant who famously stated, "Act so that in your own person as well as in the person of every other you are treating mankind also as an end, never merely as a means" (Kant, 1938, orig. 1865, p. 47).

23. Sen (1989), p. 55.

24. These are taken *word-for-word* from Nussbaum (2011), but see also Nussbaum (2000).

25. Nussbaum (2011) stated: "I envisage the account of Central Capabilities and of the threshold as a source of political principles that can be translated into a set of (minimally) just political institutions. I have particularly connected the capabilities list to the part of a nation's written constitution (or of its unwritten constitutional principles, if it has no written constitution) that elaborates citizens' fundamental entitlements" (p. 166).

26. See Nussbaum (2011).

27. UNDP (1990), p. 9.

28. One important characteristic of the HDI is that it is a *relative measure* in that all scores are measured in relation to the best-scoring country. As a consequence, decreases in the HDI

can reflect the improvement of other countries in the included indicators rather than worse indicators in the country in question. This is not in the spirit of moral minimalism.

29. In an early work on the capabilities approach, Sen (1989) stated, "Given clarity regarding the ends (avoiding, in particular, the pitfall of treating human beings as means), the social and economic instrumentalities involved in the ends-means relations can be extensively explored" (p. 55). Likewise, Nussbaum (2000) wrote that "we should not look just to the total or the average, but to . . . each and every person" (p. 56).

30. This and subsequent quotes from Sen (1987), p. 15.

31. See, for example, Sen (1981).

32. Sen (1989), p. 47.

33. Nussbaum (2011).

34. See, for example, Crocker (2008).

35. Sen (1987), p. 15.

36. Nussbaum (2000), p. 69.

37. To take one example, Nussbaum (2011) spoke of "delivering capabilities" in the form of "health care and education" (p. 65). Healthcare and education are *not capabilities*. They are basic services that hopefully will contribute to capabilities.

38. To take one example, Crocker (2008) emphasized the concept of commodity fetishism throughout his book on development ethics but nevertheless stated: "Because all humans are equal in dignity, we have certain moral obligations to each of them. One such obligation is to (try to) provide the conditions, including commodities and other material conditions, for all people to have those freedoms (capabilities) necessary to be able to be in charge of their own lives or have autonomy" (pp. 220–221).

39. World Bank (2011a).

40. World Bank (2011a).

41. Katherine Boo (2012) described a multitude of real-world tragic choices in her *Beyond the Beautiful Forevers*, a book on life in a Mumbai slum. Here is one example concerning a young boy Sunil who is worried that he is not growing due to a lack of food: "He took the sandals from the feet of his sleeping father and sold them to Abdul for food. He had consumed five vada pav by the time his father woke to thrash him. Another day, he'd sold his father's cooking pot. His own sandals he'd exchanged for rice, after which there was little left to sell. The hunger cramps could be treated by hits off discarded cigarettes. Lying down also helped. But nothing soothed his apprehension that the hunger was stunting his growth" (p. 35).

42. Roma and Pugh (2012).

43. It is also remarkable how little attention is paid to how to *achieve* capabilities beyond goal setting, constitutions and legislation. Nussbaum's recent book is entitled *Creating Capabilities* (2011), but actually says *very little* about their actual creation and the role of basic goods provision in this process.

44. This is the implicit conclusion of philosopher David Braybrooke (2005), who in attempting to combine the capabilities approach with basic needs thinking stated that "I can only speculate that the strategy of getting basic needs met first, before putting full moral effort into achieving the capabilities in the second level of construction, is more likely to be successful" (p. 219).

45. The early, more polite part of the debate was recorded in Mehta and Chatterjee (2011). The Bhagwati book was Bhagwati and Panagariya (2013), while the Sen book was Drèze and Sen (2013).

46. For an example of the acrimony of the debate, see Bhagwati (2013).

47. Sen (2013).

48. Sanitation hardly makes an appearance in Bhagwati and Panagariya (2013).

49. Banerjee and Duflo (2011), p. 267.

50. For an example of this point of view, with empirical evidence, see Suri at al. (2010).

3

Basic Goods

The premise of this book is that *basic goods*, namely those goods and services that meet basic human needs, are at the center of human progress. The approach views basic goods as the *ingredients of well-being* in that they allow human beings to be secure, healthy, literate, and able to participate effectively in their societies. They are the material prerequisites of capability expansion and can help to support growth processes. Basic goods provision is part of minimalist approaches to ethics and systems of basic human rights, namely subsistence rights. Significant deprivations in basic goods and services are widespread, and we face significant challenges to overcoming these deprivations. Basic goods might not be *what matters* above all else, but they nonetheless *matter a great deal*. The purpose of this chapter is to understand why this is so.

Economists tend to be radically agnostic when it comes to types of goods and services. Wanting to avoid "paternalism," they generally resist giving one set of goods priority over another because households should be left to decide what to consume. From this point of view, any deprivations in basic goods provision can be best addressed on the demand side with cash transfers to poor households. Relatedly, in standard assessments of economic welfare, all legally consumed goods get lumped together as welfare enhancing. Rice, prenatal care, whiskey, cigarettes, and handguns all end up being treated as desirable components of household consumption and as therefore contributing to well-being.

The basic goods approach views this economic tradition as unhelpful. It regards prenatal care as fundamentally different from whiskey because it meets a basic need, contributing directly to the health of a mother and her child. In the basic goods approach, prenatal care and other basic goods are *treated differently* than other nonbasic goods and *given priority* in policy deliberations. The approach also recognizes that some types of consumption (cigarettes and handguns) can be harmful rather than beneficial. In this way, the approach reflects Adam Smith's and Alfred Marshall's distinction between needs and wants in a way that becomes relevant to policymaking.

Some of these distinctions reflect the problem of what ethicists call *nonprudential desire* (discussed in the Appendix to this book). The philosopher James

Patrick Griffin succinctly described this problem when he stated that "the trouble is that one's desires spread themselves so widely over the world that their objects extend far outside the bound of what, with any plausibility, one could take as touching one's well-being."[1] Given this problem, what is the alternative? We have already met one in Chapter 2 in the form of the capabilities approach. However, Griffin had a different suggestion, namely to define well-being in terms of basic needs fulfillment. In his definition, *"well-being is the level to which basic needs are met so long as they retain importance."*[2] Griffin's suggestion was the beginning of the basic goods approach, and to pursue it further, we need to rediscover needs.

Rediscovering Needs

As mentioned in Chapter 1, the economist Alfred Marshall maintained a distinction between needs and wants. Marshall's student (and later colleague) Arthur Pigou also recognized this distinction and specified needs in terms of a minimum standard composed of food, health services, educational services, and housing.[3] Modern economics has largely cast aside the distinction between needs and wants and treats needs as just another type of want or preference. Despite attempts to downplay their role, however, needs do make an appearance now and then and have been shown to have empirical validity. This body of thought is described in the Appendix.

There are other traditions that emphasize the role of human needs. As every psychology student knows, Abraham Maslow described a hierarchy of needs that began with the physiological, moved through safety, love/belonging and esteem, and ended with self-actualization. Indeed, Maslow explicitly set such needs apart from desires, stating that "basic needs are *more* common-human than superficial desires or behaviors."[4] In the realm of social theory and social policy, needs were put on center stage by Len Doyal and Ian Gough who stressed that needs are both "universal" and "knowable." In their work, Doyal and Gough stated that "basic human needs . . . stipulate what persons must achieve if they are to avoid sustained and serious harm."[5] In this way, they showed that the needs concept indeed fits into the realm of social theory and policy.

Moral philosophers also have occasionally considered basic human needs. For example, David Braybrooke noted that "the concept of needs differs top and bottom from the concept of preferences."[6] Braybrooke defined basic needs as things that are "essential to living or to functioning normally" and presented his own list of such needs.[7] In doing so, as with Pigou, he emphasized the role of a "minimum standard of provision" that helps to define a limit to moral obligations or, to look at it from the other end, what he termed "moral capacity." In a similar fashion, David Copp used basic human needs as the foundation for the development of a right to an "adequate" standard of living that would command a priority in government action.[8] He drew on David Braybrooke's list of basic needs, acknowledged some "vagueness" in the concept, but argued that more precision was not realistic.

As I demonstrate, the moral philosophy tradition of basic needs implies that the basic goods approach is a type of ethics. More specifically, it fits within the *ethical minimalism* school of thought. These and other considerations also imply that the basic goods approach is tied to certain conceptions of human rights, namely that of *subsistence rights*. These ethical and human rights considerations are an important component of the basic needs approach.

Drawing on these varied traditions, I consider basic needs as being *developmentally related* to the human condition and *verifiably* so. For a need to be authentic, it must support the life of the human organism.[9] Or, to put it another way, any serious deprivation of basic needs has negative ramifications for the human organism. Therefore, although an individual may claim a "need" for cigarettes, objective evidence would dispute this.[10] In this way, the basic goods approach is a type of "objective" ethics and would therefore tend to fall into what ethicists sometimes call "objective list theory." In objective list theory, before we can put something on our list of *what matters*, we must provide a "claim of realism" to demonstrate that it *actually matters* in an objective sense.[11] The basic good approach makes such a claim.

In placing objective needs at the center of things, the basic goods approach does not necessarily rule out more expansive approaches. Indeed, needs themselves can be conceived of in more expansive terms as playing a central part of larger schemes of quality of life, or even be seen as part of subjective well-being.[12] The focus on basic needs defined objectively, and the goods and services that address them, is a question of emphasis meant to draw attention to current and future imperatives to provide missing basic goods. It is an exercise in what Braybrooke termed *precautionary priority* to ensure that there is access to the ingredients of well-being.[13]

There are counterarguments to an approach based on basic needs and basic goods. For example, in their book *Poverty, Work and Freedom*, David Levine and Abu Turab Rizvi argued that "so far as we respect individual freedom, we cannot know in advance what makes any particular individual's life worthwhile, because what makes a life worthwhile in a society of individuals remains to be determined by those individuals themselves."[14] These authors also questioned the extent to which the mere specification of basic needs provides enough information as to how those needs can be satisfied. As a consequence, these authors stressed the "unknown" aspect of deprivation that reflects individual differences and creative freedom, invoking a type of individuation argument discussed in Chapter 2. Nevertheless, even here there is some overlap. These authors conceived of deprivation in terms of "a lack of something vital for living" and emphasized this lack in absolute rather than relative terms.[15]

Levine and Rizvi also raised the concern that even those who have basic needs fulfilled were still poor. They stated "We may survive physically while losing the meaning that life has had, or is meant to have, for us. When this happens, we are still poor, though our basic needs may be satisfied."[16] The authors are correct in this assertion. We do not mean to imply here that the mere provision of basic goods *alleviates* poverty, only that it makes it *less severe*. Basic goods provision is therefore only a first step among many.

There is a related concern, expressed in different ways, that minimal thresholds or floors could become maximal ceilings. That is, once the most basic goods have been delivered, there is no longer any implied social responsibility. This "floors become ceilings" concern was also raised by political scientist and ethicist Audrey Chapman in the human rights context.[17] This is an important concern, but again the approach is only focused on first steps as an imperative deserving the utmost attention. It is in no way a comprehensive agenda, merely an agenda far from being fulfilled.

For the remainder of this book, I am going to treat human needs as real and verifiable. To take a stark but important example, nearly six million infants and children perish each year before the age of five.[18] It would seem strange and disrespectful to say that these individuals perish because of a failure to meet their wants or preferences. In the normal use of term, preference failure does not lead to death. Strictly speaking, perhaps, the children would have preferred to *live*, but is this really the issue? As Braybrooke noted, "questions about whether needs are genuine, or well-founded, come to the end of the line when the needs have been connected with life and health."[19] Indeed, any serious analysis of the phenomenon of infant and child mortality indicates that there are specific *causes* contributing to the premature mortality: respiratory and diarrheal infection, malarial infection, and poor nutrition to name a few. These seem more like failures to meet basic needs than failures to meet wants or preferences. Or more specifically, they seem like failures to provide basic goods and services with which to keep these children alive and well.

What Are Basic Goods?

What specifically do I mean by basic goods? First, basic goods include both basic *goods* and basic *services*. In fact, in some instances, it is difficult to completely disentangle goods and services from each other. The provision of health services requires goods (syringes), and the provision of food requires services (transportation). As a consequence, our use of the terms *goods* and *services* is always somewhat incomplete. Second, as previously discussed, basic goods and services are identified with reference to objective human *needs* that are developmentally related to the human condition in that they support the life of the human organism. More succinctly, basic goods satisfy basic needs.

Third, basic goods and services are often *multifunctional* in that they make contributions beyond their direct intent. Education services provide the information and skills to better maintain health. Health services make it more likely that a child will be able to attend school and be educated. Electricity makes it more likely that medicines can be kept at an appropriate temperature to prevent illness. Clean water supports good health. In these ways, the increased provision of various basic goods has a mutually supporting nature, and the multifunctional nature of basic goods and service provision is what makes them so important in the growth-capabilities nexus.

A preliminary list of basic goods is presented in Table 3.1. This is not necessarily a complete list but focuses on some of the most essential goods and services that are emphasized in ongoing discussions in development policy. This list includes nutritious food, clean water, sanitation, health services, education services, housing, electricity, and human security services.[20] Each of these goods and services is motivated in the table with reference to the needs it addresses. One potential objection to this list is that the needs addressed are stated in terms of outcomes that are similar to the capabilities/human development paradigm. This, however, is exactly the point. There is nothing wrong with the *aspirations* of the capabilities approach. Its limitation is to be found in its suppression of the *determinants* of these aspirations, what it calls *material preconditions*. The purpose of Table 3.1 is to feature these determinants.

The basic goods listed in Table 3.1 are *underprovided*. Or to put it another way, there are significant numbers of individuals who are deprived of them. Recall the following facts from Chapter 1:[21]

- Food: Approximately 800 million people suffer from chronic hunger in the sense that they are not well-nourished enough for an active life.
- *Water*: More than 700 million people do not have access to an improved drinking-water source.
- *Sanitation*: Approximately 2.4 billion individuals do not have access to clean and safe toilets, and nearly one billion individuals practice open defecation.
- *Health services*: Approximately six million infants and children die each year, largely due to preventable causes.
- *Education services*: Approximately 250 million of the 650 primary school-age children (nearly 40 percent) have not mastered basic literacy and numeracy, and there are more than 750 million illiterate adults.
- *Housing*: A much-quoted but *unverifiable* statistic is that at least one billion people lack access to adequate housing, with approximately 100 million of these being homeless.
- *Electricity*: Approximately 1.1 billion people live without access to electricity.
- *Human security services*: Half a million people die each year as a result of armed violence.

Table 3.1 **Basic Goods and Services**

Basic Goods and Services	*Needs Addressed*
Nutritious food	Food is needed to meet minimum caloric requirements. Beyond this, key vitamins and minerals are important for minimal health. Additional micronutrients support health and ward off potential infections.
Clean water	Water is required for basic health and survival. This includes water for drinking, sanitation, hygiene, food production, and cooking.
Sanitation	Sanitation is critical for the prevention of a multitude of diseases and is seen as intrinsic to human dignity.
Health services	Basic health services (primary healthcare) and associated products are required for survival and minimal health.
Education services	Basic education services (primary and secondary) are a prerequisite for participation in modern human life as well as of being able to remain healthy. Educated parents, particularly mothers, make child survival and health more likely.
Housing	A minimal level of housing quality is important to protect individuals against the elements and to provide space for food preparation and hygiene. Beyond this, it is generally essential for effective participation in human life.
Electricity	Electricity contributes to refrigeration (which can improve food storage and preserve medicines), radio and television (which can potentially provide critical information), and air conditioning (shown to improve health in very hot environments).
Human security services	Basic security services are critical to maintaining bodily integrity and the prevention of injury. They are also critical to functioning societies (based on minimal levels of trust), to the functioning of markets, and to the provision of all other basic goods and services.

These deprivations have dramatic impacts on the well-being of those deprived. This takes place in the form of reduced life expectancies (including nearly six million children perishing each year), severely compromised quality of life, wasted human potential, and reduced economic performance. They also constitute an *injustice* that needs to be addressed in the form of a violation of acknowledged subsistence rights.

Minimalist Ethics

As described in Chapter 2, the capabilities/human development approach spawned the new field of development ethics.[22] But the capabilities approach to development ethics is not the only possible one. An advantage of the basic goods approach relative to the capabilities approach is its relationship to what is called a *common* and *minimalist* ethics. The notion of "common" used here is what ethicist Sissela Bok referred to as being "easily recognized across societal and other boundaries" and "so clear-cut as to offer standards for critiquing abuses."[23] The notional of "minimal" was described by the political philosopher Michael Walzer, as "a simplified . . . morality" based on "mutual recognition among the protagonists of different fully developed cultures."[24] It also has been described by philosopher Henry Shue as the "morality of the depths" or "the line beneath which no one is allowed to sink" and by philosopher David Braybrooke as the "rock bottom" of ethics.[25] The basic goods approach asserts that there is a set of basic goods provisions that are *both* common *and* minimal, on which little disagreement can be expected and that represents a common, ethical minimum.

There are arguments that no such common, minimalist ethics exist, that all ethics are context specific. However, the basic goods approach suggests, for example, that a Muslim citizen in Pakistan who lacks shelter in the winter months due to an earthquake, as well as the Christian citizen of Honduras who similarly lacks shelter due to a mudslide, would both agree that the basic good of housing is of utmost value. Likewise, a Hindu Indian and an Animist West African, both suffering from malaria, would agree that bed nets are of value. It is precisely such real and existing overlaps in values that make common, minimalist ethics both possible and urgent.

Decades ago, this common, minimalist ethics was linked to basic needs. Consider this description from the basic needs approach of the 1970s:[26]

> The basic needs approach recognizes that countries will have different requirements as a result of differences in their economic, social, political, and cultural characteristics. Nevertheless, there are certain minimum levels of personal consumption and access to public services that can be regarded as everywhere essential . . ., and in these cases it is possible to define targets in physical units on a global basis.

In this way, the basic goods approach promotes a *narrowly defined* universalism, rather than a *comprehensive* universalism, all that is achievable in terms of agreement and overlap in values when it comes to provisioning. As noted by Sissela Bok, both comprehensively universalist and overly relativistic arguments fall into *premature closure*. This is characterized by "either holding one particular set of values to be so self-evident as to require no further justification or allowing the rhetoric of moral incommensurability to block every inquiry concerning them."[27] The common, minimalist ethics of the basic goods approach avoids both types of premature closure. The approach also avoids "proceduralist" remedies to relativist concerns. Proceduralist ethical systems invariably and inevitably smuggle in additional sources of values to buttress procedural success. Instead of invoking procedure, the common, minimalist approach identifies what is most urgent directly and explicitly.[28] In this way, it focuses attention on highest-ranked priorities taken up in the second part of the book. As such, the approach is proximate to a sense of justice. This is not justice in a well-worked-out theoretical sense. Rather, it is a "common, garden variety justice" that calls for extreme shortfalls in basic goods provision to be immediately addressed as a matter of subsistence rights.[29]

Subsistence Rights

There is a long-standing reluctance to extend conceptions of human rights from the realm of negative or political rights the realm of positive or economic rights.[30] However, this reluctance has been forcibly shown to be illogical by the philosopher Henry Shue in the realm of a subset of economic rights, namely subsistence rights.[31] As demonstrated by Shue, and as common sense suggests, even negative, political rights (e.g., freedom from violence or freedom of political participation) require positive action in the form of the provision of basic human security services, legal services, and judicial services. Further, it is impossible to exercise such rights when severely deprived of basic subsistence goods. Simply put, there are no functioning political rights for the prematurely dead.[32] This reflects Shue's concept of *basic rights*, namely, those rights that must be fulfilled so that other rights can be enjoyed. *Basic goods are basic rights*, and basic goods provision is a basic subsistence right.[33]

Despite an overall reluctance to recognize subsistence rights, there is a relatively long-standing tradition of trying to implement a system of minimal thresholds defined in terms of basic goods and services. The reason for this is that there is a link between human needs and human rights. Once we allow for the reality of human needs, we naturally begin to consider at least a minimum threshold of provision as a right.[34] As a consequence, conceptions of human rights have been developed in terms of basic needs and their concomitant basic goods and services for some time now. We saw one example of this in Cambridge economist Arthur Pigou's minimum standard specified in terms of food, health services, educational services, and housing.[35] Another example was the development economist Frances Stewart who spoke of the "need to ensure that everyone has access to enough basic goods and services to maintain a level of living above a basic minimum, as a prime objective of economic development."[36]

More recently, economic rights scholars Shareen Hertel and Lanse Minkler stated that "despite (the) evidence of unfathomable suffering experienced by much of the world's population, military security and political freedoms capture the most attention. . . . But a different kind of freedom and a new kind of security need to share center stage."[37] What Hertel and Minkler advocated is the right to freedom from deprivation as part of a new concept of human security, freedom from want as well as freedom from fear. This hoped-for outcome requires the universal basic goods provision.

As it turns out, freedom from basic goods deprivation is recognized within the existing human rights framework of the United Nations. This begins with the 1948 Universal Declaration of Human Rights (UDHR),[38] which addresses basic goods and services in Articles 25 and 26. Article 25 states that "Everyone has the right to a standard of living adequate for the health and well-being of himself and of his family, including food, clothing, housing and medical care and necessary social services." Article 26 of the UDHR extends this to educational services, stating that "Everyone has the right to education. Education shall be free, at least in the elementary and fundamental stages. Elementary education shall be compulsory. Technical and professional education shall be made generally available and higher education shall be equally accessible to all on the basis of merit."

The 1966 International Covenant on Economic, Social, and Cultural Rights (ICESCR)[39] reiterates what was stated in Article 25 of the UDHR. Article 11 of the ICESCR recognizes "the right of everyone to an adequate standard of living for himself and his family, including adequate food, clothing and housing" and "to be free from hunger." In elaborating on food security, Article 11 also calls for countries: "To improve methods of production, conservation and distribution of food by making full use of technical and scientific knowledge, by disseminating knowledge of the principles of nutrition and by developing or reforming agrarian systems in such a way as to achieve the most efficient development and utilization of natural resources" and "Taking into account the problems of both food-importing and food-exporting countries, to ensure an equitable distribution of world food supplies in relation to need."[40] I discuss food security in Chapter 4.

In the case of water and sanitation, the United Nations General Assembly passed a 2010 Resolution on the Human Right to Water and Sanitation[41] that recognized "the right to safe and clean drinking water and sanitation as a human right that is essential for the full enjoyment of life and all human rights." So rights to water and sanitation are emerging within the UN system. I discuss water and sanitation in Chapters 5 and 6, respectively.

Article 12 of the ICESCR addresses health and recognizes "the right of everyone to the enjoyment of the highest attainable standard of physical and mental health."[42] As part of this right, steps should be taken to "assure to all medical service and medical attention in the event of sickness."[43] In somewhat parallel fashion, Article 13 of the ICESCR addresses education and recognizes "the right of everyone to education."[44] As part of this, Article 13 reinforces Article 26 of the UDHR, stating that "primary education shall be compulsory and available free to all. Secondary education in its different forms, including technical and vocational secondary education, shall be made generally available and accessible to all by every appropriate means, and in particular by the progressive introduction of free education." Health and education are studied in Chapters 7 and 8, respectively.

With regard to housing, both Article 25 of the UDHR and Article 11 of the ICESCR recognized the right to housing as part of a larger right to a standard of living. In 1991, the UN Committee on Economic, Social and Cultural Rights[45] further recognized the right to adequate housing in General Comment 4 on the Right to Adequate Housing and extended it beyond mere shelter to "the right to live somewhere in security, peace and dignity." I discuss housing in Chapter 9.

In these ways, the current system of human rights reinforces and institutionalizes the basic goods provision imperative and places the basic good approach within the larger framework of subsistence rights. Despite the reluctance to embrace such "second generation" subsistence rights, the logic of these subsistence rights is sound, and they are an integral part of the current human rights system. Further, there is emerging work that explicitly utilizes the basic goods framework as part of subsistence rights.[46] What is missing is substantially greater recognition of the previously mentioned concept of human security.[47]

Objections to subsistence rights can and are made on the grounds that the minimum thresholds involved in subsistence rights only apply to environments in which deprivations are rampant. But this can be addressed by employing thresholds that rise with levels of GDP per capita. However, we should be aware that, although deprivations might not be *rampant* in countries with high levels of GDP per capita, they certainly *do exist*. For example, there is a great deal hunger, lack of access to clean water, lack of access to basic medical care, and lack of access to adequate shelter in the United States, a country that leads the world in GDP per capita. So even here, minimal subsistence thresholds are relevant.

Recall from Chapter 2 that the capabilities approach envisions implementation via minimum thresholds established in a constitutionally enshrined system of human rights. The considerations reviewed here suggest that, in large measure, defining minimum thresholds in terms of basic goods and services is both more important and more practical than doing the same for Nussbuam's list of ten capabilities. Practically speaking, do we want human rights systems defined in terms of capabilities to play or in terms of access to clean water? Do we want human rights systems defined in terms of the use of senses in a "truly human way" or in terms of access to basic healthcare? Consensus and progress is much more likely if we conceive of human rights in terms of access to water and basic healthcare than in terms of play and the use of senses. Further, in defining human rights in this way, we are more likely to support capabilities expansion. Once again, focusing on determinants rather than outcomes is the way forward.

The basic goods approach to subsistence rights is also emerging within increased concerns with sustainability. For example, Narasimha Rao and Paul Baer have used the approach to estimate what they call "decent living standards" and associated "decent living emissions."[48] Invoking subsistence rights, they suggested that levels of decent living emissions could be interpreted as emissions *entitlements* that become relevant in setting country obligations in climate change agreements. Their list of basic goods included: food, safe water and sanitation, shelter, healthcare, education, clothing, television, refrigeration, and mobile phones. Rao and Baer's set of subsistence rights is more extensive than the one used here, indicating that the basic goods approach is not hard-and-fast but rather something that can be deployed in a somewhat-flexible manner.

Finally, some aspects of basic goods as subsistence rights relate to a useful index of social and economic rights, namely the Index of Social and Economic Rights Fulfillment (SERF Index).[49] The SERF Index measures the extent to which countries fulfill economic and social rights obligations, and most of its measures relate to basic goods and services. These include the following: food, health services, education services, and housing. The housing dimension actually measures provisions of water and sanitation, rather than housing directly, but this is still very relevant. Creatively and importantly, the SERF Index employs achievement possibility frontiers (APFs) that assess the performance of rights fulfillment in terms of a country's level of GDP, the latter used as an indicator of fulfillment capacity. This gives a sense of the extent to which more progress is often possible at given levels of GDP per capita.

All of the previous considerations lead us to consider minimal levels of basic goods provision as subsistence rights. It is worth noting, however, that this falls short of the entire agenda of economic and social rights. The right to work, the right to health itself, and the right to social security broadly defined are not part of the basic goods approach.[50] This is not to say that these other elements of economic and social rights do not have merit, but just that they do not fall within the realm of the basic goods approach. Our concern here is more narrowly focused on a specific set of subsistence rights.

Basic Goods and Growth

Suppose we do indeed pursue a development strategy that focuses on universal basic goods provision. There would be a worry among some economists that this would take away from conventional growth-oriented strategies and that this would have negative repercussions for achievable growth levels. To use an elementary economic concept, basic goods provision carries with it an *opportunity cost*. Indeed, we have seen this sort of worry expressed in criticisms of Amartya Sen's prescriptions for India as being too focused on human development objectives rather than growth objectives. The standard argument is that the focus on basic goods provision will undermine growth, which in turn undermines the very basic goods provision that we seek. But is this always the case?

In an article on Indonesia published in 2014, the pro-growth *Economist* magazine stated: "Over the next six years Indonesia will add 15 million people to its workforce. The World Bank says it should be trying to achieve growth rates of 9 percent. For that, Indonesia needs much better education, health care and infrastructure."[51] If basic goods provision is so damaging to growth, why are the first two items on *The Economist*'s list basic services listed in Table 3.1? Let us take another example of *The Economist* discussing the challenges of addressing the "chronically poor" in Latin America. On the short list of ways to meet this challenge is what *The Economist* refers to as "basic services," and these include clean water, sanitation, education, and better policing (human security services).[52] Is there really such a contradiction between the provision of basic goods and services and growth?

The answer seems to be *no*, provided that we are really concerned with *basic* goods and services provision and not more expansive lists of things we would ideally like to see.[53] Furthermore, there are good reasons to view basic goods and services provision as actually contributing to growth prospects as suggested by *The Economist*. For example, the delivery of educational services contributes to the stock of human capital, which has been shown to potentially increase growth rates. A better-educated public is in a better position to leverage the institutional quality that is available and to make use of opportunities for entrepreneurship. A better-educated public is also in a better position to make better choices in the health arena, particularly for their children. Basic health services, clean water, and sanitation would all support this and contribute to worker productivity. So would basic housing. Human security services (peacekeeping and policing) would support the institutional environment and allow individuals to actually make use of opportunities present in that environment.

Similar arguments apply to the issue of institutions and growth briefly discussed in Chapter 2. It is all well and good to invoke property rights and enforceable contracts as key elements of institutional environments, but individuals have a difficult time in *realizing* these potentials without access to basic goods and services. If you are too sick to get to the provincial courthouse, you cannot enforce your property rights. If you cannot read a contract (or a constitution), you cannot hope for its enforcement.[54] It may well be naïve to assume that individuals can make use of institutions without access to certain basic goods and services. And if they cannot make use of the institutions, those institutions cannot contribute to growth.

There is also evidence that basic goods considerations will become more relevant over time, due to advances in information and communications technologies or what is sometimes called the knowledge economy. Economic ethicist Albino Barrera addressed this issue and suggested that the satisfaction of basic needs via certain types of basic goods provision was actually a *prerequisite* of the productive efficiency on which growth in the knowledge economy depends.[55] He went further and identified the market failures that could prevent this from naturally occurring via market-based transactions. The central reason for this is that issues of nutrition, health services, and education services are also issues of *human capital formation* in which time horizons are very long (even reaching across generations) and returns uncertain. This makes the optimal consumption of these basic goods much less than fully known. Because there are positive interpersonal and intertemporal externalities involved, there is no guarantee that the private consumption decisions with respect to these particular basic goods will be either individually or socially optimal. Efforts to nudge provision levels forward can therefore overcome these market failures.

Empirical evidence suggests that basic goods provision does indeed support growth outcomes. In the case of education, this was once in doubt due to measurement errors. But once these errors have been properly addressed, it becomes clear that education supports growth.[56] Although less attention has been given to health and growth, the same positive relationship seems to hold.[57] The evidence thus suggests that human capital in the form of education and health, the outcomes of basic goods provision, supports growth. As a consequence, the worry that basic goods provision will compromise growth-oriented development strategies does not seem to be well founded. In truth, the provision of *all* goods and services entail opportunity costs. One thing that distinguishes *basic* goods and services from others is that the *net* opportunity costs tend to be lower than for other goods and services due to their contributions to human capital formation.

Having made this argument, however, there is a need to be honestly cognizant of some important caveats. There are no doubt *conditions* under which the provision of basic goods and services best support growth and indeed capabilities expansion and human development. As shown in Chapter 7, for example, there are many examples of the failed provision of primary healthcare services. There are even examples of healthcare workers behaving in abusive ways to patients, as well as examples of corruption in healthcare systems.[58] And as shown in Chapter 8, there have been many concerns about the poor delivery of and corruption in education services.[59] There is also empirical evidence that the lack of quality in educational outcomes impedes growth.[60] From even these two examples of basic services, we can see that poorly delivered basic goods may not support growth. The corruption issue also shows that, just as a modicum of basic goods delivery is a precondition to individuals making use of quality institutional environments, a modicum of quality institutions can be necessary for basic goods delivery. This situation also can arise with some types of property rights. So, for example, it would be difficult to provide sufficient food and adequate housing in an institutional environment without well-defined land rights. The same also may be true for sanitation systems that extend beyond single-family pit latrines. In these ways, basic goods and institutional environments are mutually dependent on each other to support growth processes.

I have been primarily concerned here with the extent to which basic goods provision inhibits or supports growth. I also have stressed that growth can support basic goods provision. But it needs to be recognized that there are instances where growth can *impede* some types of basic goods provision. For example, some environmentalists might want to add clean air to the list of basic goods in Table 3.1, and there are a number of cases in which growth has significantly compromised air quality. Although estimates vary, a recent study has suggested that at least three million individuals die prematurely each year as a result of poor air quality, with perhaps one third of these deaths occurring in China where air quality is notoriously bad.[61] The basic goods approach allows for observation of such cases where the growth-provision relationship breaks down.

Providing Basic Goods and Services

Although this book argues that a focus on basic goods and services provision is a good start in conceiving of *what matters*, it is important for us not to be naïve about the process of provisioning. Many calls for the recognition of basic needs and basic goods provisioning, as well as for the recognition of subsistence rights, are rather silent on the actual *means* by which the provisioning is to take place. Sometimes this silence is explicit, other times implicit.[62] One aim of this book is to move beyond this silence and to address provisioning problems. It will not be conclusive in every case, but I hope to shed light on some of the relevant issues.

The basic goods provision problem was nicely described some time ago by the noted development economist Frances Stewart:[63]

> The actual achievement of satisfactory conditions of life is the outcome of a complex and lengthy chain of developments in the economic system. At the end of this chain is an interaction between a set of goods and services (the basic needs goods) and a person, leading to a certain condition of human life, which may be defined as satisfactory or unsatisfactory according to the agreed criteria of fulfillment of basic needs. The chain of events leading to this outcome consists of all those aspects of the economic system which result in the availability of some level and quality of basic needs goods and all those events leading to

household distribution of cash income, subsistence income, and access to public goods which together determine each household's full income, (or entitlements), which they may use to acquire basic needs goods.

As suggested in this quotation, basic goods provision is a matter of supply and demand. In this, basic goods provision is like the provision of any other good or service. It just happens to be more important. The supply side is a natural focus that tends to attract more attention. This is where impending shortages or intriguing technological developments can be found. However, the demand side of basic goods markets can matter as well and can be more subtle.

In Chapter 2 I was critical of the capabilities approach being resistant to allowing for tradeoffs among valued human development outcomes. So, for instance, in the Nussbaum variant of the approach, the capabilities to play and to maintain bodily integrity are not subject to tradeoffs. Because basic goods and services are ultimate determinants of capabilities, it would make more sense to say that there were no tradeoffs among their provision than in the case of capabilities. But I will not make this claim. Indeed, the needs-based nature of the basic goods approach suggests that the provision of some basic goods can be situationally more important than the provision of other basic goods and that this can depend on circumstances. For example, it may not be possible to provide secondary schooling to refugees. Food, water, sanitation, temporary housing, and human security service will be the priorities for provision efforts in this case.[64] The same priorities may arise in circumstances of natural disasters or extreme budgetary constraints. Such appropriately considered tradeoffs in basic goods provision can be a practical and central part of the basic goods approach. What Martha Nussbaum called "tragic choice" is unfortunately part of the provisioning process in some circumstances.

Technological Optimism

In many cases, supply side issues in basic goods provision are matters of technology. As a consequence, one key focus in the remainder of this book will be technological issues. However, there is a need for caution with regard to a claim that technology and technological entrepreneurship can solve everything, a claim I term *technological optimism*. In the view of technological optimists, new groundbreaking innovations, old-fashioned entrepreneurship, new-fangled social entrepreneurship and techno-philanthropy are reasons for optimism about the supply side of basic goods provision. For example, one recent source of this genre stated that "Abundance for all is actually within our grasp."[65]

Technological optimism certainly has some trends to draw on. Who would have predicted the ubiquity of mobile phones a couple of decades ago? In some developing countries, mobile phone penetration rates approach 100 percent with extraordinary benefits in the areas of health, market information, and mobile banking. On the other hand, in some countries, there are more mobile phones than latrines and toilets, and the best mobile phone app will not protect you against diarrheal infection. Given that our modern S-trap flush toilet was invented in 1775 and the history of flush toilets goes back millennia, it can be seen that there are barriers to the adoption of crucial technologies. Even in the United States, over a million people do not benefit from this technology.[66] And there are cities where over one hundred people (typically slum-dwellers) share a single latrine, an even more elementary technology.

One problem with technological optimism is the tendency to exaggerate potential. At one point, the Segway human transporter was going to revolutionize transportation. After a few years, it became clear that it was going to revolutionize shopping mall policing. There are now claims that the inventor of the Segway, Dean Kamen will revolutionize clean water production with his Slingshot. There are similar claims that water and food provision challenges can be largely solved through desalination and (smart, solar-powered) hydroponics. Following on these ideas, Qatar announced in 2012 a big push for domestic food security based on such technologies. The idea was to use these technologies to significantly boost domestic food production between 2012 and 2024. By 2014, the Qatari government had dropped these ideas. If this package of technologies cannot be developed in financially rich Qatar, how will it work in financially constrained and politically fragile Mali?[67]

The fundamental problem with technological optimism is the assumption that technologies diffuse quickly. The vision here is often described as a *stock* of technology that can be freely drawn on by all people of the world.[68] Or it is sometimes described as a public good that can be supplied at very low marginal cost. A better vision of technology is not as a stock but as a *flow*, a flow that can be *restricted* for any of a number of reasons: inadequate demand, lack of information, contextual factors, poor institutional environments including lack of human security, lack of access to supporting technologies including spare parts and other necessary inputs, and intellectual property protection. From the flow perspective, without work to remove restrictions, even simple technologies (toilets, latrines, metal silos) do not diffuse as quickly as we might like.

With regard to the potential of technological entrepreneurship, local conditions will always matter. As economist Phil Auerswald emphasized, "a fundamental prerequisite for prosperity in any given place is that the returns to productive entrepreneurial activities must be greater, on average, than the returns to unproductive and destructive entrepreneurship."[69] The problem here is that many environments support the returns to *destructive* entrepreneurship. These environments are those with widespread institutional failure, pernicious greed, and a lack of human security services. Without a modicum of security and a lack of corruption, destructive entrepreneurship can and does prevail.[70] Although entrepreneurs do not always wait for optimal conditions to act, it is difficult to expect *widespread* productive entrepreneurship without basic security, basic housing, clean water, sanitation, and basic literacy and numeracy. The obvious rebuttal to this point is that entrepreneurs could actually innovate to provide these basic goods and services. Indeed they *could* and *do*, but there has been ample evidence from many different parts of the world that this does not always happen.

This can be seen in the widely cited work on slums by Benjamin Marx, Thomas Stoker, and Tavneet Suri.[71] There has been a tendency to see slums as hives of entrepreneurship, and this is no doubt true to a significant extent. But the lack of basic goods and services is a persistent damper on this process. These authors cited poor hygiene, lack of sanitation services, and lack of access to clean water as contributing to poor health. Poor health, in turn, has economic impacts on the families involved, either through medical bills or through the inability to work. Access to housing, of course, is another issue that defines slums. All of these factors contribute to slum-based entrepreneurship being less magical than previously thought. With just under one billion people currently living in slums and perhaps two billion people forecasted to live in them by the end of this century, these persistent problems raise questions about optimistic entrepreneurial scenarios.

I am not suggesting here that technology and entrepreneurship do not play critical roles in the provision of goods and services of all kinds, including basic goods and services. They do. What I am saying is that technology and entrepreneurship cannot be invoked as factors to *solve* the problem. Solving the provision problem will also include political processes, the redirection of existing resources, and multilateral action at the global level. A number of different realms need to work together effectively, not just technology and entrepreneurship.

Demand Side Issues

As previously stated, there is a reluctance in modern economics to recognize basic needs and, therefore, basic goods. Even when these are acknowledged, there is a default position that is often invoked, namely that basic goods provision can be fully addressed through demand-side *cash transfers* to the deprived. It is argued that this is the most direct and efficient means of basic goods provision.[72] It is also argued that to go beyond cash transfers in the provision process is to venture into a paternalistic relationship vis-à-vis deprived individuals and households. I consider the paternalism argument in the Paternalism section and focus on the effectiveness issue here. It can be shown that although cash transfers may very well have their place as a starting point, other provision options can also be relevant.

Cash transfers put resources directly into the hands of basic goods deprived individuals.[73] However, as described earlier in our consideration of basic goods and growth, when it comes to basic goods and services, informational constraints and market failures can abound. These can render *unconditional* cash transfers less effective in providing basic goods and services than might be supposed. For example, in the realm of health services, development economist Charles Kenny noted that: "A major reason behind poor health in developing countries is that people are not using available technologies, through lack of knowledge or incentives."[74] This can be as simple and critical as a lack of understanding of the germ theory of disease but can also reflect education levels and cultural practices. To the extent that a lack of demand for essential basic goods reflects a lack of education, increasing supplies of basic educational services can be crucial. Education can also reduce the impact of cultural factors that retard the use of some basic goods. Unconditional cash transfers may not be enough to address these issues.

Another issue is that unconditional cash transfers are received in a no-strings-attached form and therefore do not involve any incentives to engaged in constructive activity. To make this observation is not to invoke a Victorian-like posture to deprived individuals. Rather, it is to recognize that there are many constraints on these individuals and that conditioning cash transfers on some productive activities can function as a useful nudge. This recognition is one reason that many national governments have embraced *conditional* cash transfer (CCT) programs rather than unconditional cash transfers. These programs effect cash transfers conditional on certain actions on the part of parents in the health and educational realms. They provide families with balances on smart cards provided that children are enrolled in school and have received basic health services such as vaccinations. CCT programs can both help overcome informational constrains and provide incentives for constructive activity. Further, there is accumulating evidence that CCT programs have positive outcomes, and these are considered in the following chapters.[75]

Paternalism

As noted earlier, there is a claim that basic goods provision policies that go beyond unconditional cash transfers are paternalistic. Let us recognize that this is a possibility. Nonetheless, there are two things to keep in mind. First, some degree of paternalism is *always* involved in policy choices, including the choice to only pursue unconditional cash transfers. The question is when and what kind of paternalism is desirable. This is a topic of much discussion in moral philosophy and medical ethics, and is not something that has been fully resolved.[76] But there is no established principle that some minimal degree of paternalism is to always be avoided.

The second thing that needs to be recognized is that most high-income countries have paternalistic systems *in place* that are taken for granted and that support the lives of many of the individuals lucky enough to reside there, free of the constant burden of routinely making potentially life-and-death decisions. Consider the following from the World Bank:[77]

> Poor people around the world are forced to make many, many choices—most of them bad—every time a child falls sick: where do they get the firewood to boil the water, where should they get sugar, should they take the child to the doctor who could be five hours away, how much will the doctor charge, should the mother wait for the husband if the child needs to be carried? Each choice can have devastating consequences if things don't pan out.

These types of realities and their absence for many people in higher-income countries have been recognized by Abhijit Banerjee and Esther Duflo:[78]

> It is true that we who are not poor are somewhat better educated and informed, but the difference is small because, in the end, we actually know very little, and almost surely less than we imagine.
> Our real advantage comes from the many things that we take as given. We live in houses where clean water gets piped in—we do not need to remember to add Chlorin to the water supply every morning. The sewerage goes away on its own—we do not actually know how. We can (mostly) trust our doctors to do the best they can and can trust the public health system to figure out what we should and should not do. We have no choice but to get our children immunized. . . . In other words, we rarely need to draw upon our limited endowment of self-control and decisiveness, while the poor are constantly being required to do so. . . .
> It is easy, too easy, to sermonize about the dangers of paternalism and the need to take responsibility for our own lives, from the comfort of our couch in our safe and sanitary home. Aren't we, those who live in the rich world, the constant beneficiaries of paternalism now so thoroughly embedded into the system that we hardly notice it?

So although we need to recognize the reality of potentially paternalistic interventions, we also need to be aware of the limits of claims of paternalism. The fact of the matter is that some degree of paternalism is hard-wired into most systems of modern economies. We should also note that, because it focuses on determinants and not on outcomes, the basic goods approach runs less of a risk of paternalistic overreach than the capabilities approach.

Is Success Possible?

Basic goods deprived people are often very poorly served by the systems that are supposed to deliver basic goods and services. Among others, this was noted in the World Bank's 2004 *World Development Report* and considered by the coordinators of that report Shantayanan Devarajan and Ritva Reinikka.[79] As an example, Devarajan and Reinikka hinted at the potential difficulties using the example of education:[80]

> The diverse body of stakeholders in public education includes parents and children, teachers and their unions, taxpayers, potential graduate employers, society as a whole, private school, and various groups favoring or opposing specific components of the curriculum. These principals have diverse preferences and objectives. Parents want "good education" and day care for their children, teachers and unions want higher pay, taxpayers want low costs, employers want vocational skills, society wants good citizens, and private schools compete for pupils and some public funds. Many of these objectives are mutually conflicting.

This education example shows that the provision of basic goods and services does not necessarily come easy. Even if rights are correctly recognized for the basic good and even if there is a technology that can be helpful, success is not assured. There can be interests opposed to the very changes that need to take place to ensure provision. To put it another way, basic goods provision is *political*. It involves persistence, persuasion, lobbying, cajoling, and shaming. In corrupt environments, it may well involve arrests and prosecutions.

Despite these complications and difficulties, however, evidence suggests that forward progress is possible and in a number of different ways. For example, some time ago the World Bank examined the provision of health, nutrition, and population services to poor clients.[81] The specific basic goods and services examined included bed nets, reproductive health services, HIV/AIDS counseling, obstetric services, tuberculosis detection, maternal and child health services, and nutrition supplements across a wide range of national settings and delivery strategies (including by governments, NGOs, and the private sector). Although not all programs assessed were as successful as initially hoped, "compared with the record of most current health, nutrition, and population programs, most of the initiatives . . . produced marked improvements in reaching the poor that sometimes approached the dramatic."[82] This study suggested that a key first step towards success is the recognition of the extent to which existing delivery system exclude the most deprived. Second, there is a need for flexibility and experimentation with room for monitoring and adjustment where failures arise. There is no one-size-fits-all approach to basic goods provision.

We must also keep in mind that help in basic goods provision can come from the *private sector*. Indeed, in the early 2000s, a small revolution occurred in the world of international business that has important implications for basic goods provision. This is the notion of the "bottom of the pyramid" or "base of the pyramid" (BoP) introduced by the late University of Michigan business professor C. K. Prahalad and his associates.[83] This BoP concept noted that there was a vast market of poor individuals who individually possess only very small amounts of purchasing power but collectively (at perhaps four billion individuals) represent a very large market. The BoP idea alerted everyone, but particularly the private sector, to the fact that there was money to be made from providing basic goods and services to poor people, engaging in what was called the "great leap downward."[84]

Since the introduction of the concept, numerous case studies have emerged of successful BoP strategies. Many more such cases will emerge. For us in this book, it is a reminder that, although there is *public responsibility* to ensure that basic goods and services are universally provided, there is also a potentially beneficial *private interest*. More important, global corporate strategy of certain types can and should play a role in basic goods provision. The entire burden does not need to be on the public sector.

BoP business strategies can dovetail nicely with the emerging phenomenon of *frugal innovation*. Frugal innovation involves developing varieties of durable goods that are simpler, cheaper, and therefore more accessible to low-income households. In a *New York Times* article, Sarika Bansal stated,[85]

> The concept challenges innovators to do more with less. In general, the creators of frugal innovations strive for them to be affordable, sustainable, lightweight and rugged. Wherever possible, they should be made locally with renewable materials. Perhaps most important, they should be developed with the end user in mind, taking into consideration things like power outages in her village, the distance she must walk to seek medical assistance and religious customs she considers sacred.

Examples of relevant frugal innovation are small, inexpensive refrigerators (with battery backup for power outages), mobile banking, low-cost water purifiers, low-cost solar power, clean birth kits, new brick presses for affordable housing, and hand-held medical diagnostics devices. The Massachusetts Institute of Technology's D-Lab (Development Through Dialogue, Design, and Dissemination) is one center for this approach. The combination of frugal innovation with BoP business strategies can help ensure success in basic goods provision.

Summary

Basic goods are those goods and services that objectively meet basic human needs. They are the preconditions for much of what we potentially value in life, be it well-being, human flourishing, or capabilities expansion. They also comprise a system of narrowly universal, minimalist ethics, and thereby, of subsistence rights within the larger human rights system. Basic goods consist of nutritious food, clean water, sanitation, health services, education services, housing, electricity, and human security services. The basic goods approach argues that basic goods provision should be *given priority* over other sorts of provision, that we should embrace the objective of the *universal provision of basic goods*.[86]

A focus on basic goods provision can support both growth processes and capabilities expansion or human development, bridging the gap between these two perspectives and agendas. Delivery systems for basic goods and services are inevitably complex, with no one-size-fits-all solution to recommend. But potential success has been demonstrated in a variety of contexts using a broad range of approaches, both public and private.

The challenges of basic goods provision are vast, however. In Part II of this book, I address a number of these challenges and attempt to suggest some tentative ways forward in the face of increasing populations in the very same regions where current deprivations are most concentrated. There we can see how the concepts and principles developed in this chapter apply to each of the basic goods and services I identified.

Notes

1. Griffin (1986), p. 17.
2. Griffin (1986), p. 42 (italics in original).
3. See Pigou (1932), p. 759.
4. Maslow (1943), p. 390.
5. Doyal and Gough (1991), p. 50. See also Dean (2007, 2009) who emphasized the role of a "politics of need" in social policy. Dean (2010) stated: "Human need represents a pivotally important concept and, arguably, the single most important organizing principle in social policy. It is pivotal in the sense that it connects the understanding of our *interdependency* as human beings with arguments about the rights that we can assert against each other. Although it remains, potentially, an elusive concept, human need is the concept from which other eminently practical and strategic approaches can flow. Or, to put it more precisely, it is through contests over human need that social policy is made" (p. 2).
6. Braybrooke (1987), p. 5.
7. Braybrooke (1987), p. 31.
8. See Copp (1992).
9. For example, as stated by Griffin (1986), basic needs are "what we need to survive, to be healthy, to avoid harm, to function properly" (p. 42). As Copp (1992) put it "The matters of basic need . . . are things a person requires regardless of his goals or desires" (p. 250). Our use of the notion of need here relates to what Dean (2010) called both "absolute need" and "basic need" and what Corning (2000) referred to as "ground zero."

10. Or, as stated by David Copp (1992), "There is obviously a distinction between a preference and a basic need. I need a nutritious diet regardless of what kind of diet I prefer. And although I prefer chocolate ice cream to vanilla, I do not need ice cream at all" (p. 251).

11. For one source on objective list theory, see Arneson (1999).

12. Doyal and Gough (1991) had a more expansive treatment of needs, and the same goes for Copp (1992). More recently, Costanza et al. (2007) defined quality of life as "the extent to which objective human needs are fulfilled in relation to personal or group perceptions of subjective well-being" (p. 269).

13. As Braybrooke (1987) emphasized "Would it not be foolish . . . in the absence of any effective rival concept, to belittle needs because they solve only part of our difficulties? They will have solved the most important part" (p. 180).

14. Levine and Rizvi (2011), p. viii.

15. Levine and Rizvi (2011) stated that "if you are poor your problem is that you lack something vital for living. This does not become a problem because others have what you do not; it is a problem regardless of the circumstances in which others find themselves" (p. x).

16. Levine and Rizvi (2011), p. 2.

17. Chapman (2007), p. 154.

18. United Nations Children's Fund ([UNICEF] 2013, 2015).

19. Braybrooke (1987), p. 31.

20. One can make an argument that *clothing* should be included in this list. I have excluded it to keep the book to a manageable size. One can also argue that the emphasis on electricity should be expanded to include energy deprivations more broadly. Once again, I am restricting the focus.

21. See Chapter 1 endnotes for citations.

22. For a very useful review of development ethics, see Crocker (2008).

23. Bok (2002), p. 1.

24. Walzer (1994), pp. 17, 39. Similar considerations can be found in Hampshire (1989).

25. Shue (1996), p. 18 and Braybrooke (1987), p. 131.

26. Lisk (1977), p. 186.

27. Bok (2002), p. 49.

28. Proceduralism (also known as contractarianism) sets out steps by which "reasonable" or "cooperative" procedures can unearth ethical principles. Walzer (1994) noted that "the procedural minimalism turns out to be rather more than minimal" (p. 12). Blackburn (2001) noted that the proceduralist approach "just disguises the real source of values, which must lie elsewhere" (p. 126). Gould (2004) criticized the approach for being "excessively cognativist" and for "translating substantive moral norms into matters of procedural decision" (p. 93).

29. Walzer (1994), p. 2.

30. See, for example, *The Economist* (2007).

31. See Shue (1996).

32. Hertel and Minkler (2007) also made just this point: "Virtually all conceptual justifications for human rights apply to the basic economic right to an adequate standard of living. Suppose that any individual was not entitled to an adequate standard of living. She would not be entitled to be free from malnutrition, would not be entitled to be free from the exposure to the elements, and would not be entitled to be free from crippling illness. Such an individual would not be assured of the minimal conditions necessary to be autonomous (self-legislating), or a purposeful agent because she could not fulfill her own plans or objectives, or be free from deprivations. The claim becomes most obvious in the case of people who die from malnutrition, exposure, or sickness" (p. 5). See also Copp (1992).

33. Shue (1996) made a distinction between security rights and subsistence rights. For simplicity here I consider security rights as one kind of subsistence right to be met via the provision of human security services. I take up this issue in earnest in Chapter 11.

34. See, for example, Braybrooke (1987) and Osiatyński (2007). More generally, Dembour (2010) outlined four approaches or schools to human rights thought: the natural school, the deliberative school, the protest school, and the discourse school. In this book, I do not

directly associate with one of these schools of thought, but the basic goods approach is probably most closely tied to the deliberative and protest schools.

35. See Pigou (1932), p. 759.
36. Stewart (1989), p. 348.
37. Hertel and Minkler (2007), p. 1. See also Goodhart (2007) and Chapter 11.
38. United Nations General Assembly (1948).
39. United Nations General Assembly (1966b), p. 7.
40. The United States has not ratified the International Covenant on Economic, Social and Cultural Rights.
41. United Nations General Assembly (2010), p. 2.
42. United Nations General Assembly (1966b), p. 8.
43. As I discuss in Chapter 7, there is a tension present here between the right to health *itself* (qualified by "highest attainable") and the right to health *services*.
44. United Nations General Assembly (1966b), p. 8.
45. United Nations Committee on Economic, Social and Cultural Rights (1991).
46. In the case of human rights to water, see Jeffords and Shah (2013). More generally, see Rao and Min (forthcoming).
47. See Kaldor, Martin, and Selchow (2007).
48. See Rao and Baer (2012).
49. See Randolph, Fukuda-Parr and Lawson-Remer (2010) and https://serfindex.uconn.edu/.
50. On this broader economic and social rights agenda, see Minkler (2013).
51. *The Economist* (2014g).
52. *The Economist* (2015a).
53. As shown in Chapter 7, this distinction becomes important in the realm of healthcare services as a distinction between providing primary healthcare and providing *health itself*. The latter is no doubt something we would ideally like to see, but it falls outside of the basic good approach.
54. In a dissection of the Afghanistan case, for example, *Financial Times* columnist Gidean Rachman (2012) noted that the country's institutional superstructure in the form of a new constitution is of less value than had been anticipated because three quarters of the Afghan population cannot read it. On the role of education (cognitive skills) and institutions in growth processes, see Hanuschek and Woessmann (2008).
55. Barrera (2007).
56. See Cohen and Soto (2007), for example. For the specific case of Latin America, see Hanuschek and Woessmann (2012).
57. See Pio (1994). For empirical evidence on the contribution of health to growth, see Weil (2007) and Barro (2013).
58. See, for example, Filmer, Hammer, and Pritchett (2000); O'Donnell (2007); and Chapter 3 of Banerjee and Duflo (2011).
59. See, for example, Barrett (2011) and references cited in Chapter 8.
60. See Hanuschek and Woessmann (2012) for the case of Latin America, for example.
61. See Lelieveld et al. (2015). On China see *The Economist* (2015e).
62. For example, in their fundamental contributions, Braybrooke (1987); Copp (1992); and Shue (1996) established the logic of basic subsistence rights but are vague on the actual challenges of provision. The same could be said of the basic needs approach to development as formulated by Streeten (1979).
63. Stewart (1989), p. 361.
64. See, for example, *The New York Times* (2017).
65. Diamandis and Kotler (2012), p. 9.
66. See Ingraham (2014).
67. See, for example, Chapters 8 and 9 of Diamandis and Kotler (2012). On Qatar, see Fuchs (2012) and *The Economist* (2014b).
68. Olson (1996).
69. Auerswald (2012), p. 21.

70. As Katherine Boo (2012) observed regarding women entrepreneurs in her *Beyond the Beautiful Forevers*, a book on life in a Mumbai slum, "for the poor of a country were corruption thieved a great deal of opportunity, corruption was one of the genuine opportunities that remained" (p. 28).

71. Marx, Stoker, and Suri (2013).

72. From a different ideological perspective, unconditional cash transfers also find support from some parts of the human rights community as a way of achieving a *basic income guarantee*. At the surface, these human rights researchers are saying something similar to the economists, but there are also significant differences. In particular, in the human rights tradition, the basic income guarantee is conceived of as a way to liberate individuals and households from the vagaries of labor markets, as well as to meet subsistence rights. See, for example, Goodhart (2007).

73. As discussed in Chapter 6 of Goldin and Reinert (2012), the same can be said of international remittances.

74. Kenny (2011), p. 129.

75. See Lomelí (2008) and Fiszbein and Schady (2009).

76. See, for example, Vandeveer (1986).

77. World Bank (2011a), p. 136.

78. Banerjee and Duflo (2011), pp. 68–70.

79. See World Bank (2003) and Devarajan and Reinikka (2004).

80. Devarajan and Reinikka (2004), p. 154.

81. See Gwatkin, Wagstaff, and Yazbeck (2005).

82. Gwatkin, Wagstaff, and Yazbeck (2005), p. 58.

83. See Prahalad and Hart (2002); Prahalad and Hammond (2002); and Hart and Christensen (2002).

84. We can get of sense of the spirit of the idea from C. K. Prahalad and Stuart Hart (2002), who stated, "It is time for multinational corporations to look at globalization strategies through a new lens of inclusive capitalism. For companies with the resources and persistence to compete at the bottom of the world economic pyramid, the prospective rewards include growth, profits, and incalculable contributions to humankind. Countries that still don't have the modern infrastructure or products to meet basic human needs are an ideal testing ground for developing environmentally sustainable technologies and products for the entire world" (pp. 2–3).

85. Bansal (2014).

86. This is what Braybrooke (1987) referred to as the *principle of precedence*, in which matters of need are prioritized over matters of preference only.

PART II

CHALLENGES

4

Food

When most people think of basic goods, they think of food. Food is a crucial part of what sustains us as human beings, both biologically and socially, and is closely tied to the wonderful multitude of human cultures. But despite the diversity of food cultures around the world, we can identify the objective human *needs* behind them, and these needs are what make food a basic good. For example, although there is disagreement as to the actual amount, it is clear that human beings have minimum caloric requirements.[1] Beyond these caloric needs, there are also requirements for key vitamins, minerals, and other micronutrients for minimal health and to help ward off infections. For this reason, we need to make a distinction between food and *nutritious* food. In most (not all) contemporary circumstances, the nutrition density of food is actually of greater concern than caloric intake.[2] This distinction is becoming increasingly important as traditional food systems are replaced by more industrialized food systems in what is called the *nutrition transition*. This ongoing process does not always contribute to positive health outcomes and is indeed implicated in increasing levels of obesity and noncommunicable disease.[3]

Food deprivation is currently widespread and, despite the claims of technology optimists, likely to remain so. At the time of this writing, just under 800 million (one in nine) people suffer from chronic hunger in the sense that they are not well nourished enough for an active life.[4] This is down from over one billion in 1990, a decrease as a percent of total global population from 14 to 11 percent. Currently, approximately one in four children in low- and middle-income countries suffers from stunting as a result of these deprivations.[5] These global figures mask regional differences presented in Table 4.1. For example, one in four residents of sub-Saharan Africa are undernourished, with the total number of undernourished individuals in that region having *increased* from 1990 to 2014. And the absolute number of undernourished individuals is highest in South Asia where approximately one in six individuals are affected.

Beyond these failures to meet caloric requirements, vitamin and mineral deficiencies abound. Table 4.2 gives an approximate sense of this problem. Vitamin and mineral deficiencies, particularly of the top four (iron, zinc, iodine, and

Table 4.1 **Undernourishment by Region (given in millions of persons and percentages)**

Region	Number (millions)		Percentage of Population	
	1990–1992	*2012–2014*	*1990–1992*	*2012–2014*
Africa	182	233	28	20
Sub-Saharan Africa	176	220	33	23
Eastern Africa	104	124	47	32
Asia	742	512	24	12
South Asia	291	281	24	16
Eastern Asia	295	145	23	10
Latin America and the Caribbean	66	34	15	6

Source: FAO (2015).

vitamin A) can cause severe health problems, even contributing to death. Other deficiencies (calcium, sodium, vitamin B9, vitamin C, and vitamin D) can cause any of a number of health problems. When we include all of these deficiencies, we encounter even more widespread levels of deprivation, on the order of two billion individuals worldwide.[6]

Deficiencies in basic vitamins and minerals as well as other micronutrients make individuals more susceptible to many infectious diseases. This is particularly true of children where deaths from infectious diseases tend to be most concentrated.[7] For example, the United States Center for Disease Control reports that improved vitamin A nutrition can prevent up to 2.5 million child deaths per year.[8] What is more, infectious diseases can rob an individual of nutrition. We therefore have a two-way causality or, in many deprived situations, a downward spiral in which undernutrition and infectious diseases interact with often deadly outcomes.[9] Nutritious food is therefore a critical basic good for maintaining health. Unfortunately, nutrition deprivation is widespread, contributing to a lack of *food security* for many millions of individuals.[10]

How Many Need to Be Fed?

The twentieth century was an era of unprecedented population growth. World population increased from under two billion in 1900 to approximately six billion in 2000. The world reached seven billion people in 2012. United Nations projections suggest that we will add approximately two billion people by 2050 and

Table 4.2 **Nutritional Deprivations**

Micronutrient/ Vitamin	Deficiency Effects	Number Affected (where available)
Top four		
Iron	Anemia, impaired cognitive development, and increased susceptibility to infectious diseases	Approximately 4 billion iron deficient and approximately 2 billion anemic
Zinc	Infections, diarrhea, impaired brain and motor functions, and increased susceptibility to infectious diseases	Deficiencies responsible for approximately 400,000 deaths each year
Iodine	Hypothyroidism (goiter), brain damage (including mental retardation), and pregnancy complications	Millions deficient
Vitamin A	Blindness due to corneal lesions, increased susceptibility to infectious diseases, and potential organ failure	Deficiencies cause approximately 500,000 children to go blind each year
Others		
Folate/folic acid	Spina bifida and anencephaly	At least 225,000 children a year
Calcium	Rickets, osteoporosis	
Sodium	Nausea and fatigue	
Vitamin B9	Birth defects	
Vitamin C	Scurvy and increased susceptibility to infectious diseases	
Vitamin D	Rickets	
Beta-carotene	Increased susceptibility to infectious diseases	
Selenium	Increased susceptibility to infectious diseases	
Copper	Increased susceptibility to infectious diseases	
Riboflavin	Increased susceptibility to infectious diseases	

Source: Bhaskaram (2002); the United States Center for Disease Control (https://www.cdc.gov/immpact/micronutrients/index.html); and *The Economist* (2011b).

an additional two billion by 2100 for a total world population of approximately eleven billion.[11] So humankind faces a central question: given the fact that we currently *fail* to provide adequate nutrition for nearly 800 million people, can we provide nutrition for an *additional* four billion individuals by 2100? Most current answers to this question are as follows: "Malthusian doomsday scenarios were always wrong in the past, so yes, we can adequately feed an additional 4 billion people by 2100. And technology will help us do it." This is the response we need to assess.[12]

The additional four billion people challenge is serious because many of these individuals will live in places that are already struggling to provide adequate nutrition as well as other basic goods. Current United Nations forecasts suggest that approximately three billion of the additional individuals will reside on the African continent, which outside of South Asia, is the place where basic goods deprivation is most concentrated.[13] And another one billion individuals will be in Asia, including South Asia, the second area where basic goods deprivation is most concentrated. As the United Nations Food and Agricultural Organization (FAO) put it, "The majority of countries whose population growth is expected to be fast in the future are precisely those showing inadequate food consumption and high levels of undernourishment. Most of them are in sub-Saharan Africa."[14]

We do want to avoid simplistic Malthusian claims about our inability to feed people. In the past, these *have* turned out to be wrong. We can see the limitations of these simplistic approaches by revisiting Paul Ehrlich's famous 1968 book *The Population Bomb*. Here the author claimed,[15]

> The battle to feed all of humanity is over. In the 1970s the world will undergo famines–hundreds of millions of people are going to starve to death in spite of any crash programs embarked upon now. At this late date nothing can prevent a substantial increase in the world death rate.

This did not happen. In fact, there *were* "crash programs" in the form of the Green Revolution in agriculture and declining fertility rates in a large number of countries. But the question is whether we can conjure up an equivalent happy scenario for the remainder of the 21st century in the face of a new set of factors: climate change, significantly depleted fisheries, limited additional agricultural lands, soil degradation, declining growth in agricultural yields, water shortages (to be discussed in Chapter 5), depleted phosphate mines, and foreign land grabs (what is politely called "agricultural investment") in Africa and elsewhere.[16] Despite the soothing words of the anti-Malthusians, caution suggests that we should at least entertain the *possibility* that it may not be as easy this time around.

There has been some confusion with regard to the required increase in food production to meet both increased populations and increased demand from rising incomes. One standard statement is that the FAO estimated that we will need to *double* food output by 2050. This statement has appeared in many places, including in the pages of *The Economist*. But that statement is wrong. The 2006 FAO report in question actually put the required increase at various levels depending on the food groups involved, typically between 50 and 70 percent.[17] In addition, there was a *more recent report* from the FAO indicating the required increases were approximately 50 percent for cereals and 75 percent for meat.[18] The doubling of food output by 2050 is not necessary, but are we going to increase food output sufficiently?

The FAO's most recent projections suggested that the absolute number of malnourished people will decline steadily from the current level of 800 million to approximately 300 million in 2050. This is indeed a relatively happy scenario. There are things that could get in the way, however, as the FAO acknowledged. First, the scenario is based on the United Nations projections of population. There is emerging evidence that these might be low in the case of Africa, precisely where most food security issues are concentrated.[19] Second, there is a great deal of uncertainty about the potential role of climate change in disrupting agricultural output. If some of the more dire predictions turn out to be true, the happy scenario would need to be revised. Third, there can be any number of potential plant blights that could emerge in the remainder of the 21st century. Fourth, political and energy issues (including conflict and biofuel demand) are great unknowns.[20]

The role of such uncertainties can be clearly seen in the recent case of Syria. The headlines of the Syrian uprising and subsequent civil war have been all about politics. Lurking in the background to the political events, however, was a drought during the years 2006 to 2010. The drought struck the northeastern Jezira region that was long considered the nation's "breadbasket" and was the focus area for agricultural development projects including significant increases in land areas under (unsustainable) irrigation. The Jezira region also was characterized by severe basic goods deprivation that was exacerbated by the drought and depleted groundwater resources.[21] These difficulties eventually led to a massive migration of hundreds of thousands of residents out of the Jezira region to southern cities in the search for better fortunes. Many of these migrants ended up in what were in effect refugee camps around the cities of Damascus and Aleppo. This humanitarian crisis was one significant cause of the political crisis that began in 2011 and continues at the time of this writing with a very significant refugee crisis.

This disastrous case contains elements present in many other countries as well: lack of resource management, increased population pressure, climate change, basic goods deprivation, and consequent lack of human security. With regard to climate change, there is increasing evidence that, outside of higher latitudes, this process is placing downward pressure on agricultural yields.[22] It is conceivable that a number of these elements could come together in a pernicious manner in some specific regions such as the Sahel region of Northern Africa, precipitating political crises that spill back on food security.[23] Given human predilections to mismanagement and conflict, it would not be wise to rule out such possibilities.[24] And with such possibilities, how can we be sure that we can meet what has been identified in the United Nations system as the *right to food*?

The Right to Food

As discussed in Chapter 3, the right to food is part of the current United Nations system of human rights. Recall that Article 25 of the UDHR states that "Everyone has the right to a standard of living adequate for the health and well-being of himself and of his family, including food, clothing, housing and medical care and necessary social services."[25] Further, Article 11 of the ICESCR recognizes "the right of everyone to an adequate standard of living for himself and his family, including adequate food, clothing and housing"[26] and "to be free from hunger." Also recall that Article 11 of the ICESCR calls for countries: "To improve methods of production, conservation and distribution of food by making full use of technical and scientific knowledge, by disseminating knowledge of the principles of nutrition and by developing or reforming agrarian systems in such a way as to achieve the most efficient development and utilization of natural resources" and "Taking into account the problems of both food-importing and food-exporting countries, to ensure an equitable distribution of world food supplies in relation to need."

The right to adequate nutrition is a *basic right* as identified by philosopher Henry Shue.[27] This reflects the fact that, as noted by Susan Randolph and Shareen Hertel, "realization of the right to food is essential to the fulfillment of *other* human rights."[28] The 1999 General Comment 12 on the ICESCR specified the right to food in terms of universal "physical and economic access at all times to adequate food or means for its procurement."[29] It also specified this right to food in terms of availability, access, and utilization. The FAO suggested that states "should promote adequate and stable supplies of safe food through a combination of domestic production, trade, storage and distribution." It also suggested that the right to food depends on the presence of adequate safety nets to protect vulnerable populations and to address crises and disasters, and it explicitly linked the right to food to the basic goods water, sanitation, and health services.[30]

The right to food touches on a very large number of policy realms. Randolph and Hertel effectively characterized these realms in terms of availability, access, and utilization as presented in Table 4.3. The range of policies here is large, from the presence of storage facilities to global food aid policies. Cultural factors also

Table 4.3 **Components of the Right to Food**

Right to Food Component	Selected Policy Areas
Availability	Amount of cultivated and irrigated land
	Agricultural and trade policies
	Storage, transport, and processing
	Research and development and rural extension
	Food aid policies
Access	Income distribution and poverty
	Access to land, credit, and agricultural inputs
	Food prices
	Access to extension services
	Safety nets
	Levels of education and health
	Levels of conflict
	Gender equity
Utilization	Access to water, sanitation, and health services
	Food safety programs
	Prevalence of disease
	Knowledge levels of nutrition, health, and sanitation

Source: Adapted from Randolph and Hertel (2013).

can come in to play with regard to gender equity. General Comment 12 allows for diversity in the way that different country governments approach these policy areas provided that these governments ensure "at the very least, the minimum essential level required to be free from hunger." So there is no required, one-size-fits-all approach imposed from the outside.

Much of the remainder of this chapter focuses on the *availability* issue, considering a number of supply-side factors, including land, water, and agricultural yields. I pay particular attention to sub-Saharan Africa because that is where it appears the most acute issues will arise. In the realm of *access*, Randolph and Hertel correctly noted that the prevalence of poverty is a critical factor. These researchers stated, "Poverty is among the more important factors that affect access, and may well be the most important factor. Poor households have limited access to land, productive inputs, food production technologies, and credit. They are also likely to have limited education and be the most vulnerable to civil strife."[31] This is where *shared* or *inclusive* growth can make a real difference.[32] As was emphasized in Chapters 1 and 3, this is not automatic but must be nurtured through policies to ensure wide ownership of assets and appropriate redistribution of incomes. *Utilization* issues, particularly the provision of water, sanitation, and health services, will be covered in ensuing chapters.

Global Policy Environment

In principle, an open world economy would support the goal of meeting the right to food and promoting food security. In particular, international trade should be able to address any country-level mismatch between demand and supply, and foreign direct investment could bring necessary resources and technologies to where they are most needed. Unfortunately, a number of considerations suggest that there are limitations to these positive outcomes. As emphasized by a number of observers, rich-world agricultural subsidies place a significant constraint on developing-country farmers, thereby compromising food availability.[33] The same is true of tariff escalation, which inhibits developing-country producers from moving down value chains in food production into higher value added products.

In principle, trade liberalization efforts can support food security and agricultural development concerns, but this is clearly not always the case.[34] For example, the Uruguay Round's Agreement on Agriculture[35] was largely designed with rich country interests in mind. This contributed to an environment of mistrust that has persisted to the current agricultural negotiations in the stalled Doha Round of multilateral trade negotiations. In the area of global finance, some markets (particularly bonds and commercial bank lending) can be characterized by significant market imperfections.[36] To the extent that such imperfections also affect food commodity markets, the outcomes could be detrimental for food security.[37] In the case of foreign aid, food aid remains a somewhat successful realm of endeavor, but much more can be done to direct it to better nutritional outcomes.[38]

Although in general we can hope that processes of globalization will support the provision of food and the promotion of food security, this outcome is far from guaranteed in the current global environment. For this reason, simply invoking global integration as a factor in promoting food security is not always valid.

Land, Water, and Yields

There is more land to be cultivated to increase food production in the face of expanding populations. The FAO has estimated that there is an additional 1.4 billion hectares of additional, cultivable land available.[39] But this organization and other researchers also emphasized that very little of this can actually be counted on to increase production.[40] Much of it is highly concentrated in a handful of countries, and these are not necessarily the countries where increased food demands will take place. Of course, international trade can address this mismatch between demand and supply, but even then lack of access, lack of infrastructure, concerns over deforestation, and the presence of disease (e.g., malaria) make relying on significantly increased amounts of land impractical.

In the case of water, further constraints emerge. Agriculture demands approximately 70 percent of the world's supply of freshwater resources. Additional water resources for irrigation are by-and-large not located where they are needed for additional cultivation. Even where they are coincident with needs, as I discuss in Chapter 5, they are often in declining availability. Therefore, along with additional lands, additional water cannot be counted on to increase production in most cases. So with both land and water in limited supply, we must turn to other means of increasing agricultural output.

Despite our association of technology with manufacturing, agriculture is a technological process in which a great amount of innovation has occurred. There was the end of the fallow system and the introduction of nitrogen-fixing crops in the 18th century, the development of chemical fertilizers and agricultural transport revolutions in the 19th century, and further innovations in fertilizer and the widespread introduction of tractors in the 20th century. And most recently, the Green Revolution technologies beginning in the 1960s introduced brand-new (semidwarf) varieties of basic grain plants.[41]

All of these innovations have had significant impacts on agricultural yields. Assessment of yield in the current era typically focuses on data since 1960. Most reasonable assessments of past yield trends since 1960 show these to be *linear*.[42] Importantly, a linear trend line implies declining growth *rates*. In addition, there is emerging evidence that, for a number of important crops and countries, this linear relationship has broken down and given way to *yield plateaus* where biological limits have been reached.[43] Thus, there seems new territory to explore with regard to agricultural yields where the past may not be a good guide to the future.

Biotechnology versus Agroecology

The way forward in providing basic goods in the form of nutritious food is partially blocked by a highly politicized debate between advocates of biotechnology on the one hand and agroecology on the other.[44] This current debate has its roots in a past debate between the father of the Green Revolution, Norman Borlaug, and the mother of the agroecology movement, Vanda Shiva. This difference of views is alive today in the claims on part of the biotechnology (agroscience and agroindustry) community that the way forward is through the continued genetic modification of crop varieties, and the claims of others that the way forward is through the application of agroecology. These two communities do no rub along well together, particularly when the issue at hand is genetic modification or genetic engineering.

Without calling a halt to the biotechnology-based approach to sustaining agricultural yields, we do need to give agroecology the chance it deserves. Why? First, there is a general principle of diversifying approaches to reduce the risks of failure in a single approach. Second, agroecology involves the reduced use of water and energy inputs, two increasinglybinding constraints. Third, agroecology tends to hold more carbon in biomass than biotechnologybased agriculture and therefore tends to limit agriculture's own contribution to global warming, which is substantial.[45] Fourth, agroecology is less intensive in negative environmental externalities associated with high levels of fertilizer and pesticide use. Fifth, agroecology has shown it can (if not *always* will) work.[46] It is also important to note that agroecology is not antiscience. It is simply a different form of science that might prove to be equally promising.

So a cautious approach is to move forward on both biotechnology and agroecology to further examine how they can contribute to increased agricultural yields in a sustainable manner. Moving beyond the tension between the two approaches for the foreseeable future could allow the continued assessment of how each can contribute to the goal of food security.

An African Green Revolution

If one thing emerges from considerations of increased populations and potential problems of food insecurity, it is the need for attention to the African continent. This is the where up to three billion individuals will be added and happens to be the place where the Green Revolution largely did not occur. Consider Figure 4.1. This plots cereal yields between 1961 and 2014 for high-income ("developed") countries as a whole and for five "developing" regions: Latin America and the Caribbean, South Asia, East Asia and the Pacific, the Middle East and North Africa, and sub-Saharan Africa.[47] The two lowest series are for the Middle East and North Africa, and sub-Saharan Africa. The case of sub-Saharan Africa is the most concerning. Here, cereal yields in metric tons per hectare were 0.8 in 1961 and 1.5 in 2014. In other words, in a half century, barely nothing has improved.

It is possible to look at this poor record in a more positive light. One way of interpreting the sub-Saharan Africa yield stagnation is in terms of a *yield gap*. This represents a potential improvement that can be drawn on if conditions were more favorable. As shown in Figure 4.1, it should be possible to increase yields in sub-Saharan Africa from 1.4 metric tons per hectare to perhaps three metric tons per hectare as in South Asia. This change would provide at least twice as

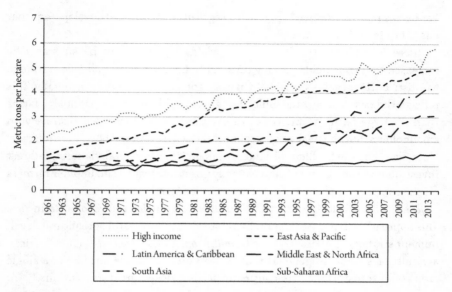

Figure 4.1 Cereal yields (metric ton per hectare) for high income countries and selected developing regions, 1961 to 2014. Source: World Bank, World Development Indicators.

much food. This is both an opportunity and a challenge. It is an opportunity because there is room for improvement right where we need it. It is a challenge because it is not always clear *how* this improvement will take place.

It is always risky to use past models for current problems, and this is the case for agricultural development in Africa. To be more specific, a Green Revolution in Africa cannot be modeled on the Green Revolution in Asia. Instead, it should be characterized in the following three ways:

- It should be primarily based on *smallholder farmers*.
- It should be *multicrop*, not single crop.
- It should be primarily *agroecological*.

Attention should be given to Africa's *smallholder farmers* who compose approximately three-quarters of Africa's farmers. To ignore them would perpetuate the rural poverty that stands in the way of food security and thereby exacerbate the very deprivations that need to be overcome. It would replicate the less-successful agricultural development of Latin America rather than the more successful case of East Asia. East Asia's hidden success was actually its initial focus on broad-based agricultural development rather than its more well-known manufacturing exports. And a significant part of Latin America's failure has been a poorly conceived approach to agricultural and rural development that has led to inequitable outcomes.[48]

There is evidence that smallholder yields in Africa can be substantially increased.[49] Even if yields initially turn out to be lower for smallholder farmers, the distributional gains would help in basic goods provision more generally. This reflects the fact that income multiplier effects are larger for smallholder farms than for large farms.[50] This is not to say that we need to focus *exclusively* on smallholders, but the neglect of smallholders in Africa would be a grave mistake. Note also that the problem of large, commercial agricultural via foreign direct investment (to be discussed later) already poses a threat to smallholder farmers on the continent and a bias toward (very) large farms.

The Green Revolution in Asia was primarily a single-crop revolution in rice. This approach will not work in Africa. Instead, any successful agricultural development strategy in Africa needs to be *multicrop*. As *The Economist* put it, "African agriculture is so heterogeneous that no leap forward in the farming of a single crop could transform it. The continent needs a dozen green revolutions."[51] To be more specific, forward progress needs to address *multi-agroecological systems*. One study actually identified *seventeen* distinct agroecological systems in Africa that were further reduced to four main types: the *maize-mixed system*, based primarily on maize, cotton, cattle, goats, poultry, and off-farm work; the *cereal/root crop-mixed system*, based primarily on maize, sorghum, millet, cassava, yams, legumes, and cattle; the *irrigated system*, based primarily on rice, cotton, vegetables, rain-fed crops, cattle, and poultry; and the *tree crop-based system*, based primarily on cocoa, coffee, oil palm, rubber, yams, maize, and off-farm work.[52] Even with these four systems (no less seventeen), there will simply not be a single approach to the problem of increasing yields.

Initially, the need to account for multiple agroecological systems may seem to be a drawback. But it does have one significant advantage. A problem inherent in the single-crop Green Revolution was that it further reduced the range of foods being consumed by emphasizing the already-dominant trio of wheat, rice, and corn. A new Green Revolution that focuses on a number of different crops could have substantial nutritional benefits by supporting more diverse diets and thereby ensuring a supply a more micronutrients to those who need them most. This would also help to mitigate the worst characteristics of nutrition transitions as they take place.[53]

Within a multipronged approach to improving yields, researchers have identified a number of important elements.[54] First, there needs to be a comprehensive approach to identifying new varieties of plants that are suitable to particular local environments in which there has been the input and feedback of the local users of the new varieties, the farmers themselves. Second, there needs to be a very careful look at the supply of nutrients and water to the farmers and their multiple crops. This needs to include a variety of mixes of organic and inorganic fertilizers appropriate for specific environments, as well as smart irrigation that is also locally tailored. Third, pest and disease control needs to be approached on a biological basis, with a reduced role for pesticides and herbicides vis-à-vis standard, modern agriculture. This is partly an issue of the plant varieties themselves but also requires integrated pest management. Finally, there needs to be a comprehensive look at storage, transportation, and delivery systems from the perspective of loss reduction. Currently, a great deal of Africa's crops is wasted due to lack of appropriate infrastructure.

None of this is going to be easy, and it is made all the more difficult because of the need to respond to multiple agroecological systems simultaneously. But the evidence suggests that it can be done using primarily (not exclusively) science-based, *agroecological* principles. A recent review points to successes around the continent in a variety of areas, including crop varieties, agroforestry, soil conservation, integrated pest management, livestock and fodder crops, and aquaculture.[55] The range of experiences with agroecological farming improvements in Africa is accumulating quickly and is surprisingly vast. So despite the inherent difficulties, there is now much to draw on.[56]

Recall from Chapter 2 the notion of technological optimism. Exhibit A for this idea is the rapid adoption of mobile phones in low-income countries and their use for myriad applications, including mobile banking. There is potential for applications of mobile phones in agricultural extension. This is particularly important for agroecology-based innovations that tend to be quite knowledge intensive. There might be a way of marrying mobile phone success with agroecology innovation. Recent evidence from Gujarat India suggests that mobile-phone-based agricultural extension can be effective. The examined case was essentially a "hot line" that put farmers in touch with extension agents.[57] Although preliminary, the results suggest that farmers do indeed have a demand for information via mobile telephony and that this information affects farmer behavior. It therefore does seem likely that mobile phones can deliver agricultural extension services in support of agroecological development.

Infrastructure and Waste

Infrastructure is important for the provision of food because the trip from farm to table is a difficult one in many places. This contributes to the problem of *food waste*. Most estimates of food waste globally suggest that up to one third of food is wasted.[58] In high-income countries, this is not an infrastructure problem but rather a problem of how food is retailed and consumed. In low- and middle-income countries, food waste is a problem of infrastructure that robs up to 500 calories per person.[59] It also wastes any inputs that went into the wasted food such as water, energy, and fertilizers. So along with increasing yields, decreasing waste is critical for the provision of food.

The list of factors contributing to food waste in low- and middle-income countries is relatively long and includes lack of storage facilities on farms (silos and other granaries), poor road networks, poor transport vehicles, lack of refrigeration facilities, lack of electricity, and poor packaging. More important, waste is distributed across the food value chain. This variety of factors is described in Table 4.4 and makes addressing food waste a challenge because there are so many actors and processes involved. However, there is evidence that, the lower is per capita income (and hence the greater is nutrition deprivation), the more food waste is concentrated earlier in the value chain (in the production-to-processing stages).[60] This insight can help to focus efforts at reducing food waste.

So where to begin? Perhaps the best place is with poorer, smallholder farmers. Efforts to eliminate waste can be combined with efforts to increase yields. Poorer smallholders are the individuals who face the greatest challenges early in the food value chain and the greatest food insecurity. Simultaneously, however, efforts need to be made to improve transport infrastructure between smallholder farmers and their primary markets. But progress can be made immediately and effectively at the level of smallholder farmers by deploying simple metal silo technologies. These simple technologies have a number of critical advantages:[61]

- Maintaining the quality of the stored grain.
- Avoiding or reducing the need for insecticides.
- Significantly reducing postharvest losses.
- Better enabling smallholder farmers to adapt to fluctuating grain prices.
- Preventing rodents and other pests/pathogens that can harm consumer health.
- Being built locally with easily available materials, contributing to the rural nonfarm economy.

There is no reason why current efforts to disseminate this simple silo technology cannot be significantly extended, addressing issues of finance, knowhow, and access to materials. This is an area where multilateral developing institutions, public–private partnerships, and NGOs can all play a role. It is also a potential case of the "bottom of the pyramid" or BoP strategy discussed in Chapter 3 and to be carried out by the private sector.

Silos do not solve all of the problems, however. This can be seen in the case of milk, for example, which spoils very easily.[62] A way to address this problem has emerged from a collaboration among Global Good, the Bill and Melinda Gates Foundation, SNV Ethiopia, and the Kenya-based Ashut Engineers Limited. This collaboration spawned a much-improved Mazzi milk jug (cost US$5.00) that will

Table 4.4 **Food Waste Along the Value Chain in Low- and Middle-Income Countries**

Stage of Food Value Chain	Sources of Food Waste
Harvesting	Crops left in field or eaten by birds and rodents; poorly timed harvest
Threshing	Poor threshing technology
Drying, transport, and distribution	Poor transport infrastructure; losses to spoiling and bruising
Storage	Pests, disease, spillage, and contamination
Processing	Poor process technology and contamination
Product evaluation and packaging	Discard, inappropriate packaging, losses to rodents, lack of refrigeration
Marketing and distribution	Damage during transport, poor handling, lack of refrigeration
Postconsumer	Lack of refrigeration and cooking fuel

Source: Adapted from Parfitt, Barthel, and Macnaughton (2010).

be produced in Ethiopia and distributed throughout East Africa.[63] The Mazzi milk jug was designed with smallholder dairy-farmers in mind and explicitly tries to respond to their whole value chain. It appears to be another example of ways forward in effectively reducing food waste.

Land Grabs

An emerging and critical issue for food security is foreign "agricultural investment" or what may be more accurately called *land grabs*. These are taking place on large scales in the Congo, Ethiopia, Ghana, Kenya, Madagascar, Malawi, Mali, Mozambique, Nigeria, Senegal, Sierra Leone, Sudan, Tanzania, Uganda, Zambia, and Zimbabwe, in other words, all over the African continent. The investing (land-grabbing) countries are Saudi Arabia, the United Arab Emirates, China, and India. To understand the potential impacts of land grabs, consider what the normally reticent World Bank has said about this practice:[64]

> Large-scale expansion of cultivated area poses significant risks, especially if not well managed. As the countries in question often have sizable agricultural sectors with many rural poor, better access to technology and markets, as well as improved institutions to improve

productivity on existing land and help judiciously expand cultivated area, could have big poverty impacts. Case studies illustrate that in many instances outside investors have been unable to realize this potential, instead contributing to loss of livelihoods. Problems have included displacement of local people from their land without proper compensation, land being given away well below its potential value, approval of projects that were only feasible because of additional subsidies, generation of negative environmental or social externalities, or encroachment on areas not transferred to the investor to make a poorly performing project economically viable.

This is World Bank speak for "There is a big problem here!" This trend has been described as "geopolitical," and it is. The use of the term *land grab* suggests that there is are nonmarket elements to the process as indicated by the World Bank, and this is often the case.[65] It is also important to recognize that the country governments involved often play facilitating roles in response to agribusiness and other firms who benefit from the transactions.[66] In some instances, the impetus for land grabs is the set of issues to be discussed in Chapter 5, namely water scarcity. This has been the case for Saudi Arabia and the United Arab Emirates, for example. Because most of the activity is in sub-Saharan Africa, the problem will make increased food output in Africa for Africans all the more difficult. This represents a failure of national and global governance taking place on the African continent.[67]

We also need to be cautious with emerging arguments that agricultural investment is an important way to close the sub-Saharan Africa yield gap shown in Figure 4.1.[68] Although this may indeed be the case, the way the yield gap would be closed would not be in a manner that would benefit smallholder farmers on the continent or help to provide more nutritious food to those who need it. Without increased oversight of these ongoing land grabs (and intervention where necessary), ensuring the adequate provision of food for an additional three billion individuals on the African continent will be difficult.

Fisheries

Approximately three billion people rely on fish for 20 percent of their protein intake, and over four billion rely on fish for 15 percent of their protein intake.[69] Fish consumption also provides a number of essential micronutrients and therefore comprises an important type of nutritious food. This food source is under stress, however, with at least one third of global fish stocks and two thirds of high-seas fish stocks being over-exploited.[70] The world is beginning to run out of fish at the same time that is going to host four billion more persons. Most of these fish are harvested from the oceans, and the oceans themselves are under unprecedented stress through human exploitation and mismanagement. This is an example of what economists call a "common pool resource" in which overuse is to be expected. Although we do have the United Nations Convention on the Law of the Sea (UNCLOS), it does not sufficiently address conservation issues. There is also a United Nations Fish Stock Agreement, but whereas 165 countries (not including the United States) have ratified UNCLOS, only eighty have ratified the Fish Stocks Agreement. Another developing issue is the movement of fish stock toward higher latitudes in response to climate change, further depleting fish stocks at lower latitudes.[71]

Fish capture has plateaued for many years now, with increased demand for fish being satisfied by aquaculture or fish farming. It is important to keep in mind, though, that farmed fish rely on food that ultimately must come from the sea or inland waters. Aquaculture is also very prone to disease outbreaks. Thus there are limits to its continued expansion on a sustainable basis to replace traditional ocean catches. To some extent, these limits can be relaxed by including more plant matter in farmed fish diets, but the limits remain.

What is needed to ensure the future supply of fish? First, the environmental components of the UNCLOS must be strengthened through what is known as an "Implementing Agreement."[72] Second, closer attention must be paid to our marine scientists rather than to our politicians. When these scientists give us warnings, they must be heeded.[73] Third, there must be a *mandatory* global registry of fishing boats to help curtail the quarter of the annual global catch that is actually illegal. Fourth, there must be a dramatic curtailment of the approximately US$35 billion spent each year by rich countries subsidizing their fishing fleets. Fifth, attention needs to be paid to the negative externalities of modern agriculture in the form of fertilizer runoff. This has contributed to over 400 dead zones in the oceans where there is essentially no life at all.[74] This issue tilts the biotechnology versus. agroecology debate previously discussed in the direction of agroecology.

Livestock

The expanded consumption of livestock-based food sources poses a challenge to the sustained, universal provision of food. Although it does not make sense to condemn livestock-based diets in general, there are a number of reasons why the transition to these diets (the "livestock revolution") is problematic. First, about one third of total cereal production is dedicated to livestock feed (in high-income countries it can be closer to three-quarters), and the FAO projects a significant expansion (on an absolute basis) of cereal feed production in developing countries.[75] Second, on a caloric basis, the transformation of these cereals into meat is inefficient (only on the order of 10 percent), and particularly so for the case of intensively raised (as opposed to grazed) cattle. Third, livestock production is one of world's largest users of land, both directly and indirectly through feed cereal cultivation. For these three reasons, livestock production competes with direct consumption for the world's cereals. Fourth, relevant for the next chapter, livestock production is very water intensive and therefore inefficient in that respect as well. Fifth, the nutrition transition to livestock-based diets, along with increased consumption of sugar and fat, is having substantial impacts on health in the form of the "diseases of affluence" such as diabetes, high blood pressure, heart disease, and obesity.[76] Sixth, the intensive production of livestock is associated with significantly negative environmental externalities, largely in the form of point-source pollution.

For these reasons, we need to be very cautious toward the increased role of meat-based diets. As noted by Randolph and Hertel, "the global increase in per capita meat consumption . . . reflects growing food security for some and reduced food security for others."[77] This is not a call for the *elimination* of livestock. When not raised intensively, poultry and pigs can be a very efficient source of protein, vitamins, and minerals and therefore play a critical role in diets. But intensive cattle and pig production needs to come under *very close scrutiny* with subsidies removed wherever they exist.[78] More broadly the sustained traditions of largely plant-based diets and the return to these diets where they have been largely abandoned can play a tremendous role in freeing up resources for basic food provision. Indeed, by one estimate, the cereals used for livestock could provide enough calories to feed over three billion people.[79]

Demand Side Issues and Provisioning Processes

As is apparent from these discussions, the supply side of food provision is a complicated matter. On top of this, there are a few key *demand side complications* to consider as well. The first is that basic-goods deprived individuals and families may not have full information with regard to what constitutes *nutritious* food. Nutrition is a relatively new science and tends to be characterized by a lack of consensus (and fads) as it gets translated into popular information sources. Understanding of basic vitamins was not complete until the mid-1900s, while understanding of the full range of micronutrients is still an ongoing process. The notion that a slum-dwelling parent would have absorbed this information in a complete way is not realistic. The other problem (if "problem" is the right word) is that poor people, like all people, seek to enjoy themselves. One way of enjoying oneself is to forgo nutritious food for "tasty" food. This issue was graphically captured by George Orwell in a famous quote from his book *The Road to Wigan Pier*, describing conditions in Great Depression England:[80]

The basis of their diet . . . is white bread and Margarine, corned beef, sugared tea, and potato–an appalling diet. Would it not be better if they spent more money on wholesome things like oranges and wholemeal bread, or if they even . . . saved on fuel and ate their carrots raw? Yes it would, but the point is that no human being would ever do such a thing. The ordinary human being would sooner starve to death than live on brown bread and raw carrots. And the peculiar evil is this, that the less money you have the less you are inclined to spend it on whole-some food. . . . When you are unemployed, you don't *want* to eat dull wholesome food. You want to eat something a little *tasty*. There is always some cheap pleasant thing to tempt you.

Another way of enjoying oneself is to purchase things *other than food* even when your diet is fall less than ideal. These could include televisions, festivals, videogame parlors, and much more.[81] It is not that the poor are stupid in this regard. It is just that they are very much like the nonpoor in their behaviors. Indeed, the pursuit of something tasty is part of what drives increasing obesity rates in both rich and poor countries.

In Chapter 3, I considered the extent to which cash transfers or conditional cash transfers are sufficient to address basic goods provisioning. I noted that the types of informational and behavioral issues that were encountered here in the case of food might limit the effectiveness of these provisioning mechanisms. In a review of this issue in their well-received book *Poor Economics*, Abhijit Banerjee and Esther Duflo concluded that "It is probably not enough just to provide the poor with more money, and even rising incomes will probably not lead to better nutrition in the short run."[82] Providing money with conditions, however, can help, and there are other policy interventions that can be useful as well.[83]

One area of consensus is the importance of focusing on pregnant mothers and their infants. Malnutrition among pregnant women is widespread among women in India and sub-Saharan Africa.[84] Evidence suggests that programs that improve the nutrition experience for these individuals have positive repercussions for both health and education throughout the children's lives.[85] These types of positive outcomes are worth supporting with government activity to enhance positive food choices for poor families, including rural families. Estimates suggest that substantial progress in improving maternal and child nutrition could be achieved at a cost of US$10 billion per year, approximately the monthly expenditure of the United States for the Iraq War.[86]

A next step would be school feeding programs. Although the results of assessments of these programs are not uniform, there is evidence that they contribute to both nutritional outcomes and to school enrollment. Some studies suggest that they also contribute to cognitive development, but this is not universally the case.[87] Combining school feeding programs with deworming and micronutrient supplementation can help to boost the positive impacts of such programs. In some circumstances, it is also possible to use local smallholder farmers as suppliers for school feeding programs, an approach known as home-grown school feeding (HGSF).[88]

Another route to helping to overcome demand-side constraints is a process known as *biofortification*. This involves increasing the nutrient density of staple crops in ways that might be unknown to the consumer. This is a project pursued by HarvestPlus (AgroSalud in Latin America), part of the global Consultative Group for International Agricultural Research (CGIAR). The crops and nutrients being addressed are beans (iron), cassava (vitamin A), maize (vitamin A), pearl millet (iron), rice (zinc), sweet potato (vitamin A), and wheat (zinc). Preliminary assessments suggest that such an approach holds promise.[89]

Despite previously mentioned concerns of Banerjee and Duflo, in a number of countries, more comprehensive systems of food provisioning are often part of broader anti-poverty schemes, including direct food transfers, the cash transfers, and CCTs discussed in Chapter 3, as well as food for work and cash for work programs. Evidence does suggest that cash transfers are spent on food and contribute to increased food security, although there is also some evidence that the poorest prefer food transfers to cash transfers.[90] In addition, the use of biometrics and smart cards to ensure that the transfers are going to the right individuals seems to be a very promising targeting of technology.[91] Such programs, and continued local experimentation, need ongoing assessment.

These examples suggest that there are viable ways forward to making some immediate progress in expanding basic goods provisioning in the case of nutritious food. Pursuing these potential avenues and assessing their relative merits are both imperative to meet emerging food security challenges.

Summary

About 800 million people currently lack access to basic goods in the form of nutritious food. Despite relatively optimistic scenarios with regard to a forecasted decline in this number even in the face of projected population increases, it is best to be cautious. Many things could interfere with this happy outcome. The lowest and stagnant agricultural yields are to be found in Africa, particularly sub-Saharan Africa. These yield gaps must be reduced if Africa is to successfully host an additional three billion citizens. Although larger farms and standard, biotechnological approaches to agricultural development should not be ignored, emphasis also needs to be placed on smallholder farmers and agroecological approaches, as well as simple storage technologies to reduce food waste. At the same time, attention needs to be quickly placed on ensuring that further degradations to global fish stocks are avoided. Subsidies to fishing and to intensive livestock production need to be steadily withdrawn. On the demand side, we cannot be certain that households will always pursue nutritious choices, but a focus on pregnant mothers and their infants, as well as school feeding programs, can help. Evidence also suggests that food and cash transfers can sometimes play a helpful role.

Notes

1. Depending on the source, caloric requirements vary between approximately 2,200 and 2,700 calories.
2. See, for example, Chapter 2 of Banerjee and Duflo (2011) who stated that "the problem may be less the quantity of food than its quality, and in particular the shortage of micronutrients" (p. 39). Micronutrients were also recognized in General Comment 12 of the 1996 World Food Summit (United Nations High Commissioner for Human Rights, 1999).
3. On the "nutrition transition, see Popkin (1993). For the case of the United States, see Olshansky (2014). Globally, approximately 1.4 billion people are overweight, and this can be seen as another form of malnourishment. See, for example, Swinburn et al. (2011).
4. FAO (2014, 2015).
5. See Black et al. (2013).
6. See *The Economist* (2014h).
7. See Bhaskaram (2002). This author nicely summed up the relationship of nutrient deficiencies and infectious disease as follows: "Micronutrient deficiencies and infectious diseases often coexist and exhibit complex interactions leading to the vicious cycle of malnutrition and infections among underprivileged populations of the developing countries, particularly preschool children. . . . Certain of the micronutrients also possess antioxidant functions that not only regulate immune homeostasis of the host, but also alter the genome of the microbes, particularly in viruses, resulting in grave consequences like the resurgence of old infectious diseases or the emergence of new infections" (p. 40).
8. See http://www.cdc.gov/immpact/micronutrients/index.html.
9. See Katona and Katona-Apte (2008).
10. The standard FAO definition of food security is as follows: "Food security exists when all people, at all times, have physical and economic access to sufficient safe and nutritious food that meets their dietary needs and food preferences for an active and healthy life."
11. For evidence that these United Nations population projections have validity, see Gerland et al. (2014). These authors concluded that "there is an 80% probability that world population . . . will increase to between 9.6 billion and 12.3 billion in 2100" (p. 234). For the most recent estimates, see United Nations (2015a).
12. For a review, see Goldin (2014).
13. See Guengant and May (2013); *The Economist* (2014c); and United Nations (2015a).
14. FAO (2012a), p. 2.
15. Ehrlich (1968), p. xi.
16. Many of these issues are discussed in the remainder of this chapter and in Chapter 5 on water. On the phosphorus issue, see Neset and Cordell (2012) and Van Vuuren, Bouwman, and Beusen (2010).
17. See FAO (2006).
18. See FAO (2012a).
19. See Guengant and May (2013) and *The Economist* (2014c).
20. On the potential relationships between population growth and conflict, see Goldstone (2002).
21. See de Châtel (2014) and Beck (2014).
22. See Inter-Governmental Panel on Climate Change (2014).

23. See Raleigh (2010) and Hendrix and Salehyan (2012) for this possibility. For a more general discussion of food security and conflict, see Barrett (2013). *The Economist* (2017a) reported on twenty million people being at risk of starvation in Nigeria, Somalia, South Sudan, and Yemen, largely due to conflict.

24. Despite the prominent role of climate change skeptics in the United States, the United States Center for Naval Analysis Military Advisory Board (2014) issued yet another warning about the "threat multipliers" inherent in climate change. It stated, "In many areas, the projected impacts of climate change will be more than threat multipliers; they will serve as catalysts for instability and conflict. In Africa, Asia, and the Middle East, we are already seeing how the impacts of extreme weather, such as prolonged drought and flooding—and resulting food shortages, desertification, population dislocation and mass migration, and sea level rise—are posing security challenges to these regions' governments" (p. 2).

25. See United Nations (1948).

26. See United Nations (1966b), p. 7.

27. Shue (1996).

28. Randolph and Hertel (2013), p. 21, emphasis added.

29. United Nations High Commissioner for Human Rignts (1999).

30. Again, see FAO (2005).

31. Randolph and Hertel (2013), p. 47.

32. See, for example, Suri et al. (2010).

33. See, for example, Peterson (2009) and Goldin and Reinert (2012).

34. See, for example, Matthews (2014).

35. World Trade Organization (2018), Annex 1A.

36. See, for example, Goldin and Reinert (2012), particularly Chapter 4 and references therein.

37. See, for example, Ghosh (2010).

38. See, for example, Haddad and Isenman (2014). Also, as noted by Goldin and Reinert (2012), for example, "Concerns are often raised about the efficacy of foreign food aid, . . . which may ultimately serve to undermine the markets of domestic growers while at the same time providing a captive source of demand for producers in the donor country" (p. 115).

39. FAO (2012a).

40. See also Godfray et al. (2010).

41. See Chapter 7 of Smedshaug (2010).

42. See, for example, FAO (2012a) and Grassini, Eskridge, and Cassman (2013).

43. See Grassini, Eskridge, and Cassman (2013) and Pretty (2008).

44. De Schutter (2010) defined *agroecology* as follows: "As a set of agricultural practices, agroecology seeks ways to enhance agricultural systems by mimicking natural processes, thus creating beneficial biological interactions and synergies among the components of the agroecosystem. It provides the most favourable soil conditions for plant growth, particularly by managing organic matter and by raising soil biotic activity. The core principles of agroecology include recycling nutrients and energy on the farm, rather than introducing external inputs; integrating crops and livestock; diversifying species and genetic resources in agroecosystems over time and space; and focusing on interactions and productivity across the agricultural system, rather than focusing on individual species. Agroecology is highly knowledge-intensive, based on techniques that are not delivered top-down but developed on the basis of farmers' knowledge and experimentation" (p. 6). Agroecology is sometimes referred to as "conservation agriculture."

45. The Inter-Governmental Panel on Climate Change (2014) listed "sustainable agriculture and forestry" as a mitigating factor for climate change.

46. See, for example, Pretty et al. (2006), a review of nearly 300 projects in the developing world.

47. By construction, the "developing" regions are confined to the developing countries within them. So, for example, the East Asia and Pacific region does not include Japan.

48. See Kay (2002); Davis (2004); and *The Economist* (2017g).

49. See Pretty, Toulmin, and Williams (2011). Tscharntke et al. (2012) also noted that "smallholders rather than large-scale commercial farmers are the backbone of global food security" (p. 54).

50. See De Schutter (2010).

51. *The Economist* (2016c), p. 14.

52. See InterAcademy Council (2004).

53. See, for example, Frison et al. (2006).

54. See, for example, InterAcademy Council (2004).

55. Pretty, Toulmin, and Williams (2011). See also De Schutter (2010).

56. For further evidence on the potential for forward progress, see *The Economist* (2016c).

57. See Cole and Fernando (2012).

58. FAO (2011a). See also Parfitt, Barthel, and Macnaughton (2010).

59. World Bank (2014).

60. FAO (2011a).

61. See Tefere et al. (2011).

62. Global Good reported, "In Kenya alone, approximately 80 percent of the country's milk is produced by more than a million small-scale farmers who rely on it for subsistence and, in many cases, income. Unfortunately, this milk often spills or spoils before it can be sold. This is due in part to the fact that farmers have limited options available for collecting, storing and transporting milk. Traditional milk pails can be kicked over during milking and gather contaminants that accelerate spoilage. From these pails, farmers often pour milk into repurposed jerry cans that break easily and are difficult to clean" (http://www.intellectualventures.com/news/press-releases/global-good-partners-with-organizations-in-africa-to-support-local-dairy-fa).

63. See http://mazzican.com.

64. World Bank (2011b), p. xlii.

65. See Anseeuw et al. (2011). The authors defined land grabs as being characterized by one of the following elements: "(i) In violation of human rights, particularly the equal rights of women; (ii) not based on Free, Prior and Informed Consent of the affected land-users; (iii) not based on a thorough assessment, or are in disregard of social, economic and environmental impacts, including the way they are gendered; (iv) not based on transparent contracts that specify clear and binding commitments about activities, employment and benefits sharing, and; (v) not based on effective democratic planning, independent oversight and meaningful participation" (p. 11).

66. Nally (2015) noted that "While states have a role in facilitating land grabs it is clear that the big player is private capital" (p. 3).

67. For more on this issue, see Cotula (2012) and Nally (2015).

68. Again see World Bank (2011b).

69. FAO (2012b).

70. *The Economist* (2014a). *The Economist* (2017d) reports even more dire statistics, namely that "almost 90 percent of wild stocks are fished either at or beyond their sustainable limits" (p. 11).

71. See Inter-Governmental Panel on Climate Change (2014).

72. Efforts to do this in 2012 (at the Rio+20 meetings) failed largely thanks to the United States (not even a UNCLOS signatory) and Russia.

73. For example, *The Economist* (2014a) reported: "For decades scientists warned that the European Union's fishing quotas were too high, and for decades fishing lobbyists persuaded politicians to ignore them. Now what everyone know would happen has happened: three-quarters of the fish stocks in European waters are over-exploited and some are close to collapse" (p. 52).

74. See Diaz and Rosenberg (2008).

75. FAO (2012a). The developing-country share of feed production will be over half by 2050. Developing countries already produce more meat than developed countries. See also *The Economist* (2017d).

76. See, for example, Popkin, Adair, and Ng (2012).

77. Randolph and Hertel (2013), p. 53.

78. On the increasingly intensive nature of pig production in China and its implications for global feed grain demand, see *The Economist* (2014i).

79. United Nations Environmental Program (2009). This estimate adjusts for the loss of the caloric value of the meat itself.
80. Orwell (2001, orig. 1937), p. 88.
81. The ICESCR recognizes the right "to take part in cultural life," and this was reiterated in General Comment 21 of the Committee on Economic, Social and Cultural Rights (CESCR) (United Nations Economic and Social Council, 2009). Festivals might be one such cultural right, and this raises a possible trade-off in meeting both subsistence and cultural rights.
82. Banerjee and Duflo (2011), p. 39.
83. For one study supporting the potentially positive impacts of CCTs on the consumption of nutritious food, see Attanasio and Mesnard (2006).
84. See, for example, Coffey (2015). In percentage terms, the malnutrition among pregnant women is significantly worse in India than in sub-Saharan Africa.
85. See Victora et al. (2008) and Maluccio et al. (2009).
86. See Bhutta et al. (2013).
87. See Bundy et al. (2009) and Jomaa, McDonnell, and Probart (2011).
88. Home-grown school feeding programs are currently being explored by the World Food Program, the Gates Foundation, and the New Partnership for Africa's Development.
89. See Bouis et al. (2011), for example.
90. See Miller, Tsoka, and Reichert (2011) on Malawi and Ahmed, Quisumbing, and Hoddinott (2007) on Bangladesh. The latter authors reported that some very poor women prefer food transfers to cash transfers to ensure that their husbands do not make off with some of the cash.
91. See, for example, Gelb and Decker (2012).

5

Water

Water is the quintessential basic good.[1] If a person does not consume water for a week, he or she will most likely die. It is unfortunate that water is also the basic good with the most pressing provision challenges in the 21st century. Indeed, we do not need to wait for further climate change and a world population of ten to eleven billion to encounter the water provision problem. It exists right now. Approximately 700 million people do not have access to an improved drinking source.[2] A standard projection within the United Nations is that, by 2025, nearly two billion individuals will be living in countries or regions with absolute water scarcity, and approximately five billion will be living in water-stressed environments of one type or another.[3] Even if these United Nations projections prove to be somewhat overestimated, the scale of the problem is vast.

The lack of access to clean water varies substantially by region of the world. As is evident from Figure 5.1, the majority of individuals without access to clean water reside in sub-Saharan Africa, East Asia, and the Pacific and South Asia. These three regions account for approximately 600 of the over 700 million people without access to clean water. Recall from Chapter 4 that these are also the regions where food provision problems are most pressing. Some specific examples of significant water scarcity are as follows:

- China is in the midst of a serious water crisis. For the country as a whole, water scarcity is at 400 cubic meters per person, while in Beijing, it is just 100 cubic meters per person. The overuse of water in China is actually causing thousands of rivers in the country to simply disappear with remaining rivers being increasingly polluted.[4]
- Himalayan glaciers supply water to one billion individuals in South Asia and parts of China. The best evidence suggests that these glaciers are beginning to melt. Although the future date of their potential disappearance has been a cause for controversy, the fact that they are indeed melting appears to be incontrovertible, posing a potentially severe if somewhat long-term problem for these regions.[5] Indeed, the effects are already being felt in Pakistan.[6]

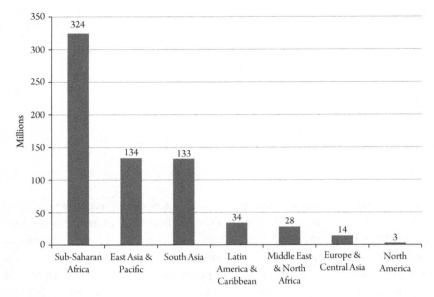

Figure 5.1 Lack of improved water source, 2015 (millions of people). Source: World Bank, World Development Indicators.

- Saudi Arabia uses over one million barrels of oil a day (out of a total production of about eight million barrels of oil per day) to power desalination plants for the Kingdom's drinking water, a mere fraction of its total water use.[7] Even with this substantial energy use to provide drinking water, the country is using groundwater resources at an unsustainable rate.
- The government of Iran has declared water to be a national security issue and is drawing up contingency plans for water rationing for the over twenty million people living in the greater Tehran metropolitan area. As a visible symptom, the increased use of water from rivers flowing into the famous Lake Urmia has caused one of the largest salt water lakes on the planet to drastically shrink in size down to only 5 percent of its original volume.[8]
- In Australia, a major agricultural exporter, drought in the Murray-Darling Basin has had a detrimental impact on agricultural output and exports, particularly to South and Southeast Asia. Further drought episodes (potentially due to climate change) could pose a significant threat to Australia's sustained agricultural exports.[9]
- Per capita water resources in Yemen have fallen to approximately 100 cubic meters per person per year, one tenth of the water poverty level and one fifth of the absolute water poverty level.[10] As discussed further in Chapter 11, recent political conflict has made addressing the water scarcity issue difficult, and it is not inconceivable that Yemen's capital, Sana, will simply run out of water.[11] This increasing water scarcity has, in turn, contributed to the conflict.[12]

- In the United States, the years 2013 to 2014 found the large state of California facing what, by some estimates, was the worst drought in half a millennium.[13] This had Californians literally praying for rain, threatened California's huge agricultural sector, and involved a number of communities running completely out of water. Although this situation improved in 2017, long-term trends are still a concern.
- Beginning in 2010, Djibouti faced significant drought and water scarcity problems. Impacts of these include failed wells, reduced agricultural output and internal refugee flows that all caught the attention of aid and disaster-relief organizations.[14]
- Despite the image of monsoons and their role in India, this country is dependent on groundwater resources for the bulk of its irrigation and drinking water. Estimates suggest that 60 percent of these groundwater resources will be degraded by 2035 with anticipated significant health consequences.[15]
- The state of São Paulo in Brazil hosts one fifth of the country's population. Beginning in 2014, São Paulo began to experience the worst drought since 1930.[16] Many reservoirs were at unprecedentedly low capacity, in one case even drying up completely. Some schools have been forced to close due to lack of water, and some hydropower stations may need to curtail their generation levels.
- Egypt is entering into a water crisis with it per capita water supply falling each year. The country is expected to reach absolute water scarcity by 2025, but there are many villages and even hospitals that are already completely running out of water.[17]

Lack of access to clean water contributes to a number of health problems. The consumption of contaminated water leads to a significant disease burden, robbing individuals of health and potentially life itself. For example, diarrheal disease, often caused by the consumption of contaminated water is responsible for up to two million deaths per year, most of these being infants and children.[18] In turn, improvements in water quality bring significant benefits. For example, in the case of the United States, one study estimated that the economic return on clean water improvements in the late nineteenth and early twentieth centuries was over 20 to 1. This same study also estimated that these improvements were responsible for almost half of the total reduction in mortality in major cities, approximately three quarters of the infant mortality reduction, and almost two thirds of child mortality reduction.[19] Similar, if less dramatic, results have been estimated for Argentina.[20] In addition, some observers see a minimum level of water security as a precondition for sustained growth.[21] Finally, lack of access to clean water imposes a water fetching burden on affected communities, and this burden falls most heavily on women with both economic and health consequences.[22] For all of these reasons, clean water is a good investment.

The health contributions of clean water, as well as its economic returns, suggest that the under provision of this basic good is problematic. More and more, however, the under provision of clean water is also assessed in terms of a failure to meet basic subsistence rights. To understand this, we need to briefly consider the evolution of the recognition of the right to water.

The Right to Water

Clean water directly addresses a fundamental human need. Recognizing this and starting some time ago, there were calls for the establishment of water as a human right and the identification of *minimum thresholds* in which to define this right.[23] Despite these early calls, the major milestones in recognition of the right to water have been relatively recent.[24] In 2003, CESCR[25] issued General Comment 15 on two articles of the ICESCR, namely Article 11 on the right to an adequate standard of living and Article 12 on the right to health. In this comment, the CESCR stated that "the human right to water entitles everyone to sufficient, safe, acceptable, physically accessible and affordable water for personal and domestic uses" *and that* "the human right to water is indispensable for leading a life in human dignity. It is a prerequisite for the realization of other human rights." In this way, the CESCR echoed the work of Henry Shue on basic rights as discussed in Chapter 3.[26] As I emphasized in that chapter, basic goods are basic rights.

In adopting a basic subsistence rights approach, the CESCR stipulated obligations to respect (not to interfere), protect (to prevent third parties from interfering), and fulfil (to take positive steps at provision) the right to water. In particular, General Comment 15 set out government obligations to "ensure access to the minimum essential amount of water that is sufficient and safe for personal and domestic uses"[27] and "to take measure to prevent, treat and control diseases linked to water." As such, General Comment 15 is very much in line with the minimum ethics approaches discussed in Chapter 3. The CESCR also stipulated that the many components of the United Nations, as well as the World Bank and the International Monetary Fund, should cooperate with one another to ensure the universal provision of clean water.

In 2010, two additional actions were taken within the United Nations system concerning the right to water. The United Nations General Assembly passed a resolution (A/RES/64/292)[28] acknowledging clean drinking water as a human right. In addition, the United Nations Human Rights Council passed a resolution (A/HRC/RES/15/9)[29] affirming drinking water as a human right and confirming this right as legally binding on states. The Human Rights Council acted again in 2014 with a further resolution (A/HRC/RES/27/7).[30] This resolution "Reaffirms that the human right to safe drinking water and sanitation is essential for the full enjoyment of life and to all human rights, and recalls that it is derived from the right to an adequate standard of living and is inextricably related to the right to the highest attainable standard of physical and mental health, as well as to the right to life and human dignity."[31] In doing so, the Human Rights Council linked the right to water with a number of other central subsistence rights concerns. Finally, an increasing number of countries recognize the right to water as part of their constitutional environmental rights.[32]

These subsistence rights developments are important steps, but they do not automatically lead to improvements in *provision*. Indeed, one recent review of the human right to water noted a number of potential stumbling blocks:[33]

> While the UN's 2010 Resolution has provided opportunities to realize equitable access to safe water and sanitation, policymakers will face a series of obstacles in implementing the human right to water and sanitation through global water governance, national water policy and water and sanitation outcomes. Despite avenues for implementation, realization of the right to water and sanitation may be hampered by diverse factors, including (i) lack of political will, (ii) financial constraints, (iii) limited access to infrastructure, (iv) lessened administrative capacity for implementation, coordination and monitoring of rights based policies, (v) insufficient technical capacity to ensure water and sanitation polices are followed, (vi) incomplete information on populations without access and (vii) challenges of water scarcity compounded by climate change.

As I noted in Chapter 3, it is always important to focus on determinants rather than outcomes to best ensure progress. But as can be seen here, there are real constraints to improving the determinants in the case of clean water provision. One key constraint, mentioned earlier, is climate change.

Climate Change, Water Availability, and Human Security

Climate change is going to have a significant impact on the ability to provide water as a basic good. One set of observers stated that "Water is the principal medium through which the societal stresses of climate change will be manifested."[34] In its 2014 report, the Intergovernmental Panel on Climate Change (IPCC) suggested that changes in precipitation patterns and melting snow and ice (including glaciers) will alter hydrological systems and reduce water availability. In subtropical regions, the IPCC expected reduced availability of both surface and groundwater resources and increased competition for water among sectors. In addition, the *quality* of water is expected to decrease with increased concentrations of sediment and pollutants. The report also suggested that there will be increased risks of the loss of rural livelihoods as a result of declining availability of drinking water and water for irrigation, particularly in semi-arid regions.[35]

Some described the 2014 IPCC report as distinctive, but it really just ratified what we previously knew about climate change trends and water availability. There also has been a movement that has been notably skeptical of the IPCC and its work. This is indeed unhelpful given the magnitude of the potential impacts of climate change on water availability. The skepticism appears to be part of a larger dismissal of science as a means of inquiry with an important role in informing public policy. Its continued presence and influence on policy processes (subsidized by specific interests) bodes ill for our ability to confront the challenges of climate-changed-induced water scarcity and the satisfaction of the right to clean water.[36]

So although access to clean water is a basic subsistence right, the insights of climate science, as well as the population projections discussed in Chapter 4, suggest that meeting this subsistence right will become increasingly difficult. Technological change will help to address some of this difficulty, and I describe some of these technologies here. But as always, technological fixes and the technological optimism surrounding them need to be carefully assessed rather than exaggerated.

As indicated in Table 3.1 of Chapter 3 and as discussed in detail in Chapter 11, human security is an important basic good or service. Unfortunately, humans are prone to violence, and the armaments to support this violent behavior are widely available even when other basic goods and service are not. There have been many suggestions that "water is the new oil" and that "future wars will be fought over water." If this is the case, climate-change-induced water scarcity, in combination with significantly increased populations, could do grave damage to human security. Empirical research suggests that water scarcity can indeed lead to conflict, and we saw an example of this in the case of Syria (discussed in Chapter 4) and in Yemen (discussed in Chapter 11).[37] This is the bad news. The good news is that evidence also suggests that institutions in the form of treaties drawn up for managing water resources mitigate the impact of water scarcity on the likelihood of conflict.[38]

So the answer to the water and human security conundrum partly lies in international relations, actually in a subfield known as international riparian relations that considers the design of river treaties. The more effort put into such institutional arrangements, the less likely will be water-inspired conflict. This is important because, once conflict begins, it is difficult to stop. And as conflict accelerates, the more difficult it becomes to provide a whole host of basic goods and the more severe the human suffering that takes place. Better to put the institutions in place now than to wait for conflict to occur.

Water and Food

In Chapter 4, I examined the challenges of providing food as a basic good. As mentioned there, agriculture demands approximately 70 percent of the world's supply of freshwater resources, and expanding agriculture in response to population increases will put water resources under increased stress. In addition, for the most part, additional water resources are not located where they are most needed for the expanding cultivation. These developments are going to make the provision of both nutritious food and clean water all the more difficult. As stated by one set of researchers on the subject, "water scarcity remains the primary constraint to global food production."[39] For this reason, climate change, water security, and food security are all now intimately tied to one another.

Although action on climate change is imperative, we also need to think in terms of adaptability. This can take place at many levels. As stated by the FAO, "Given the trends in agricultural demand for water—as driven by population, income growth and changing diets—a recurring challenge for agricultural water management is the question of *how to do more with less*."[40] These adaptations will need to take place at the farm level and include crop varieties, cropping patterns, water storage and management, and irrigation technologies. But higher-level adaptations also will need to be made with regard to overall water systems (including river basins), water allocation, and drought relief.

One specific effort underway is achieving more "crop per drop." This needs to take place across agricultural systems and across the divide of rain-fed and irrigated agriculture, as well as across smallholders and large commercial farms. A relevant initiative in this area is the system of rice intensification (SRI), an agroecology approach that attempts to reduce the water intensity of rice cultivation. Given that rice cultivation uses up to one third of total water use, SRI could make a significant difference.[41] SRI involves changing the way rice seedlings are transplanted, increased use of organic matter, modified and reduced irrigation, selective use of chemical fertilizers, and modified weeding. Water savings can range as high as 50 percent, and the technique has been successfully applied in over forty countries with increased yields (and incomes) being the norm. Lessons learned from SRI are being applied to wheat (system of wheat intensification or SWI), sugarcane (sustainable sugarcane initiative or SSI) and the Ethiopian grain teff (system of teff intensification or STI). Indeed, all of this is converging on a practice sometimes referred to as system of crop intensification (SCI). There is emerging evidence that this innovation will spread out among an increasing number of crops, both saving water and increasing agricultural yields.

An additional technology that can reduce the demand for water in food production systems is computer-assisted or "smart" irrigation. We have all seen irrigation systems (agricultural or residential) operating in the rain or launching plumes of water that evaporate in high heat. Smart irrigation can make sure this does not happen. It also can go further and tailor irrigation to soil and weather conditions. Wireless networks of sensors can detect local soil moisture, evapotranspiration, and solar radiation conditions. This, along with information on weather forecasts, can be used to optimize irrigation patterns. These technologies are spurring the private sector to enter into this emerging sector and provide a variety of products to farmers, as well as to residential and commercial properties. Smart irrigation is just one aspect of an emerging technology field knows as "precision agriculture." Evidence suggests that the water savings involved in precision agriculture can both significantly reduce water consumption (by perhaps 20 to 30 percent) while increasing yields.[42]

As discussed in Chapter 4, because meat is much more water intensive than grains, its increased consumption puts a significant strain on water resources. Limiting the "livestock revolution" will therefore be important to the provision of water as a basic good. This is largely the realm of consumer sovereignty and therefore not strongly responsive to policies. But to the extent possible, limiting livestock consumption is a necessary part of any attempt to achieve more "crop per drop." At a minimum, subsidies to the intensive livestock production should be steadily withdrawn.

The Industrial Ecology of Water

Although we are not always aware of it, there can be a great deal of water *embedded in* the products we consume, something that is referred to as "virtual water." In some cases, the amount of this virtual water embedded in a product can be high. Most consumers would be surprised to learn that their hamburger contains 2,400 liters of virtual water or that their T-shirt contains 2,000 such liters.[43] As a consequence of virtual water and international trade, product demand in one country can be transmitted across the globe as demand for water abroad. So even if a consumer does not live in a water-stressed environment, his or her consumption can have a detrimental impact in such environments.

These considerations bring us to the issue of industrial ecology and its impact on water availability. Water use encompasses the whole value chain, from natural resource extraction to final product delivery. As *The Economist* noted, "five big food and beverage giants—Nestlé, Unilever, Coca-Cola, Anheuser-Busch, and Danone—consume almost 575 billion litres of water a year, enough to satisfy the daily water needs of every person on the planet."[44] This gives us a sense of the vast scale of industrial water demand and the potential for saving virtual water through conservation. Indeed, businesses are slowly waking up to the fact that water use in their entire value chains is going to eventually impact them. The same *Economist* article reported: "José Lopez, the chief operating officer of Nestlé, notes that it takes four litres of water to make one litre of product in

Nestlé's factories, but 3,000 litres of water to grow the agricultural produce that goes into it. These 3,000 litres may be outside his control, but they are very much a part of his business." Where subsidies exist for the industrial and commercial agriculture use of water, they need to be seriously reconsidered to provide incentives for necessary conservation.

Nanotechnology

Overall, this book takes a cautious approach to technologists' claims to have "solved" problems through technological fixes. But this overall skepticism does not mean that we should ignore all potentially advantageous technological advances. In the area of water security, nanotechnology is one such advance. Nanotechnology involves the manipulation of matter at a very small scale, from the supramolecular down to the atomic. Among the technologically savvy, nanotechnology is a *big thing*. This potential big thing just might help in the provision of a few basic goods, but particularly so in the case of water.[45]

Relevant applications of nanotechnology to water security include: smart irrigation in the form of nanosensors, wastewater purification, and desalination. In the realm of smart irrigation, nanosensors can detect soil moisture to ensure that water is applied only when and where it is needed. As just discussed, if this technology were widely deployed, it would put a dent in the vast amounts of water used for irrigation. With regard to wastewater purification, there are nanotechnology applications in the areas of the adsorptive removal of pollutants, catalytic degradation and disinfection, and membrane filtration and desalination. There are applications of these technologies to the provision of drinking water (e.g., the removal of arsenic from groundwater), but also to the treatment of wastewater short of drinking water quality for use in agriculture. Although we do not want to second-guess the progress of science in these areas, membrane filtration appears to be the nanotechnology with the most relevant application to water treatment.

Water treatment issues are always front-and-center in water provision. But a new dynamic will emerge as water becomes scarcer over time. People will be forced to try to obtain water from more questionable sources, water that is compromised in some way. The list can include storm water, contaminated fresh water, brackish water, wastewater, and seawater. This is an area where nanotechnology can make a difference and why it could become increasingly relevant.[46] I summarize the relevant technologies in Table 5.1.

Technology optimists tend to suggest that nanotechnology has the water problem largely *solved*.[47] As usual with this group, this is an overstatement. First, nanotechnologies are, like many emerging technologies, dense in intellectual property protection. Indeed, one source described nanotechnology intellectual

Table 5.1 **The Application of Nanotechnology to Water and Wastewater Treatment**

Technology Type	Description	Applications and Readiness
Adsorption	Removal of organic and inorganic contaminants	Nanoadsorbents can be incorporated into existing water treatment systems if an additional separation unit is added to recover the nanoparticles. Applications to arsenic removal have been commercialized.
Membranes and membrane processes	Providing a physical barrier to remove unwanted elements	Incorporation of nanomaterials into membranes can improve their functionality in a number of dimensions. Application to water treatment is just starting.
Photocatalysis	An oxidation process that removes trace contaminants and microbial pathogens	Can enhance biodegradability of contaminants but is still largely in research laboratory stages.
Disinfection and microbial control	Removing microbes without producing harmful by-products	Useful for disinfection, membrane biofouling control and biofilm control. The nanomaterial Nano-Ag is being commercialized.
Sensing and monitoring	Monitoring contaminants at low levels of concentration	There is some current use, and research is underway on nanomaterials.

Sources: Qu, Alvarez, and Li (2013) and Sastry, Shrivastava, and Rao (2013).

property protection as a "thicket."[48] Intellectual property protection is what makes innovation possible but it is also what can slow down the *application* of new technology. This is one reason why, in this book, I consider technology to be a potentially restricted flow rather than a freely available stock, and this metaphor applies to nanotechnology.

Second, the journey from laboratory to commercial application can be a long one, and in the case of nanotechnology, sober scientific assessments are cautious.[49] Third, there is also the fact that, given that this is a rapidly moving research area, we are not well aware of any *downside risks*, particularly of nanomaterials.[50] By definition, we are talking here about tiny molecules or even smaller particles. The health and safety properties of these molecules and particles are largely unknown, and there are no existing systems in place to address any potential risks. For this reason, fast progress could actually be unsafe until further information and experience become available.

So an honest assessment of the role of nanotechnology in water security is that there is great deal of *potential*. In particular cases, applications are already being commercialized. But there is still quite a way to go before nanotechnology *solves* the water provision problem. A lot more research still needs to be done, more commercialization attempts need to be made, and public policy systems need to be put into place before this particular technological fix is widely applied.

Desalination

Desalination is a crucial part of water security in some countries. The International Desalination Association reports that there are more than 17,000 desalinations plants in the world in approximately 150 countries serving over 300 million people.[51] Most of us think about desalination in terms of seawater, but there are many locations where desalination can also address brackish water far from the sea. That said, the large-scale application of desalination is limited in landlocked countries.

Roughly speaking, there are two approaches to desalination: multistage flash (MSF) and reverse osmosis (RO). As a result of a number of innovations, the energy intensity of RO desalination has been significantly reduced.[52] A major leap, however, is to be found in the combination of RO with renewable energy sources. This is sometimes referred to as renewable energy sources desalination or RES–DES. Whether wind energy, photovoltaic or solar thermal technologies are most appropriate depends on the location and plant characteristics, but the evidence so far is the RES–DES holds out some promise.[53]

To cite one example, Barefoot College in India operates a solar-powered, RO desalination plant in India to desalinate brackish groundwater. It produces 600 liters of water per hour for six hours a day, serving 1,000 people.[54] This is the type of local and sustainable solution that could be made more widespread without great difficulty. At the other end of the scale, Saudi Arabia is building the world's largest solar-powered, RO desalination plant in Al-Khafji, Saudi Arabia. This project is a joint effort of the King Abdul-Aziz City for Science and Technology and IBM in the Joint Center for Nanotechnology Research. The plant will be based on concentrated photovoltaic technology. It is expected to serve 100,000 people, and Saudi Arabia plans a number of additional solar-powered plants for the future.[55] These two examples give a sense of the ability to adjust the scale of the RES–DES solution to the problem at hand.

As with the case of applying nanotechnology, RES–DES inspires technology optimists to claim that the clean water provision problem is largely solved.[56]As is the case with nanotechnology technologies (some of which new desalination technologies embody), the journey from laboratory to commercial application can be a long one. Some of the new technologies are still being debated in research journals, and the disposal of salt brine can be both problematic and expensive. So, no doubt, there will be real progress, but once again, the problem may be less than "solved."

Storage

Given the increased variability of waters supplies that are expected as climate change progresses, water storage technology becomes increasingly important. This association between variable supply and the need for storage can arise in other contexts as well, including in Chapter 10 on electricity. In the case of water, consider the following from one set of researchers on the subject:[57]

> Even relatively small volumes of water storage can, by safeguarding domestic supplies and supporting crops and/or livestock during dry periods, significantly increase agricultural and economic productivity and enhance people's well-being. For millions of smallholder farmers, reliable access to water is the difference between self-sufficiency in food and hunger. Water storage can also contribute to electricity generation and providing water supply to commercial and industrial enterprises. Consequently, it has an important role to play in poverty reduction, sustainable development and adaptation to climate change.

Water storage capacity differs dramatically around the world. Consider the data presented in Figure 5.2. These statistics are unfortunately dated, but they give a sense of the large differences in available storage capacity and identify where water storage shortfalls are most acute, namely, the Middle East and North Africa, sub-Saharan Africa and Asia, regions where water issues are most pressing.

The data in Figure 5.2 should not make us jump to the conclusion that *large* storage infrastructure is what is required in all cases. Although large infrastructure-financed dams might have their place in some circumstances, there is a *range* of storage options available, from the mammoth to the very small. As emphasized by the International Water Management Institute, we are better off thinking in terms of water storage options along a continuum of scale and across both surface and subsurface approaches.[58] These include traditional reservoirs (of all sizes), ponds and tanks (of all sizes), aquifers or groundwater, soil moisture, and natural wetlands. In some circumstances, it is small tanks, ponds, and reservoirs that are the right tool for the job.[59] Choosing the most

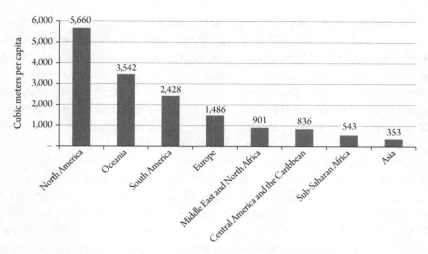

Figure 5.2 Per capita water storage capacity (cubic meters per capita).
Source: W. R. White (2005).

appropriate approach to water storage can help to increase water security, allow
for better adaptation to climate change, help to address the provision of food
through increasing agricultural yields and even reducing poverty.[60]

There can be potential drawbacks to water storage. In some locations, standing water can provide breeding environments for mosquitos that carry malaria,
dengue fever, and yellow fever. This also can be the case for freshwater snails
that carry schistosomiasis parasites.[61] Where water storage tanks are used, covering these can be very helpful. Where small ponds are used, varying the level of
water stored as much as is possible might help. The increased use of malaria bed
nets might need to accompany the increased use of water storage in vulnerable
areas. This is an unfortunate dilemma related to water storage in some health
environments.

Portable Solutions

A number of portable water filtration and storage options have emerged in recent years. For example, the British engineer and inventor Michael Pritchard
observed the water supply problems that followed the Asian tsunami in 2004
and Hurricane Katrina in 2004 and felt that something could be done to alleviate these problems. He eventually produced what he called the LifeSaver
Bottle.[62] The LifeSaver Bottle uses a pump and activated charcoal filtering to
remove bacteria, viruses, parasites, and fungi from the water within. It also has
a prefilter to remove sediments.[63] Although the LifeSaver Bottle is popular with
backpackers and soldiers, its developers take its humanitarian goals seriously.

Beyond the LifeSaver Bottle, there is the LifeSaver Jerrycan and the LifeSaver C2 and M1. The Lifesaver C2 and M1 utilize nanomaterials and are scaled for school, hospitals, and humanitarian camps. These larger models are also water storage systems and are being sold in Asia out of a distribution center in Borneo, East Malaysia. A single filter system for the C2 or M1 can filter up to two million liters of water before needing replacement. As the company points out, these larger systems, while providing clean water, also save families on costs of fuel previously used to boil water to ensure it is safe to drink.

Other companies are also active in portable water treatment. LifeStraw is a small water filter for personal use. As with the case of Lifesaver, LifeStraw is scaling up with LifeStraw Family 1.0 and 2.0 and LifeStraw Community products.[64] Tata Swach is another water purifier system developed by Tata Industries in India that uses a combination of rice husk ash and nanomaterials (silver particles).[65] The portable aqua unit for lifesaving (PAUL) is a backpack-based water filtration system for use in disaster and humanitarian relief operations.[66] Thus there are many emerging options for portable water filtration and storage that can have positive impacts around the world.

Infrastructure and Institutions

As we can see from the technology and storage issues discussed here, in many circumstances, improving the delivery of clean water requires upgrades in water service *infrastructure*. This can be particularly true in water-insecure environments (often rural) where the opportunities to make basic infrastructure investments have not occurred. In the water policy field, the word "infrastructure" is always followed by the word "institutions." As stated by David Grey and Claudia Sadoff, "The only demonstrated path to achieving water security at a national scale has been through investment in an evolving balance of complementary institutions and infrastructure for water management."[67] This is to prevent outcomes such as the often-cited example of the proliferation of bore holes, drilled pipes, and water pumps leading to groundwater mining in the absence of effective institutions. There is a temporal mismatch here, however, in that infrastructure needs are pressing *now*, while institutional development is notoriously *incremental*. Also, the appropriate qualities of both infrastructure and institutions are always location specific. Grey and Sadoff expanded on this:[68]

> Infrastructure will not deliver high, sustained returns if it is not well designed and managed and managers will not be able to optimize the use of the resource without adequate (natural or man-made) infrastructure. Similarly, strong institutions and sustainable governance will also directly contribute to appropriate investment in and proper operations

and maintenance of, sound and reliable water infrastructure. For effective water management, institutional design needs to ensure inclusion, accountability and equity and be flexible enough to adapt to change, such as in technologies and social policies. Experience again and again demonstrates that investments in institutions and infrastructure must be made in concert, with their relative weight or priority a question of degree only.

That said, some countries with pressing water needs have almost no infrastructure at all, particularly in rural areas. In such cases, initial focus may need to be on very basic infrastructure rather than the nuances of management.

Demand Side Issues and Provisioning Processes

In my discussion of food in Chapter 4, I noted that basic-goods deprived individuals and families may not have full information with regard to what constitutes *nutritious* food. Informational and other issues can also adversely affect the demand for clean water. For example, it can be difficult for poor families with limited livelihood options to always remember to purchase and use an appropriate chlorine product to treat their less-than-clean water. There is also some evidence that households can have a low willingness to pay for clean water. However, there is evidence that the demand for clean water (and therefore willingness to pay) is responsive to increased information provision.[69]

The World Bank explained these demand side problems as follows:[70]

> Even if households fully understood the etiology of diarrheal diseases, the small reduction in over-all disease burden and the lack of an impact on nutritional outcomes could make it very difficult for an individual household to "infer" that clean water led to better health outcomes (for researchers, this is precisely why the impact of any intervention on mortality is impossible to detect unless samples are huge—certainly much larger than what a household would have access to). In addition, it is difficult for individuals to handle rational calculations when probabilities are small and the payoffs are huge.

Approaches such as household use of chlorine products or the previously discussed, portable water treatment devices are collectively known as *point-of-use treatment* or *household water treatment*. Despite informational and other demand problems, there is some evidence that these approaches can result in significant reductions in diarrheal infections, and this led the World Health Organization to advocate for this approach.[71] Perhaps inevitably, there were subsequent questions about the efficacy of point-of-use treatment.[72] To be more specific, in some circumstances, it is unclear how much point-of-use treatment adds to other interventions such as piped water, storage, improved sanitation, and hand washing. It may very well be that improved sanitation (discussed in Chapter 6), is a bigger priority in many circumstances, or that improved water sources and improved sanitation services need to go hand in hand as simultaneous community investments.[73] Nevertheless, subsidized chlorine products at water sources or via the distribution of coupons to mothers are still worth continued evaluation, as are continued discussion and experimentation at the community level.[74]

In assessing ways forward to provide increased amounts of clean water, we need to keep in mind that there are a variety of means through which poor individuals can and do obtain water. Water can be provided via public entities or via private firms, or combinations of these in the form of public–private partnerships. Despite ongoing debates, we should be careful before the endorsement of these over the other because there are many nuances involved.[75] There also can be a variety of *informal* water markets on which poor people rely. These range from bulk suppliers (e.g., tanker trucks) to small suppliers, including those delivering water in a variety of container types. Although these informal markets can be exploitative, the same can potentially be true of more traditional public and private provision, which both can be characterized by corruption and rent seeking.[76] Generalizations across provision mode are probably not helpful. Rather, we need to assess matters on a more case-by-case basis.

Regardless of delivery mode, the existence of the subsistence right to water does not imply that we need to ignore the *economics* of water service delivery. Rather, as stated by one researcher, "good water economics is good water politics."[77] Another way to state this is that cost recovery is essential for sustainable water provision. Fortunately, the field of resource economics provides a useful set of tools that can help to determine appropriate pricing schemes to promote the "take-up" of poor families into the system, while at the same time, ensuring cost recovery.[78] Economic analysis can support meeting the human right to clean water.

Summary

Water is the quintessential basic good and is part of emerging conceptions of subsistence rights. It is underprovided, however, and its provision is going to become even more challenging as climate change progresses through the 21st century. A number of new technologies are emerging that might make a significant contribution to expanding the provision of water. These include "more crop per drop" agriculture, smart irrigation, new means of water desalination, advanced filtration based on nanotechnology, and new water storage systems. Although these new technologies are to be welcomed and have great potential, conflict in water scarce regions such as the Sahel and the Middle East could usher in human tragedies if we are not careful.

There is some empirical uncertainty about the best approach to provide clean water, but it seems clear that without advances in sanitation services to accompany access to improved water sources, health gains will be significantly below their potential. Institutions for effective water resource management must evolve along with new infrastructure projects, point-of-use treatment must undergo continued evaluation, and cost recovery models must be continuously tailored to specific local systems. All of these efforts can help to meet the subsistence right to water.

Notes

1. See, for example, Reinert (2014).
2. WHO and UNICEF (2014).
3. See, for example, www.unwater.org. The common measure of *water scarcity* or *water poverty* is 1,000 cubic meters per person per year. *Absolute water scarcity* or *absolute water poverty* is 500 cubic meters per person per year. See Falkenmark, Lundquist, and Widstrand (1989) and White (2012).
4. *The Economist* (2013b).
5. See Clark (2013) and Inter-Governmental Panel on Climate Change (2014). The 2014 avalanche on Mount Everest that killed sixteen Sherpas was an "ice release" linked to climate change and effectively shut down the 2014 climbing season. See Narula (2014).
6. See Masood (2015).
7. See Giansiracusa (2010) and Lee (2010).
8. See Erdbrink (2014).
9. See, for example, Qureshi, Hanjra, and Ward (2013).
10. Haidera et al. (2011).
11. *The Guardian* (2012).
12. Weis (2015).
13. See Ingram and Malamud-Roam (2013) for an important work of paleoclimatology on this issue.
14. See http://www.wfp.org/countries/djibouti.
15. Wyrwoll (2012).
16. *The Economist* (2014d, 2014j).
17. See Ezz and Arafat (2015).
18. See Zwane and Kremer (2007) who pointed out that "In developing countries, in particular, surface water is often contaminated with pathogens (including bacteria, viruses, and parasites) due to contact with human and livestock waste" (p. 3). Piped water, sanitation, breastfeeding, immunization, oral rehydration therapy, micronutrient supplementation, hand washing, and point-of-use water treatment have all been shown to be effective in treating diarrheal disease. There is less agreement on the effectiveness of communal water infrastructure in rural areas according to these authors. Note that hand washing is often treated as a behavioral issue, but a family without the relevant basic goods (soap and clean water) can hardly be expected to wash their hands.
19. See Cutler and Miller (2005).
20. See Galiani, Gertler, and Schargrodsky (2005). Note that these authors consider privatization of water services in Argentina. It is not the case that privatization can be counted on to provide such benefits in all cases. See, for example, Prasad (2006) and Araral (2009).

21. See, for example, Grey and Sadoff (2007). Even volatility in water availability can affect growth, as in the case of India and monsoons.
22. See Sorenson, Morssink, and Campos (2011).
23. See, for example, Gleick (1996, 1998) and Woodhouse (2004–2005). The minimum thresholds can be set out in terms of prevention of dehydration, consumption beyond dehydration needs, sanitation and hygiene, cooking, and agriculture. For example, minimum thresholds for drinking (both for preventing dehydration and consuming beyond dehydration needs) have been set at five liters per day. Requirements for sanitation services, bathing, and food preparation have been set at twenty, fifteen, and ten liters per day, respectfully, for a total of fifty liters per day. However, as noted by Gleick (1998), this excludes water required to grow and process daily food requirements. This requirement can dwarf the direct water needs and is estimated by Gleick to be over 2,000 liters per day.
24. For a review, see Gupta, Ahlers, and Ahmed (2010); Meier et al. (2013); and Jeffords and Shah (2013).
25. United Nations High Commissioner for Human Rights (2003).
26. See Shue (1996).
27. United Nations High Commissioner for Human Rights (2003).
28. United Nations General Assembly (2010).
29. United Nations Human Rights Council (2010).
30. United Nations Human Rights Council (2014).
31. As I discuss in Chapter 7, the United Nations use of the concept of "the highest attainable standard of physical and mental health" (p. 3) falls outside of the basic goods approach.
32. As noted by Jeffords (2013), "As of 2010, out of 198 national constitutions of the developed and developing countries across every continent, 142 include at least one reference to the environment, in a broad sense. Of these 142, 125 have a specific environmental human rights provision or at least the makings of one, and 10 include a direct human right to water" (p. 330). See also Jeffords (2016).
33. Meier et al. (2013), p. 13.
34. Ranganathan et al. (2010), p. 7. The authors went on to say: "Although the exact impacts remain uncertain, in many places, even where total rainfall increases, climate change will most likely increase rainfall variability. Without doubt those who will be most adversely affected are the poor, who already struggle to cope with existing variability. They will find it increasingly difficult to protect their families, livelihoods and food supply from the negative impacts of seasonal rainfall and droughts and floods, all of which will be exacerbated by climate change" (p. 7).
35. Inter-Governmental Panel on Climate Change (2014).
36. It is interesting that the United States military has expressed exasperation with climate change skepticism. See the United States Center for Naval Analysis Military Advisory Board (2014), which stated, "We are dismayed that discussions of climate change have become so polarizing and have receded from the arena of informed public discourse and debate" (p. iii).
37. See Weis (2015) and Box 11.1 on Yemen.
38. See Tir and Stinnett (2012). For more on water conflict, see http://worldwater.org/water-conflict/.
39. Hanjra and Qureshi (2010), p. 368.
40. FAO (2011b), p. 77.
41. See the 2011 special issue of *Paddy and Water Environment* (9:1), as well as the SRI website maintained at http://sri.ciifad.cornell.edu/.
42. See, for example, Atta, Boutraa, and Akhkha (2011). For solar applications in smart irrigation, see Burney et al. (2010).
43. See Hoekstra and Chapagain (2007).
44. *The Economist* (2008).
45. Sastry, Shrivastava, and Rao (2013) reported: "Nanotechnologies are technologies which either incorporate or employ nanomaterials or involve processes performed at the nanoscale. At this scale, the physical, chemical and biological properties of materials differ fundamentally from the properties of individual atoms and molecules or bulk matter. These changes

result in unique mechanical, physical, chemical, electronic, photonic and magnetic properties of nano scale materials. The ability to manipulate matter at the nano scale can lead to improved understanding of biological, physical and chemical processes and to the creation of improved materials, structures, devices and systems that exploit these new properties. Because of this general purpose enabling nature, nanotechnology has the potential to impact all sectors of human development" (pp. 9–10).

46. See Qu, Alvarez, and Li (2013).
47. See, for example, Chapter 8 of Diamandis and Kotler (2012).
48. Sastry, Shrivastava, and Rao (2013). The authors stated, "In the water sector, the complex value chain of nanotechnology and the patent thickets present significant challenges for technology development and transfer" (pp. 11–12).
49. Consider the following recent, scientific assessment by Qu, Alvarez, and Li (2013): "There are two major research needs for full-scale applications of nanotechnology in water/wastewater treatment. First, the performance of various nanotechnologies in treating real natural and waste waters needs to be tested. Future studies need to be done under more realistic conditions to assess the applicability and efficiency of different nanotechnologies as well as to validate nanomaterial enabled sensing technologies. Secondly, the long-term efficacy of these nanotechnologies is largely unknown as most lab studies were conducted for relatively short period of time. Research addressing the long-term performance of water and wastewater treatment nanotechnologies is in great need. As a result, side-by-side comparison of nanotechnology enabled systems and existing technologies is challenging." And "Despite the superior performance, the adoption of innovative technologies strongly depends on the cost effectiveness and the potential risk involved. The current cost of nanomaterials is prohibitively high with few exceptions. . . . There are currently two approaches to address the cost issue. One proposed approach is to use low purity nanomaterials without significantly compromising efficiency as much of the production cost is related to separation and purification. Alternatively, the cost-effectiveness can be improved by retaining and reusing nanomaterials" (p. 3942).
50. This point was made by Wiesner (2013).
51. See http://idadesal.org.
52. The innovations include membrane technology, including nanomaterials, rack design, and energy recovery systems. See Peñate and García-Rodríguez (2012).
53. Again, see Peñate and García-Rodríguez (2012).
54. See barefootcollege.org.
55. See Patel (2010).
56. Technology optimists Diamandis and Kotler (2012) evoked a photograph of the earth as a "pale blue dot" of water in space, with (desalinized) oceans allowing for an abundance of clean water. The fact that desalination technologies are on "exponential growth curves" makes this abundance almost inevitable, but ironically we also need to "commit ourselves to the path" (p. 99).
57. McCartney and Smakhtin (2010), p. 1.
58. See McCartney and Smakhtin (2010).
59. This point has been made by FAO (2008), McCartney and Smakhtin (2010), and Wisser et al. (2010), among others. Wisser et al. (2010) suggested that small water reservoirs in sub-Saharan Africa could potentially double cereal output.
60. See the case of Ethiopia in Hagos et al. (2012).
61. See, for example, Boelee et al. (2013) on the cases of Ethiopia and Burkina Faso.
62. See lifesaversystems.com.
63. This device was independently tested by the London School of Hygiene and Tropical Medicine. See Donachie and Krahn (2007).
64. See vestergaard.com.
65. See tataswach.com.
66. See wasserrucksack.de.
67. Grey and Sadoff (2007), p. 569.
68. Grey and Sadoff (2007), p. 560.

69. See, for example, Ahuja, Kremer, and Zwane (2010) and Kremer et al. (2011).
70. World Bank (2011a), p. 138.
71. See, for example, Arnold and Colford (2007); World Health Organization (2007); and Ahuja, Kremer, and Zwane (2010).
72. See, for example, Schmidt and Cairncross (2009).
73. This was precisely the conclusion of the study by Komarulzaman, Smits, and de Jong (2014) for Indonesia. The authors concluded, "A critical finding is that treating water before its consumption does not significantly reduce diarrhoea risk. . . . Access to piped water on the premises is strongly associated with lower diarrhoea incidence among children under five in Indonesia. The availability of improved water at the community level only helps to reduce diarrhoea risk under specific circumstances. . . . Hence, for an optimal effect, the provision of clean drinking water should go hand in hand with the improvement of sanitation at both household and community level (p. 9)."
74. See the discussion of this issue in Ahuja, Kremer, and Zwane (2010). For an example of community involvement in evaluating point-of-use approaches, see Arvai and Post (2012).
75. See, for example, Prasad (2006) and Araral (2009).
76. See, for example, Venkatachalam (2015).
77. Araral (2009), p. 227.
78. For an explanation of this and an application in the Philippines, see Chun (2014). Chun concluded, "Differential pricing can have large effects on increasing the take-up of water services by poorer households, while ensuring cost recovery. However, the identification of various pricing strategies is just the start of the process of moving toward a more financially sustainable model. To implement differential pricing would require undertaking documentation of the income level of each household or area to map prices to consumers. Information dissemination would also have a role, to ensure that potential and current consumers can make more informed decisions on their take-up and usage of the service. However, such costs of implementation are expected to be low in comparison to the potential returns that can be achieved in increasing consumer access and the financial solvency of the provider" (p. 676).

‖ 6 ‖

Sanitation

Sanitation is something that we would rather not think and talk about. As a consequence, it often ends up at the bottom of policy agendas. This is unfortunate because improving sanitation services is actually one of the most important development policies. Why? The World Health Organization has estimated that, for every dollar spent on sanitation globally, the return is over $5.00.[1] This is the type of payback that would catch the attention of any red-blooded investor. Despite these significant returns, however, sanitation is woefully underprovided. Approximately 2.4 billion individuals (one third of humanity) do not have access to clean and safe toilets, and nearly one billion individuals practice open defecation.[2] Open defecation leads to a myriad of diseases with the consequence of lost school days for sick children and lost work days for sick adults. It also contributes to stunting and adversely affects cognitive development. Sanitation is therefore a central health and development issue as well as a basic subsistence right.

Progress in improving sanitation is slow. The 2.4 billion people without improved sanitation in 2015 is only 11 percent smaller than the 2.7 billion who lacked this basic good in 1990. The reduction in open defecation is indeed larger: from 1.3 billion in 1990 to nearly 1.0 billion in 2015, a fall of over 20 percent. Still, we are dealing with a persistent and large-scale problem, and the absolute number of people in urban areas practicing open defecation is actually *increasing*.[3] So the sanitation provision problem is both widespread and very persistent.

There is, however, a more positive way of looking at trends in sanitation deprivation. Between 1990 and 2015, almost 2.1 billion people *gained access* to improved sanitation. Likewise, we can cite the fact that, as a percentage of low- and middle-income country populations, open defecation declined from 31 percent in 1990 to 16 percent in 2015.[4] As these statistics indicate, it is population growth that is an important contributing factor to the absolute number of people deprived of sanitation services. The addition of three to four billion more individuals to the planet in the 21st century will consequently ensure the continued challenge of providing this basic good.

Where is the deprivation of sanitation services most pressing? This is addressed in Figures 6.1 and 6.2. Figure 6.1 gives the lack of improved sanitation facilities in 2015 by region in millions of persons. Figure 6.1 shows that South Asia is the region with the most individuals deprived of improved sanitation services (nearly a billion). This is followed by sub-Saharan Africa and East Asia

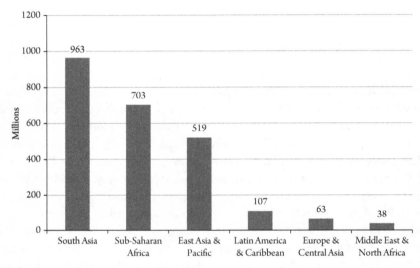

Figure 6.1 Lack of improved sanitation facilities, 2015 (millions of people).
Source: World Bank, World Development Indicators.

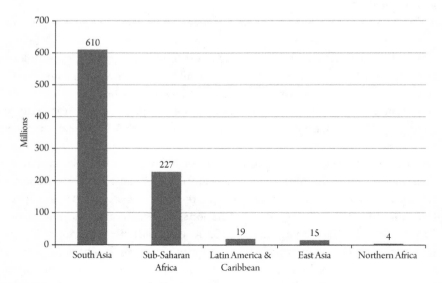

Figure 6.2 Open defecation, 2015 (millions of people). Source: WHO and UNICEF (2015).

and the Pacific with about 700 million and 500 million, respectively. These three regions are where most efforts to improve sanitation services need to be focused. Figure 6.2 looks at the specific issue of open defecation. Figure 6.2 demonstrates that, by far, the region with the most extreme deprivation in sanitation services is South Asia where over 600 million individuals practice open defecation. This is followed by sub-Sahara Africa where over 200 million engage in this practice.

Despite the persistence of the total number of individuals deprived of sanitation services, progress is possible. Figure 6.3 shows the percentage reduction in the proportion of the population engaged in open defecation for the countries with the greatest decrease in this value between 1990 and 2015. More important, two South Asian countries (Bangladesh and Pakistan) are included here, indicating that significant progress is possible in the very region where the problem is most acute. Also important is the fact that Figure 6.3 includes countries from Asia, Africa, and Latin America, indicating that significant progress is possible around the world. Note also that the growth experiences of the countries in Figure 6.3 ranged from lackluster to strong, showing that significant progress in the provision of sanitation services can be made with or without high growth rates.

The vast majority of individuals who practice open defecation reside in rural areas, accounting for nearly 900 million of the nearly one billion. For this reason, sanitation is primarily (not exclusively) a rural development issue. Years ago, rural development was a central component of development policy. It is unfortunate that this emphasis was pushed aside beginning in the mid-1980s when the focus shifted to the debt crisis, structural adjustment, promoting

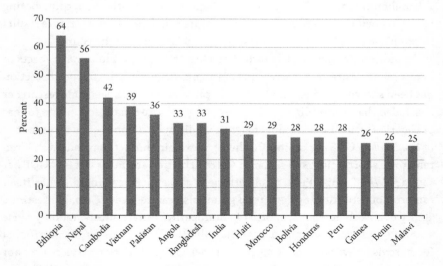

Figure 6.3 Percentage reduction in proportion of population practicing open defecation 1990 to 2015. Source: WHO and UNICEF (2015).

globalization (not necessarily a bad thing), and liberalizing markets. Part of the neglect of rural development and rural health has been a neglect of rural sanitation. A focus on sanitation could therefore be part of a rediscovery of rural development, a positive change in development policy with benefits in and of itself.

Impacts

We now have a sense of the scope of deprivation in sanitation services, but what are the impacts? Evidence suggests that they are substantial. Lack of sanitation is complicit in a host of diseases and health complications. A list of these is presented in Table 6.1 and gives a sense of the scope of the problem. This table shows that poor sanitation can exacerbate a large number of diseases, contributing to a substantial amount of sickness and a relatively large number of deaths. It is not surprising that these negative health impacts fall largely on the poor and the young.

The most important disease group in Table 6.1 is diarrheal disease (cholera, typhoid, dysentery, and diarrhea). These diarrheal diseases are one of the leading causes of infant and child deaths in the world, estimated to account for approximately 9 percent of total infant and child mortality or 580,000 infants and children a year.[5] To the extent that sanitation deprivation causes diarrhea, it also causes infant and child mortality.[6] A rule of thumb is that improved sanitation could reduce child diarrheal deaths by one third.[7] A second cause of infant and child death in the world, however, is pneumonia. Pneumonia is estimated to account for approximately 17 percent of total infant and child mortality or 1.1 million infants and children a year,[8] and poor sanitation is a contributing factor in pneumonia infections as well.[9] Sanitation deprivation therefore results in extensive poor health and mortality, particularly among the young.

In addition to these widely recognized health impacts, additional impacts of poor sanitation are being increasingly recognized. The practice of open defection has been shown to reduce child height or cause stunting. Indeed, one researcher concluded that, controlling for GDP, reducing India's open defecation rate to that of Nigeria's would increase child height in India by an amount equivalent to that of *quadrupling* GDP per capita. This helps to explain the fact that India's children tend to be shorter than sub-Saharan African children at similar levels of GDP per capita.[10] Why is this? First, fecal germs can cause diarrhea, and diarrhea itself can promote stunting. Second, fecal germs also can reduce the small intestine's ability to absorb nutrients, a form of enteropathy.[11] These effects not only cause stunting, but can also impair cognitive abilities.[12] So focusing on nutritional food provision without focusing on the provision of sanitation services may not be sufficient to improve nutritional outcomes. This point is often overlooked in

Table 6.1 **Diseases Associated with Lack of Sanitation**

Disease	Symptoms	Approximate Morbidity/ Mortality	At-Risk Populations
Cholera	Profuse watery diarrhea and vomiting, severe dehydration; about 75 percent of infected individuals do not develop any symptoms, although they can infect others for 7–14 days. In other cases, it can kill within hours.	3–5 million cases and 100,000–120,000 deaths every year.	People living urban slums, displaced people or refugees, and people with low immunity such as malnourished children or people living with HIV.
Typhoid	Fever, headache, insomnia, constipation, diarrhea, abdominal pain, and tenderness.	17 million cases.	
Bacillary dysentery	Watery diarrhea with intestinal cramps and general malaise, soon followed bloody, mucoid stools.	120 million cases and 1.1 million deaths.	Poor populations living in crowded settings and children under the age of 5.
Diarrhea	Acute watery diarrhea with or without blood.	850,000 deaths among children.	
Hepatitis A and E	Symptomatic infections most common in adults aged 15–40 years; typical symptoms include jaundice, anorexia, enlarged, tender liver, abdominal pain and tenderness, nausea and vomiting, and fever.	Hepatitis A: 1.4 million cases; Hepatitis E: 20 million cases and 70,000 deaths.	Individuals with poor sanitary conditions and hygienic practices.

(continued)

Table 6.1 (Continued)

Disease	Symptoms	Approximate Morbidity/ Mortality	At-Risk Populations
Rotavirus	Diarrhea without blood, nausea, vomiting, abdominal pain, and dehydration.	400,000 child deaths.	Poor children and low birth weight infants have an increased risk.
Amoebic dysentery	Diarrhea with blood and mucus, abdominal pain and fever.	40,000–100,000 deaths.	
Giardiasis	Nausea, epigastric pain, abdominal cramps, and diarrhea.		Healthcare workers, people eating improperly treated food or drink, individuals in contact with other infected individuals.
Roundworms	Individuals with light infections usually have no symptoms; heavier infections can cause diarrhea and abdominal pain, general malaise and weakness, and impaired cognitive and physical development.	1.5 billion cases.	
Whipworms	Diarrhea and abdominal pain, and anemia in most severe cases.	500,000 cases.	Children aged 5–14 years are particularly vulnerable.
Hookworms	Abdominal pain and anemia that becomes severe in the absence of treatment.	50,000 deaths and 900 million cases.	Anyone walking bare feet on contaminated ground.

Schistosomiasis	Abdominal pain, diarrhea, blood in stools or urine, liver enlargement in advanced cases, and kidney damage in advanced cases.	10,000 deaths and 200 million cases.	Fishing and farming populations in areas where there are poor water and sanitation conditions; women doing domestic chores in infested water, and children playing in the fields or with soil.
Guinea worm	Emergence of the worm is accompanied by swelling, burning sensation, blistering, and ulceration of the area from which the worm emerges.	Few cases and rarely fatal.	People working in the field and children.
Filariasis	Elephantiasis in late-stage disease.	120 million cases.	
Trachoma	Chronic inflammation, scarring, visual impairment, and blindness.	20 million cases with 1 million blind.	Children and women who take care of them.

Source: Roma and Pugh (2012).

discussions of food security and highlights the interrelationships among basic goods and services.

There is also at least anecdotal evidence that lack of sanitation in schools lowers school attendance and that this negative impact is larger for girls. Given that a large range of positive externalities has been associated with girls' schooling, a lack of sanitation in schools is a serious concern.[13] The empirical data on the contribution of latrines and toilets on school attendance are mixed, but common sense suggests that access to safe and clean toilet facilities could not but help in educational attainment for both girls and boys.[14] It also would help to ensure that girls and boys would get sick less often.

Development economists also have recently discovered the economic costs of sanitation deprivation. The World Bank has estimated that the economic costs of inadequate sanitation are approximately US$250 billion a year. These costs reflect ill health, lost education, environmental impacts, and lost tourism.[15] In Chapter 3, I considered the relationship between basic goods provision and growth, noting that basic goods provision and growth could be mutually supporting. In the case of sanitation, it appears that this would no doubt be the case. In fact, the World Bank (a growth-focused institution if there ever was one) claims that sanitation deprivation itself suppresses growth.[16] So those concerned about growth prospects also should be concerned about sanitation provision.

The Right to Sanitation

As we have seen, basic sanitation services are necessary for individuals, families, and communities to avoid significantly compromised health (and even death). This fact makes sanitation services a basic subsistence right. Recognition of this subsistence right largely evolved parallel to that for clean water discussed in Chapter 5. As mentioned there, in 2003, the CESCR issued General Comment 15[17] on two articles of the ICESCR[18], namely Article 11 on the right to an adequate standard of living and Article 12 on the right to health. In this comment, the CESCR stated that "Ensuring that everyone has access to adequate sanitation is not only fundamental for human dignity and privacy, but is one of the principal mechanisms for protecting the quality of drinking water supplies and resources. . . . States parties have an obligation to *progressively extend safe sanitation services*, particularly to rural and deprived urban areas, taking into account the needs of women and children" (emphasis added).

Further steps were taken in 2010 when the United Nations General Assembly passed a Resolution on the Human Right to Water and Sanitation that recognized "the right to safe and clean drinking water and sanitation as a human right that is essential for the full enjoyment of life and all human rights."[19] Also in 2010, the United Nations Human Rights Council[20] also passed a resolution affirming drinking water and sanitation as a human right and confirming this right as legally binding on states. The Human Rights Council acted again in 2014 with a further resolution, which reaffirmed "the human right to safe drinking water and sanitation is essential for the full enjoyment of life and to all human rights."[21] Finally, an increasing number of countries recognize the right to sanitation as part of their constitutional environmental rights.[22]

There is recognition that sanitation is a basic subsistence right as defined by Henry Shue and as discussed in Chapter 3.[23] As I emphasized in that chapter, basic goods are basic rights. More and more, however, there is also a recognition that sanitation helps support more traditional rights in the form of human security (discussed in Chapter 11), particularly that of women. Millions of Indian and African women without access to sanitation are forced to relieve themselves at night, and this makes them vulnerable to violence, including sexual violence.[24] In this way, sanitation is a human right in the more traditional, "negative rights" realm of being free from violence, along with being a basic subsistence right.

Options for Sanitation Service Provision

Thus sanitation deprivation is widespread and has significant detrimental impacts, including mortality, particularly among infants and children. And this deprivation is a violation of basic subsistence rights. What to do then? There is a wide variety of approaches to sanitation systems, from very simple pit latrines to industrial-sized wastewater treatment plants. Table 6.2 describes a set of options in terms of four broad stages and various options for each stage. *Toilets* include pit latrines, ecological toilets, and water-flushed and pour-flushed toilets. *Wastewater disposal and transport* include leach pits, septic tanks and drainage fields, open drains, sewer interceptor tank systems, and sewerage systems. *Wastewater treatment* includes ponds and constructed wetlands and activated sludge processes, and *final wastewater disposal and reuse* includes final wastewater disposal processes as well as wastewater and excreta reuse.

Implicit in Table 6.2 is the fact that sanitation, like all goods and services, can be viewed *in value chain* terms, consisting of collection, transport, treatment, disposal, and reuse. In many important cases, collection, transport, and treatment are done close to the site in question. That is, I am talking about pit latrines, septic tanks, and drain fields; open drains and decentralized sewer interceptor tank systems, what are collectively known as onsite sanitation systems (OSS). Also in many cases, removal services (manual or vacuum) can be a critical part of the system.[25] As pointed out by sanitation economist Sopie Trémolet, "the majority of the developing world uses onsite sanitation facilities, which requires households to regularly maintain them by hiring service providers to empty the contents of pit latrines and septic tanks and dispose of it safely."[26]

Table 6.2 **Approaches to Sanitation**

Stages	Options	Description	Advantages and Disadvantages
Toilets	Pit latrines	Single or twin pits with slab and hole; ventilated improved pit latrines (VIPs) have a vent pipe to draw away odors.	Relatively inexpensive; odors can deter use; not useful near water.
	Ecological toilets	Turn excreta into fertilizer and soil conditioner; some separate out urine and feces.	Can be prefabricated and built above ground; can involve maintenance.
	Water-flushed and pour-flushed toilets	Water is used to remove excreta into a pit, septic tank, or sewerage system.	Very sanitary; not always helpful in water-scarce environments.
Wastewater disposal and transport	Leach pits	Hold excreta so that water can slowly percolate into ground and sullage can eventually be removed.	May not be useful where groundwater tables are high; can cause health risks in dense urban area.
	Septic tanks and drain fields	A more advanced form of a leach pit with perforated pipes and gravel to promote leaching.	Safer and more effective than leach pits but requires sufficient area and certain soil conditions to be effective.
	Open drains	Uncovered channels that deliver wastewater from households to collection points.	Easy to clean; not effective for sewerage.
	Sewer interceptor tank systems	Sewerage systems with interceptor tanks that collect solid materials; can be decentralized.	Gradients can be flatter without the need to move solids through the system; less expensive than conventional sewers because pipe diameters can be smaller.
	Sewerage systems	Closed conduits to transport excreta and other wastewater to treatment plants.	Most sanitary of sanitation options but can be expensive.

Wastewater treatment	Processes	Systems to remove suspended solids, dissolved organic matter and other impurities to produce effluent of different qualities.	Can produce various grades of water up to safe drinking water; some processes can be very expensive.
	Ponds and constructed wetlands	Anaerobic ponds can be used as a first treatment of sewerage to be potentially followed by facultative and maturation ponds; constructed wetlands add specific aquatic plants to help the process.	Low cost and low maintenance; requires land resources and can produce odors.
	Activated sludge process	Many alternative processes to break down organic matter into carbon dioxide, water, and inorganic compounds.	Can ensure the removal of harmful organic matter from wastewater; requires technological sophistication and a continuous supply of electricity.
Final wastewater disposal and reuse	Final wastewater disposal	Wastewater (at whatever level of cleanliness achieved) and stormwater both need to be disposed of if not reused in some way.	If drinking quality, the water can be used in distribution systems; if not, there are potential environmental and health issues related to its disposal.
	Wastewater and excreta reuse	Wastewater can be used for agricultural purposes and, if clean enough, for household water supply; fecal sludge can be used in agricultural and energy applications.	If not clean enough, there can be negative health implications of reuse.

Sources: http://www.worldbank.org/en/topic/water, https://aguatuya.org/ and Trémolet (2013).

This is where bottom-of-the-pyramid, small businesses can and do become in-volved in service provision.

As in any value chain, each of these stages can be conceived of as a (potential) market. For each of these markets, there is a demand side and a supply side. One possibility behind the lack of sanitation services is therefore a simple lack of demand or lack of supply. But there also can be some types of what economists call "market failures" that imply a potential need for governments to become involved.[27] A number of these are identified in Table 6.3. For example, Trémolet noted that service providers emptying pit latrines can have little incentive to dispose of the latrine contents appropriately, so the government might step in to provide such an incentive with a volume-based payment at designated dis-posal sites. Of course, such sites need to be made available in the first place, and this is where the government also can be involved.

At the very end of the sanitation value chain is disposal and reuse. As Trémolet and others emphasized, if done correctly, there is unexploited poten-tial for wastewater and fecal sludge in agriculture and for fecal sludge in energy production. Exploiting these possibilities will require rethinking the sanitation system and addressing important health concerns.[28] Because many of these are new applications, there could be a role for governments in demonstrating new possibilities as well as in matching potential suppliers and users. It is clear, though, care is required to ensure the safety of such end use processes.

Increased Attention and Spending

Improving the provision of sanitation services will require increased attention to the issue and, if necessary, increased spending. Estimates are that sanitation accounts for only one fifth of the total spending in the water, sanitation, and hygiene sector (WASH).[29] Given the documented, significant returns to sani-tation investments, why are governments not spending more on sanitation? World Bank economist Shanta Devarajan addressed this question. His answer hinges on the presence of previously mentioned market failures in the form of externalities. Devarajan explained,[30]

> Even if households don't invest enough (in sanitation), why doesn't the government step in? Here is the resolution of the puzzle: Finance min-isters are constantly besieged by advocates for one activity or another who say, "My sector has all these effects on growth and poverty reduc-tion, so you should spend more on my sector." This argument is wrong. Why? Because governments have limited resources. Any expenditure by government on sanitation will come at the expense of something else (or higher taxes)—such as roads or education or health.

Table 6.3 **Potential Market Failures and Policy Options for Sanitation Service Provision**

Stages	Demand/ Supply	Market Failure	Policy Options
Access	Demand	Lack of information or access to finance; positive externalities from investing in sanitation improvements.	Information campaigns, microfinance focused on sanitation improvements, and subsidies.
	Supply	Service providers such as latrine builders are small and lacking in capabilities; utilities fail to reach all households.	Provide training and finance opportunities to service providers; introduce incentives for utilities to reach all households.
Transport and treatment	Demand	Households unwilling or unable to pay emptying fees.	Information campaigns and small subsidies to promote latrine emptying.
	Supply	Service providers that empty latrines are small and lacking in capabilities; service providers cannot find disposal sites.	Provide training and finance opportunities to service providers; build more disposal sites and provide incentive to service providers to use them.
Disposal and reuse	Demand	Lack of information and taboos regarding reuse products.	Information campaigns to make potential users of reuse products aware of their presence.
	Supply	Lack of information about reuse possibilities; limited value of reuse products.	Matching function between potential suppliers and potential users.

Source: Adapted from Trémolet (2013).

So how should governments decide what to spend on? They should spend on those things that the private sector will not spend on, or will not spend enough on. The classic example is an externality—where the benefits or costs occur to people other than the person undertaking the action. Sanitation, or its converse, open defecation, is a negative externality. People who defecate in the open not only harm their own children, but other people's children. Their incentive to invest in sanitation is less than the costs. This is the strongest case for public spending on sanitation.

Furthermore, ignoring the externality argument has serious consequences. Governments typically overspend on private goods, such as high-end medical care, at the expense of goods with externalities, such as sanitation. Rich people and medical unions have political power to lobby for spending on curative health care; others lobby for fuel subsidies (another private good). Poor people's voice for sanitation goes unheard.

Therefore many national governments need to recognize that the most productive investment they can make is often woefully underprovided and that there are sound *economic* arguments for them to step in to provide it. Sanitation provision is not only a matter of subsistence rights. It is a matter of economic efficiency.

At the multilateral level, the WASH sector was neglected for decades as multilateral aid agencies focused instead on an ever-changing set of development priorities or what has been called the "endless waltz of paradigms."[31] The foreign aid statistics of the Organizational for Economic Cooperation and Development show that the WASH sector accounts for between 0 and 9 percent of donors' contributions, with most OECD countries contributing 0 to 3 percent to this sector.[32] It makes no sense that sanitation, estimated to have a return of over 500 percent would languish as a nonpriority in development assistance. Fortunately, there seems to be some change at the World Bank. In 2014, World Bank President Jim Yong Kim drew a connection between the provision of sanitation services and the reduction of poverty, noting that progress on poverty was predicated on progress in sanitation. This followed a number of years of increased lending by the World Bank in water and sanitation.[33] This is not to suggest that we should wait until the World Bank acts to attempt to make progress on basic goods provision, but the World Bank is a leader in the global aid system and tends to set the course for other lenders.

Demand Side Issues and Provisioning Processes

We are not going to be able to move forward quickly on sanitation service provision if we use as a model the conventional sewerage systems typical of high-income countries. By and large, these will not be applicable to poor rural or densely populated urban areas. Instead, we must think in terms of *simpler* and *more varied* systems. In rural areas, private family- and community-based latrines can be an appropriate solution that prevents open defecation. In urban areas, simplified systems can involve smaller-than-usual pipe diameters, slightly reduced gradients and lower depths. Treatment plants can be more decentralized than in conventional sewerage systems, allowing for organic growth over time as populations increase. In some instances, this approach to urban sanitation may involve changes in codes and regulations. Nevertheless, the nontraditional, decentralized approach has been shown to work.[34]

A number of different organizational forms can help in the increases provision of sanitation services. These can include private firms, public entities, public–private partnerships and a variety of civil society organizations (NGOs and community-based organizations or CBOs). Mixtures of these ("institutional pluralism") are also possible and can often be helpful in serving different populations.[35] Large private companies have an important role to play in sanitation, although they are not always able to effectively serve informal settlements.[36] Public–private partnerships have their advocates and can help in some well-regulated instances but also can be associated with patronage problems.[37] Smaller and more nimble entrepreneurs also have a role to play in both rural and urban settings as an example of BoP provision. These include both fully private entities as well as social entrepreneurs associated with NGOs and CBOs.[38] Civil society organizations can play an important role in urban, informal settlements that are persistently underserved by private firms and public entities.

Much of this is on the supply side. As I mentioned in Chapter 3, however, constraints to basic goods provision also can exist on the demand side. In the case of sanitation, this can arise with beliefs such as "I have never used a toilet, but I am still alive!" One approach to this issue that has arisen has become known as community-led total sanitation (CLTS).[39] This program began in Bangladesh and has spread to many low- and middle-income countries with sponsorship from many donors. It involves the creative use of "disgust, fear, and shame" to motivate communities to abandon open defecation, building and using pit latrines. The approach is decidedly bottom-up, eschewing directives from outside of the communities involved and encouraging locally developed approaches to pit latrine construction and maintenance. Some may object to "disgust, fear, and shame" being used for changing the demand for sanitation, but health and mortality stakes can be very high. As an alternative, in the Indian context, the Sulabh organization has promoted an inexpensive, ecological toilet with a "no toilet, no bride" campaign that has had a real impact.

There is also some evidence that smaller BoP providers in the form of social entrepreneurs can have an impact on demand. According to one set of researchers, this is due to the fact that they do not only provide a product but get involved in the "delivery platform." This involvement includes face-to-face interactions via market surveys, assessing the financing requirements, understanding the broader community and its social norms, education, house-to-house visits, and the identification of leading demanders or "change leaders," and even the use of entertainment and rituals.[40] Once systems are in place, subsequent monitoring takes place to ensure that the problem of "abandoned toilets" does not ensue. The evidence from the important case of India suggests that such approaches can overcome demand-side constraints to ensure positive health improvements.

Along with educational campaigns, good old-fashioned *marketing* can help. In some cases, reasons for finally adopting improved sanitation facilities are not related to concerns for health, but with public appearance, safety, and even convenience.[41] Marketing strategies need to account for this. They also need to account for the previously discussed value-chain aspect of sanitation such as the availability of emptying services for pit latrines, as well as space constraints that can affect household demand. So along with social entrepreneurship in support of sanitation, there is a role to be played by social marketing.[42]

As can be seen from this brief discussion, there is no one-size-fits-all approach to sanitation provision and to influencing the demand side of sanitation. There is room for a variety of approaches that can be tailored to specific environments. Meeting the subsistence right to sanitation will require ongoing assessment of different approaches in different contexts.

Summary

Sanitation deprivation is extensive. Approximately 2.4 billion individuals do not have access to clean and safe toilets, and nearly one billion individuals practice open defecation. These conditions lead to a myriad of health complications concentrated among the poor and the young, as well as significant economic costs. They also exacerbate poverty and suppress growth. It is perhaps for these reasons that Mahatma Gandhi, who gave his life for Indian independence, one stated that "sanitation is more important than independence." Sanitation services are a set of interconnected stages that need to be considered together, from access to toilets and latrines all the way to final disposal and reuse. And there are a number of different organizational forms that can contribute to the provision of these services. Sanitation has been neglected both by national governments and multilateral aid agencies, although this is finally beginning to change. Nevertheless, the addition of three to four billion more individuals to the planet in the 21st century will consequently ensure a continued challenge of the provision of this basic good.

Notes

1. World Health Organization (2012).
2. WHO and UNICEF (2014, 2015).
3. All of these figures are from WHO and UNICEF (2014, 2015).
4. WHO and UNICEF (2014, 2015).
5. UNICEF (2013).
6. UNICEF (2012) reported that "Nearly 90 per cent of deaths due to diarrhoea worldwide have been attributed to unsafe water, inadequate sanitation and poor hygiene" (p. 5).
7. See Cairncross et al. (2010) and Roma and Pugh (2012).
8. UNICEF (2013).
9. UNICEF (2012) reported that "It is known that the poorest and most vulnerable children within countries are more often exposed to pathogens that cause pneumonia and diarrhoea (for example, through poor sanitation or inadequate water supplies)" (p. 8).
10. See Spears (2013). Banerjee and Duflo (2011) reported the following: "Roughly half the children (in India) are stunted, which means that they are far below the norm. One-fourth of them are severely stunted, representing extreme nutritional deprivation. . . . What makes these facts more striking is that the stunting and wasting rates in sub-Saharan Africa, undoubtedly the poorest area of the world, are only about half those in India" (p. 30). These authors do not link this pattern to sanitation, however.
11. See Kosek et al. (2013) and Lin et al. (2013).
12. See Spears and Lamba (2013).
13. For a central contribution to the issue of girls' schooling, see Schultz (2002). School attendance for girls is, in part, an issue of menstrual hygiene. On this issue, see Sommer (2010) and Dolan et al. (2014).
14. For a review, see Jasper, Le, and Bartram (2012).
15. See http://www.worldbank.org/en/news/press-release/2013/04/19/wb-confronts-us-260-billion-a-year-in-global-economic-losses-from-lack-of-sanitation.
16. See http://www.worldbank.org/en/topic/sanitation/overview. In the case of India (the country with the most severe sanitation issue) the Bhagwati–Sen argument discussed in Chapter 2 has not made enough mention of sanitation. For example, in their book on growth in India, Bhagwati and Panagariya (2013) barely mentioned this issue.
17. United Nations High Commissioner for Human Rights (2003).
18. United Nations General Assembly (1966b).
19. United Nations General Assembly (2010), p. 2.
20. United Nations Human Rights Council (2010).
21. United Nations Human Rights Council (2014).
22. See Jeffords (2013, 2016).
23. See Shue (1996).
24. See Water Aid (2013). Being unable to use a toilet or latrine during the day can also lead to distended bladders and colons, urinary tract infections, and chronic constipation.
25. For example, Jenkins and Scott (2007) reported the following for Ghana: "The bucket latrine with frequent and regular emptying service was a product-service package that worked well for decades for hundreds of thousands of Ghanaian households who lacked space and capital, until national policy called for fazing them out and public conservancy labor arrangements ended in many towns. Indeed many respondents in the qualitative work spoke positively of the bucket latrine, its major limitation being that it was now difficult to find people, and often expensive, to empty them. People valued their low cost, their limited smell due to regular emptying and the removal of feces from their home" (p. 2439).
26. Trémolet (2013), p. 278.
27. This point was made by Trémolet (2013). The notion of "market failure" is a characteristic in a market that prevents "allocative efficiency" or the provision of a good or service to the point where the marginal social benefit of the good equals the marginal social cost.

28. Trémolet (2013) noted, "Health concerns should be overcome. Existing initiatives have shown that it is possible to safely reuse sanitation by-products for agriculture, provided appropriate treatment and monitoring is in place. This would entail removing unnecessarily strict regulations and replacing them with regulations based on the results of the latest research into safe handling of sanitation by-products or adopting new regulation (when those are not already in place)" (p. 282).

29. Roma and Pugh (2012).

30. http://blogs.worldbank.org/futuredevelopment/why-should-governments-spend-sanitation.

31. See Santiso (2007).

32. See OECD (2013) for 2010 aid data. The percentages of aid budgets dedicated to water and sanitation were the following: Australia (9 percent), Austria (8 percent), Belgium (0 percent), Canada (2 percent), Denmark (5 percent), European Union (2 percent), Finland (3 percent), France (0 percent), Germany (0 percent), Greece (0 percent), Ireland (0 percent), Italy (1 percent), Japan (0 percent), Korea (0 percent), Luxembourg (1 percent), Netherlands (8 percent), New Zealand (1 percent), Norway (3 percent), Portugal (0 percent), Spain (8 percent), Sweden (3 percent), Switzerland (5 percent), United Kingdom (3 percent), and United States (0 percent).

33. The World Bank stated, "The World Bank is committed to using innovative approaches to meet the sanitation challenges: ending open defecation, improving service delivery, and closing the loop from access to sanitation facilities to sustainable disposal of wastewater and sludge management." See http://www.worldbank.org/en/topic/sanitation/overview#2.

34. See, for example, Paterson, Mara, and Curtis (2007) and http://aguatuya.org.

35. See, for example, Tukahirwa, Mol, and Oosterveer (2013).

36. In Kampala, for example, Tukahirwa, Mol, and Oosterveer (2013) reported that "solid waste service provision is contracted out to only large private companies. However, these companies have hardly been able to provide services in urban poor informal settlements. The inadequacy of these services in the poor urban settlements has prompted a large growth of NGOs/CBOs trying to fill the gap. These organizations work independently in solid waste management without formal government recognition and predominantly service the urban poor. The contribution of these organizations is hampered by government obstruction because of its preference for large private companies" (p. 207).

37. For the Ghanaian case, see Ayee and Crook (2006).

38. For the important Indian case, see Ramani, SadreGhazi, and Duysters (2012).

39. See Kar and Chambers (2008).

40. Ramani, SadreGhazi, and Duysters (2012). Assessing the Indian case, these authors stated, "Indeed, sanitation entrepreneurs agree that education is an essential ingredient for success. Not only do potential investors have to be educated on the advantages of having a toilet, but they must also be made aware of the disadvantages of open defecation. Furthermore, consumers are rarely aware that toilet use can improve health conditions only if all their neighbors also have and use toilets. The benefit of a toilet in terms of hygiene is not immediately visible to them. Therefore, awareness building is absolutely necessary to create an endogenous demand by which potential investor-households convince their neighbors and a group of households comes forward to experiment with the introduction of toilets" (p. 682).

41. For the Ghanaian case, see Jenkins and Scott (2007). The authors showed that such considerations can trump concerns about fecal–oral contamination and that the understanding of contamination processes can be lacking. Respondents tended to have a miasma theory of contamination rather than a germ theory.

42. See, for example, Kotler and Lee (2009).

7

Health Services

Recall that, in Chapter 2, I contrasted the growth perspective and the capabilities perspective on development. If there is one area where these two perspectives diverge most dramatically, it is health. Health is put front-and-center in capabilities and human development considerations, whereas it usually lingers in the background in the growth perspective. As a consequence of this creative tension, we now appropriately give life expectancy attention as a key development indicator on par with GDP per capita. And as it turns out, advances in life expectancy can take place with less growth than previously thought. This is what led Charles Kenny of the Center for Global Development to conclude that "even without *any* increase at all in GDP per capita, significant improvements in quality of life can be—and frequently have been—accomplished."[1] How can this be? Kenny explained that a basic package of primary health services is simply not all that expensive, being as low as a few percent of GDP per capita.[2] So basic health services or primary healthcare (PHC) are actually less expensive than we commonly think.

In the capabilities and human development perspective, it is health *outcomes* that matter. Hence the focus is on life expectancy. The basic goods approach, however, takes a different approach. Rather than health outcomes, it emphasizes health *determinants*, the delivery of PHC services that makes positive health outcomes possible. The focus is on health determinants rather than on health outcomes simply because the outcomes are conditional on the determinants. It is not that positive health outcomes are not important (they are very important). It is just that these positive outcomes cannot be achieved unless policy changes are made that expand the delivery of PHC services.[3]

As with food, water, and sanitation, deprivations in health services are widespread. This is evident, for example, in the fact that nearly six million infants and children died before their fifth birthday in 2015. As seen in Chapters 5 and 6, some of this is due to diarrheal disease from poor water and sanitation. But on top of this, there is also malaria, lack of treatment for respiratory infections, and a lack of prenatal and postnatal care for infants and their mothers. As demonstrated later in this chapter, it is very unlikely that this annual infant-and-child death toll will fall rapidly in the next few decades, and the accumulated death toll over decades is simply heartbreaking.

Data on access to health services are a bit sketchy, with uneven coverage of countries. But one often-used, standard measure is doctors per 1,000 population. This measure is given in Figure 7.1 for the bottom- and top-twelve countries for the most recent year available from 2010 to 2014.[4] What can be seen is an extraordinary difference in the availability of doctors, by a factor of nearly 800. It does not escape notice that some of the countries with the lowest number of doctors per 1,000 population are also those with the lowest life expectancies in the world. The data in Figure 7.1 indicate extraordinarily wide discrepancies in this (imperfect) measure of health service delivery.

To be sure, in some ways, Figure 7.1 is misleading. There are health practitioners *other than doctors* working in all countries. However, WHO suggests that a minimally functioning healthcare system requires at least 2.3 healthcare workers (doctors, nurses, and midwives) per 1,000 population.[5] Many countries (more than 50) fall below that level, often by very large amounts. More than thirty countries fall below 1.0 healthcare workers per 1,000 population. Most of the underserved countries are in sub-Saharan Africa, but the list includes countries from Latin America, Asia, and the Middle East as well.

Moving to slightly more advanced aspects of health deprivation, the *Lancet* Commission on Global Surgery estimated that there are five billion individuals without access to safe surgical and anesthesia care.[6] Intuition suggests that such care is generally expensive, but there are arguments made that this is not necessarily the case. Health researchers David Ljungman, John Meara, and Yihan Lin estimate that one third of human disease requires surgery of some sort and that US$20 billion a year would do a great deal to address this need.[7] This seems like an extraordinary amount of money before we consider that the rich countries of the world spend approximately US$150 billion on farm subsidies each year.[8]

What does a lack of access to PHC look like in practice? Here is one example from Pakistan written by investigative reporter Peter Maas concerning Mr. Emroz Khan:[9]

> Emroz Khan destroys for a living. He dismantles car engines, slicing them open with a sledgehammer and a crooked chisel, prying apart the cylinders, tearing out pistons, dislodging screws and bolts and throwing the metal entrails into a pile that will be sold for scrap. He is 21 and has been doing this sort of work for 10 years, 12 hours a day, six days a week, earning $1.25 a day.
>
> His hands and arms are gnarled works of body art, stained a rich black like fresh asphalt and ribboned with scars. As dusk falls on Cinema Road, where Emroz works in a shop that is so poor it has no name or sign, he rolls up his sleeve and asks me to put my finger along a

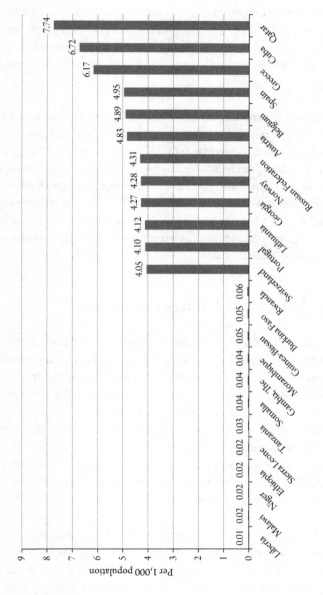

Figure 7.1 Doctors per 1,000 population for bottom-12 and top-12 countries, 2010 to 2014. Source: World Bank, World Development Indicators. Note: At the time of this writing, 2014 is the most recent year for which data are available. This table takes the most recent year from 2011 to 2014. However, some countries do not have any data for this time period.

bulge on his forearm; it feels as hard as iron. It is iron, a stretch of pipe he drove into his body by mistake. He cannot afford to pay a doctor to take it out.

"I've had it for three years," he says.

He opens his left palm and places two fingers alongside what looks like a crease, then pulls apart the crease to reveal a two-inch gash that runs an inch deep. I hadn't noticed it because the raw flesh was covered with grease, like the rest of his palm and arm. The wound is two years old.

The deprivation here is expressed as Mr. Khan's inability to walk into a hospital and have the piece of iron in his forearm removed and the gash in his hand treated. In his interview with Peter Maas, Mr. Khan commented, "That's what our life is like. It is the life of animals." Actually, with regard to access to healthcare, it is *worse* than some animals. There are many dogs and cats in the world with access to top-quality healthcare, including dental care and advanced surgeries, that is completely out of reach for hundreds of millions of human beings. Such differences bring us to investigate the extent to which healthcare, particularly PHC, is a basic subsistence right.

The Right to Primary Healthcare

As is clear in previous chapters, this book is supportive of basic subsistence rights, as well as the language in the United Nations system to support such rights. In the realm of health rights, however, I am going to *diverge* from some of the United Nations language. In doing so, I am going to make a distinction between the right to *primary healthcare* or PHC and the right to *health itself*. I am going to offer strong support to the right to PHC but argue *against* the right to health itself. Let us examine why.

As we have seen, food, water, and sanitation are three key examples of basic subsistence rights. PHC is indeed a fourth. The logic of treating PHC as a basic subsistence right was presented by political scientist Michael Goodhart:[10]

> The right to health care is fundamental for emancipation in that its denial or removal endangers one's life and well-being. To limit (or threaten) a person's access to or quality of health care would be to subject that person to a particularly cruel and callous form of dependence. . . . The right to health care is also basic. . . . Although health cannot always be guaranteed, what can and must be ensured is that all members of society are enabled to maintain their health or address health problems through access to health care.

So there are good reasons for recognizing PHC as a basic right. Article 25 of the 1948 Universal Declaration of Human Rights states that "Everyone has the right to a standard of living adequate for the health and well-being of himself and of his family, including food, clothing, housing and medical care and necessary social services, and the right to security in the event of unemployment, sickness, disability, widowhood, old age or other lack of livelihood in circumstances beyond his control."[11] This statement is fully consistent with the basic goods approach that would view PHC as a basic subsistence right.

In 1966, however, the United Nations Assembly adopted the ICESCR, which came into force in 1976. Article 12 of the ICESCR recognized a right to "the enjoyment of the highest attainable standard of physical and mental health."[12] It did emphasize "the creation of conditions which would assure to all medical service and medical attention in the event of sickness," or the provision of PHC. But the right to *health itself* (an ultimate outcome) falls beyond Henry Shue's basic rights concept and, therefore, the basic goods approach.[13] An additional divergence occurred in 1978 in the Alma-Ata Conference on Primary Health Care. The Alma-Ata Declaration defined a "fundamental human right"[14] to "health, which is a state of complete physical, mental and social wellbeing and not merely the absence of disease or infirmity." This is a giant step beyond the basic goods approach, an approach based on *minimalist* ethics of provision and not maximalist guarantees of outcomes.[15] That said, the Alma-Ata Conference did usefully elaborate on the concept of PHC, the elements of which are essential to the application of the basic goods approach to health:[16]

- "Reflects and evolves from the economic conditions and sociocultural and political characteristics of the country and its communities and is based on the application of the relevant results of social, biomedical and health services research and public health experience;
- Addresses the main health problems in the community, providing promotive, preventive, curative and rehabilitative services accordingly;
- Includes at least: education concerning prevailing health problems and the methods of preventing and controlling them; promotion of food supply and proper nutrition; an adequate supply of safe water and basic sanitation; maternal and child health care, including family planning; immunization against the major infectious diseases; prevention and control of locally endemic diseases; appropriate treatment of common diseases and injuries; and provision of essential drugs;
- Involves, in addition to the health sector, all related sectors and aspects of national and community development, in particular agriculture, animal husbandry, food, industry, education, housing, public works, communications and other sectors; and demands the coordinated efforts of all those sectors;

- Requires and promotes maximum community and individual self-reliance and participation in the planning, organization, operation and control of primary health care, making fullest use of local, national and other available resources; and to this end develops through appropriate education the ability of communities to participate;
- Should be sustained by integrated, functional and mutually supportive referral systems, leading to the progressive improvement of comprehensive health care for all, and giving priority to those most in need;
- Relies, at local and referral levels, on health workers, including physicians, nurses, midwives, auxiliaries and community workers as applicable, as well as traditional practitioners as needed, suitably trained socially and technically to work as a health team and to respond to the expressed health needs of the community."

The right to health itself was more recently endorsed in 2000 by CESCR in its General Comment 14 on the Right to the Highest Attainable Standard of Health. This Comment argued that the "right to health"[17] is not confined to the right to healthcare but "embraces a wide range of socio-economic factors that promote conditions in which people can lead a healthy life, and extends to the underlying determinants of health, such as food and nutrition, housing, access to safe and potable water and adequate sanitation, safe and healthy working conditions, and a healthy environment." Such considerations are clearly related to the basic goods approach and make clear that basic goods and services are prerequisites to any recognized "right to health." Nonetheless, the "right to health" falls outside the basic goods approach itself.

I apply the distinction between the right to PHC and the right to health itself to the previously mentioned case of Mr. Emroz Khan. The basic goods approach would argue that Mr. Khan should be able to immediately walk into a hospital and have the piece of iron in his forearm removed and the gash in his hand treated. His inability to do this is a violation of his human rights to PHC. The approach would not argue, however, that Mr. Khan must live to ripe old age or be guaranteed "complete physical, mental, and social wellbeing," because some illnesses are simply inevitable. In the basic goods approach, the subsistence right is active at the level of *health services*, but not at the level of health itself.[18]

But even if we were to recognize a right to health itself, health-related goods and services would be necessary inputs into this expanded right. The right simply will not be realized without them. Consider for example Jonathan Wolff's book *The Human Right to Health* sponsored by Amnesty International. In the introduction to this book, Wolff stated,[19]

Decent food and housing, as well as modern hygiene and sanitation remove many of the threats to infant health. The assistance of skilled midwives and doctors in birth shrink newborn mortality. And a range of medical techniques, from advanced surgery to simple powders to overcome diarrheal dehydration, can make a huge difference to survival in childhood. We do not need to make new medical discoveries or invent new vaccines or pharmaceuticals to prevent the great majority of the world's infant deaths—or adult deaths, for that matter.

So even from the perspective of the more expanded right to health itself, basic goods and services are still essential.[20] However, for the reasons just given, I persist with a more minimal conception of a basic subsistence right to PHC, but not to health itself.

Leading Causes of Death

If we are concerned about providing PHC, we need to have some sense of the most pressing *needs* for these services. One way of doing this is to consider the leading causes of death. These are presented in Table 7.1 for the world as a whole. In order of importance, the top-ten causes of death are: ischemic heart disease; stroke; lower respiratory infections; chronic obstructive pulmonary disease (COPD); trachea, bronchus, and lung cancers; Alzheimer disease and other dementia; diarrheal diseases; tuberculosis; and road injuries. Each of these is briefly described in Table 7.1, and risk factors are given. Because the causes of death presented in the table are for the world as a whole, they are averaged over low-, middle-, and high-income countries. But leading causes of death can vary significantly among these income levels. The WHO describes the difference as follows:[21]

> In high-income countries, 7 in every 10 deaths are among people aged 70 years and older. People predominantly die of chronic diseases: cardiovascular diseases, cancers, dementia, chronic obstructive lung disease or diabetes. Lower respiratory infections remain the only leading infectious cause of death. Only 1 in every 100 deaths is among children under 15 years.
>
> In low-income countries, nearly 4 in every 10 deaths are among children under 15 years, and only 2 in every 10 deaths are among people aged 70 years and older. People predominantly die of infectious diseases: lower respiratory infections, HIV/AIDS, diarrheal diseases, malaria and tuberculosis collectively account for almost one third of all deaths in these countries. Complications of childbirth due to prematurity, and birth asphyxia and birth trauma are among the leading causes of death, claiming the lives of many newborns and infants.

Table 7.1 **Leading Causes of Death, 2015**

Cause	Description	Sample Risk Factors	Mortality
Ischemic heart disease	A coronary heart disease involving the restriction of blood flow to the heart	Smoking, fat intake, high blood pressure, physical inactivity, and alcohol consumption	8.76 million
Stroke	Loss of brain function due to a disturbance in the blood supply to the brain	Smoking, high blood pressure, high blood glucose	6.24 million
Lower respiratory infections	Pneumonia and acute bronchitis	Poor nutrition, suboptimal breastfeeding, lack of access to improved water supply and to sanitation services	3.19 million
Chronic obstructive pulmonary disease (COPD)	A lung disease characterized by the obstruction of airflow in and out of the lungs. Comprised primarily of two related diseases, namely, chronic bronchitis and emphysema	Smoking, air pollution (urban and indoor)	3.17 million
Trachea, bronchus and lung cancers	Cancers of the respiratory system	Smoking	1.69 million
Diabetes mellitus	A group of metabolic diseases involving high blood sugar levels over a prolonged period of time	Poor nutrition, high blood glucose, physical inactivity	1.59 million
Alzheimer disease and other dementia	Progressive brain disorders that lead to a loss of cognitive functioning	Genetics and potentially environmental and lifestyle factors	1.54 million

Table 7.1 (Continued)

Cause	Description	Sample Risk Factors	Mortality
Diarrheal diseases	Cholera, typhoid, dysentery and diarrhea	Poor nutrition, suboptimal breastfeeding, lack of access to improved water supply and to sanitation services	1.39 million
Tuberculosis	Caused by a bacteria that mostly affects the lungs	Infection by HIV/ AIDS and tobacco use increases TB infection rates substantially	1.37 million
Road injuries	Injuries due to road traffic collisions	Poor or absent road safety systems, alcohol consumption	1.34 million

Source: www.who.int and World Health Organization (2009).

The difference in mortality profiles between high- and low-income countries suggests that health services need to be tailored to specific environments to save the most lives. It also suggests that, as incomes increase, the more "lifestyle" choices matter for mortality patterns. This reflects the shift from infectious diseases to chronic diseases or what is called the "epidemiological transition."[22] The difficulty in some countries (e.g., a number of many middle-income countries) is that health systems are confronted by both infectious diseases and chronic diseases simultaneously, a situation known as the "epidemiological backlog."[23] The epidemiological backlog can make deploying health budgets effectively quite difficult. The threat of an epidemiological backlog also makes confronting lifestyle disease all the more pressing. This is, in part, due to the "nutrition transition" discussed in Chapter 4 and, in part, due to the use of tobacco products.

The WHO estimates that tobacco use is responsible for one in ten adult deaths. This is through its impact on cardiovascular disease, chronic obstructive lung disease, and lung cancer. The case of tobacco thereby provides a useful example that clearly distinguishes the basic goods approach from the standard economic approach based on the utility of consumption (discussed in the Appendix). In the standard approach, the consumption of tobacco products generates utility and is therefore valued. In the basic goods approach because tobacco products do not address an objective need, they are not so valued. Further, because they cause objective harm, they are *disvalued*. The implication of tobacco products in one in ten adult deaths shows the importance of this disvaluing in the basic goods approach. It also helps to explain the WHO's increased attention to this issue.

Child Survival

Perhaps the most damning evidence of the global failure to provide basic goods and services is the number of children who die as a direct result. The failure to provide essential basic goods and services contributed to the nearly six million children who perish yearly as of 2015, largely from preventable causes.[24] Child mortality data contribute to both hope and despair. The hope revolves around the fact that there is clear progress being made. As shown in Figure 7.2, child mortality rates fell from 91 per 1,000 live births in 1990 to 43 per 1,000 live births in 2015.[25] Hope is also present when we consider total child mortality. As shown in Figure 7.3, this has fallen by more than one half between 1990 and 2015, from over 12 million to below six million.

But despair enters into the picture because the numbers, particularly the cumulative numbers are so high. As of 2015, 16,000 children perished daily (11 per minute). And significantly more than 200 million children died between 1990 and 2015. There is a regional aspect to this despair in that, also as of 2015, one in twelve children in sub-Saharan Africa died before their fifth birthday. Also, the trend line for total child mortality in Figure 7.3 is decreasingly negative, indicating that it is becoming somewhat more difficult to achieve further reductions in child mortality. To put it another way, child mortality is quite persistent given current trends.

Total child mortality is concentrated in certain countries. In order of importance, and as of 2015 these are the following: India, Nigeria, Pakistan, Democratic Republic of the Congo, Ethiopia, China, Angola, Indonesia, Bangladesh, and

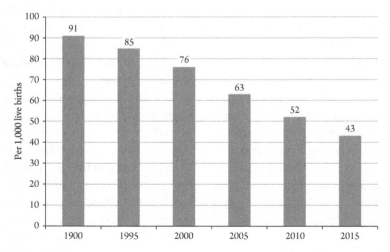

Figure 7.2 Child mortality rates (per 1,000 live births). Source: United Nations Inter-Agency Group on Child Mortality (2013, 2015).

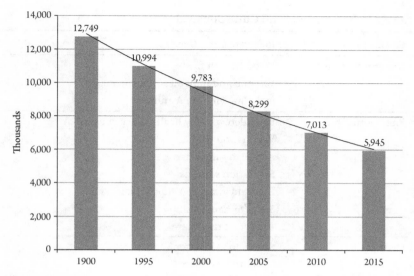

Figure 7.3 Total child mortality (thousands). Source: United Nations Inter-Agency Group on Child Mortality (2013, 2015).

Tanzania. This country concentration makes it possible to focus energies where it would matter most for saving absolute numbers of infants and children.

So by any measure, child mortality presents a pressing issue for the health policy communities. The question is *how* we can make sustained forward progress. Inevitably, emphasis will need to be placed on the provision of certain basic goods and services. The role of basic goods in reducing child mortality has been recognized by the United Nations on a number of occasions.[26] Some of the key basic goods and services are presented in Table 7.2, matched to source of child mortality. Utilizing the most simple of basic goods, soap, in handwashing has been shown to reduce infections of both diarrhea and pneumonia substantially, for example.[27] In addition to the basic goods identified in Table 7.2, however, other basic goods apply across all sources of child mortality. For example, educational services (particularly but not exclusively for girls and women) are crucial. Indeed, UNICEF estimated that progress in female education has been linked to "more than half of the recent reductions in under-five mortality."[28] UNICEF went on to report:[29]

> Mechanisms through which maternal education may have a positive impact on child survival include economic benefits acquired by the mother through education, providing access to better housing, sanitation and health care; improved immunization status of children born to better educated mothers; and other changes in usage of preventative and curative health services across the continuum of care. Education

Table 7.2 **Basic Goods and Child Survival**

Cause of Death	Relevant Basic Goods
Under nutrition	Nutrient-rich foods
	Vitamin and mineral supplements, including vitamin A and zinc
Pneumonia	Early detection by healthcare professional
	Vaccination
	Access to safe water
	Sanitation services
	Zinc and vitamin A supplements
	Soap for handwashing
	Antibiotic treatment
Diarrhea	Access to safe water
	Sanitation services
	Oral rehydration therapy
	Zinc and vitamin A supplements
	Soap for handwashing
Malaria	Insecticide-treated bed nets
	Diagnostic testing
	Artemisinin-based combination therapy

Source: United Nations Children's Fund (2013, 2015).

can also delay marriage and child-birth, which in turn has a positive impact on child survival.

Access to contraceptives is also critical through its contribution to healthy birth spacing. UNICEF reported that "maintaining a birth spacing of at least two years would cut mortality among infants by 10 percent, and would cut mortality among children ages one to four by 21 percent."[30] Important also is the presence of skilled attendants at birth in order to reduce neonatal mortality, as well as breastfeeding coaches. UNICEF noted that "globally, only two out of five newborns are put to the breast within the first hour of birth; roughly the same low proportion of 0–5 months olds are exclusively breast-fed." [31] This has not only nutritional implications but immunity implications as well as suboptimal breastfeeding is a key risk factor for both pneumonia and diarrhea.[32]

As indicated earlier, there is a *geographic* component to the provision of basic goods and services for reducing child mortality. The two leading causes of child death are pneumonia and diarrhea. More than half of the deaths attributable to these causes occur in India, Nigeria, Pakistan, and the Congo. Nigeria is also host to nearly a third of child malaria deaths. Note that India, Nigeria, and Pakistan were identified in Chapter 6 as countries with high rates of open defecation, which contributes substantially to child mortality. So as stated earlier, it will be possible to geographically concentrate efforts in reducing child mortality so as to make the most progress possible in terms of absolute numbers of lives saved. Basic health services for mothers, infants, and children, combined with efforts to improve sanitation, can work together to save young lives.[33]

I noted in the introduction that it is possible to make substantial progress on life expectancies even with little growth. Relatedly, it is possible to make significant progress on child mortality at low levels of GDP per capita. UNICEF reported a number of low-income countries that have made substantial progress in reducing child mortality. These countries include Bangladesh, Cambodia, Eritrea, Ethiopia, Guinea, Liberia, Madagascar, Malawi, Mozambique, Nepal, Niger, Rwanda, Uganda, and Tanzania. In light of this evidence, UNICEF concluded that "*at all levels of national income*, it is possible to make rapid advances in reducing under-five mortality by combining political commitment, sound strategies and adequate resources" (emphasis added).[34] Therefore, where progress is not being made, strategy and commitment are missing.

Health Services for Poor People

The provision of health services turns out to be a contentious issue almost everywhere. The medical, public policy, and health economics research literatures on the issue are vast, and the public policy debates are heated. I am going to try to substantially narrow the scope by focusing on PHC services for those who need it the most, namely, poor people deprived of these services. One area of consensus is that PHC services are grossly underprovided or, to use the term of art, *underutilized*. It is also clear that utilization is lowest where it is most needed, namely, among the poor.[35] This phenomenon is known as the "inverse care law" and applies to *public* as well as private expenditures.[36] The more you need PHC, the less you get of it. Something is definitely wrong with this picture.

As I discussed in Chapter 3, there is both a supply side and a demand side to any basic good or service, and this includes PHC. The importance of considering both supply and demand sides of PHC services was summarized by health economist Owen O'Donnell:[37]

> There are two sides to the access problem. On the supply side, good quality, effective health care may not be offered. On the demand side, individuals may not utilize services from which they could benefit. The two are obviously related. Poor quality care will arouse little interest

from the public. A high level of demand, made effective by purchasing power, will induce the provision of quality care. Solving the access problem requires tackling both demand and supply side issues.

An often-used framework for evaluating supply-side conditions is in terms of the four qualities of availability, accessibility, affordability, and acceptability.[38] With regard to availability and accessibility, differences often appear across the urban–rural divide. There is a widely recognized tendency for availability and accessibility to be concentrated in urban areas, while rural areas are distinctly neglected.[39] This reflects a more general neglect of rural development. With regard to affordability, it is tempting to say that the major issue is a lack of resources, and often this is the case. But, as I mentioned at the beginning of this chapter, PHC services are not always as expensive as often alleged. With regard to acceptability, *quality* issues (and even corruption issues) abound.[40] The aspects of poor quality have been described as follows:[41]

> Facilities open and close irregularly; absenteeism rates of doctors and nurses can be very high; staff can be hostile, even violent to patients; misdiagnosis is not uncommon; medicines are too often unavailable, sometimes due to staff pilfering for use in private practice; and there is inappropriate prescribing and treatment.

The demand side for health services is just as important as the supply side. Initially, the focus on PHC services made the assumption that the provision process was simply a technical one and that, if the services were made available, they would be consumed. Subsequently, less-than-satisfactory experience proved that this was distinctly *not the case*. Evidence suggests that poor people do spend a significant portion of their income on health, but not always in a productive fashion.[42] Knowledge appears to be important in promoting demand. This helps to explain why immunizations are not demanded even when they are essentially free, for example. For this reason, PHC and education services (discussed in Chapter 8) are mutually reinforcing.[43]

What to do? Action is required on both the supply and demand sides. On the supply side, efforts at provision need to be increased (in some instances substantially) with a focus on the most essential services of reasonable quality, distributed to match the locations of deprived individuals. On the demand side, programs need to be developed make PHC more affordable. Recall from Chapter 2 that Vietnam has a life expectancy not far below that of the United States, despite spending about 2 percent of what the United States spends per capita. Not coincidentally, Vietnam has been working since 1992 to provide basic health insurance in the form of the Social Health Insurance (SHI) and Health Care Funds for the Poor (HCFP) programs (both compulsive), as well as the Voluntary Health Insurance (VHI) program, and to incrementally make these programs as universal as possible. Evidence suggests that this has had a positive impact.[44] In particular, prepayment and insurance arrangements cover more than half the population. Partly as a consequence of these programs, immunization rates and births attended by skilled health professional rates are high, while malaria and tuberculosis infection rates are quite low.

Also discussed in Chapter 2 was the case of Costa Rica. This country has pursued a nearly universal healthcare system with contributions from labor, employers, and the government, run by the Caja Costarricense de Seguro Social (CCSS). As in the case of Vietnam, this has been effective in the universal delivery of PHC, with positive life expectancy outcomes.[45]

Short of these types of comprehensive approaches, subsidies, fee waivers, or vouchers can be targeted by age (to children and expectant mothers), by service (to immunizations and prenatal/obstetric care with demonstrated, positive externalities), and by socioeconomic group (traditionally poor minorities). CCT programs for the poor can also be tied to health service demand for children.[46] Because these are targeted to children and to both PHC and education, CCTs address a number of objectives simultaneously.

Essential Medicines

As I emphasized, basic goods are often a mixture of both goods and services. In the case of health, the services involved draw on goods of many sorts, including medicines. The WHO maintains a list of *essential medicines* that it defines as "those that satisfy the priority health care needs of the population." It further states that "essential medicines are intended to be available within the context of functioning health systems at all times in adequate amounts, in the appropriate dosage forms, with assured quality, and at a price the individual and the community can afford."[47] The list is updated periodically on the basis of reviews by expert committees and distinguishes between children and adults. The WHO program on essential medicines involves countries of all income levels. As some have recognized, the essential medicines project can be very helpful in meeting the basic subsistence right to PHC. Health policy specialist Hans Hogerzeil put it this way:[48]

> Its consistent focus on sustainable, universal access to essential medicines through the development of national medicines policies has always been in line with human rights principles of non-discrimination and care for the poor and disadvantaged. This also applies to its focus on good governance. For example, the careful selection of essential medicines, good quality assurance, procurement and supply management

and rational use all serve to optimize the value of limited government funds, and thereby empower and support governments in making basic services available to all.

So the WHO essential medicines program can be effective. However, as can be seen in Table 7.3, the list of essential medicines is long! The list includes thirty categories, with most categories including numerous subcategories. It is difficult to imagine that this list would be practical in rural health clinics trying to provide basic care. For this reason, we also need to think in terms of *shorter,*

Table 7.3 **WHO's Essential Medicine Categories**

1. Anesthetics	16. Diuretics
2. Medicines for pain and palliative care	17. Gastrointestinal medicines
3. Antiallergics and medicines used in anaphylaxis (acute allergic reactions)	18. Hormones, other endocrine medicines, and contraceptives
4. Antidotes and other substances used in poisonings	19. Immunologicals (including vaccines)
5. Anticonvulsants and antiepileptics	20. Muscle relaxants and cholinesterase inhibitors (latter to address Alzheimer's)
6. Anti-infective medicines	21. Ophthalmological preparations
7. Antimigraine medicines	22. Oxytocics and antioxytocics (for managing labor induction)
8. Antineoplastics (anticancer) and immunosuppressives	23. Peritoneal dialysis solution
9. Antiparkisonism medicines	24. Medicines for mental and behavioral disorders
10. Medicines affecting the blood	25. Medicines acting on the respiratory tract
11. Blood products and plasma substitutes	26. Solutions correcting water, electrolyte, and acid-base disturbances
12. Cardiovascular medicines	27. Vitamins and minerals
13. Dermatological medicines	28. Ear, nose, and throat medicines in children
14. Diagnostic agents	29. Specific medicines for neonatal care
15. Disinfectants and antiseptics	30. Medicines for disease of joints

Source: World Health Organization.

prioritized lists. Antibiotics and antimalarial medicines are more important than antidepressants, for example. Such shorter lists are sometimes referred to by the term "essential medicine kit" in relief efforts, but need to be more generally applied. The contents of the kit can and should vary from one application to another. After establishing the kit contents, delivery can often be challenging due to poor road infrastructure and poor communication systems. With a few notable exceptions, this seems to be a neglected issue at the forefront of providing universal access to PHC.[49] It urgently needs further attention.

Medical Brain Drain

As seen in Figure 7.1, access to doctors in many countries can be very far below that of other countries, by a factor of nearly 1,000. This situation is made potentially worse by doctors and nurses emigrating from lower-income countries to higher-income countries in a phenomenon known as *medical brain drain*. For many countries, a substantial percentage of trained doctors and nurses eventually leave their home countries. In some cases, this can involve up to one third or even one half of graduating doctors. Intuitively, we can sense that, as doctors and nurses emigrate, PHC in their home countries would suffer. And indeed, health policy researchers have sounded the alarm on this issue. For example, bioethicists Estzer Kollar and Alena Buyx stated,[50]

> Health-worker migration, commonly called "medical brain drain," is part of larger problem known as the global health workforce crisis, that is, the grossly uneven distribution of the health workforce and the critical shortage of health-workers in world regions with a high disease burden. . . . The unequal distribution of the global health workforce is exacerbated by mass emigration of doctors and nurses fleeing from poor working and living conditions, and by the increasing recruitment activities of affluent nations. Few dispute that medical brain drain presents a serious challenge for the healthcare systems of poor countries and raises important ethical questions. Despite the introduction of various policies at national and international levels, the trend is largely unbroken and more needs to be done if the harmful effects of medical brain drain are to be mitigated.

The reason for this alarm is that, in some cases, countries with a large disease burden find that their level of healthcare workers (doctors, nurses, and midwives) falls below that considered functional by the WHO (at least 2.3 per 1,000 population). For countries that fall below this level (many in sub-Saharan

Africa), losing more health workers is dangerous. This became apparent, for example, with the Ebola outbreak in West Africa in 2014.[51]

There is a lively debate on the merits of these concerns. What is clear, however, is that individual countries are up against global trends in high-skilled migration they cannot control. As a consequence, they will need to be creative. It is probably inescapable that developing countries suffering from significant outflows of health professionals will be required to pursue *two-tier* health professional training programs. This involves the introduction of basic training programs that fall short of international standards but can nevertheless have a positive impact on health outcomes. It should be noted that this is *not a first-best policy*. But such two-tier training is already a reality in some countries as a way to respond to challenges.[52] Unfortunately, this approach will need to be expanded to guarantee minimal access to PHC in countries losing health workers to emigration.

Pandemics and Antimicrobial Resistance

The world is periodically reminded of the potential threats of global pandemics. This has come in the form of the 2002–2003 severe acute respiratory syndrome (SARS), the 2009 swine flu outbreak, and the 2014 Ebola outbreak. It is worth recalling in this context that the 1918 influenza pandemic killed approximately 3 percent of the global population at that time, an equivalent of over 200 million individuals given the current world population. Indeed, one observer noted that "Influenza killed more people in a year than the Black Death of the Middle Ages killed in a century; it killed more people in twenty-four weeks than AIDS has killed in twenty-four years."[53] The slow response to the 2014 Ebola outbreak in a case of a disease that cannot be transmitted through the air, suggests that the global health system has some ways to go before we can be confident of its readiness to protect vulnerable people from the inevitable insipient pandemics of the future.

This issue is made all the more difficult due to antimicrobial resistance (AMR). AMR is defined by the WHO as "resistance of a microorganism to an antimicrobial medicine to which it was previously sensitive. Resistant organisms (they include bacteria, viruses and some parasites) are able to withstand attack by antimicrobial medicines, such as antibiotics, antivirals, and antimalarials, so that standard treatments become ineffective and infections persist and may spread to others." AMR is becoming a significant threat to modern health systems.[54] For example, tuberculosis (TB) has taken on increasingly strong AMR characteristics, even evolving into extensively drug resistant (XDR) TB that is essentially untreatable. Along with TB, other areas of AMR concern include malaria and staph infections.[55] The unfortunate AMR phenomenon is a potential global crisis that does not receive nearly the attention it deserves.

Summary

Primary healthcare is a basic good and a subsistence right. Despite some claims to the contrary, this subsistence right does not extend to the right to health itself. As is evident in the fact that nearly six million children died before their fifth birthday in 2015, PHC is underprovided. This also can been seen in the lack of healthcare providers in many countries relative to minimal WHO standards, a lack made worse by medical brain drain. The difference in mortality profiles between high- and low-income countries suggests that health services need to be tailored differently in the two environments to save the most lives. In low-income and some middle-income countries, the provision of PHC, clean water, and effective sanitation are required to make greater progress in reducing infant and child mortality. The universal stocking of minimal essential medicine kits is also critical. Despite these essential steps in basic goods provision, larger global issues of pandemics and AMR must not be forgotten.

Notes

1. Kenny (2011), p. 109.
2. Kenny (2011), p. 127. Kenny cited Loevinsohn and Harding (2005). See also Casabonne and Kenny (2012).
3. *The Economist* (2017c) reported, "Primary health care is not flashy, but it works. It is the central nervous system of a country's medical services—monitoring the general health of communities, treating chronic conditions and providing day-to-day relief. It can ensure that an infectious disease does not become an epidemic. . . . Primary care can deal with the vast majority of medical conditions. Expanding primary care tends to bring marked improvements" (p. 10).
4. No data were available beyond 2014, and some countries had no data at all.
5. The WHO actually represents this as twenty-three healthcare workers per 10,000 population.
6. See http://www.lancetglobalsurgery.org/.
7. Ljungman, Meara, and Lin (2017).
8. See, for example, Peterson (2009) and Goldin and Reinert (2012).
9. Maas (2001).
10. Goodhart (2007), p. 101. Once again, I am using the idea of a basic subsistence right in the sense of Shue (1996).
11. United Nations General Assembly (1948).
12. United Nations General Assembly (1966b), (p. 8)
13. The distinction here between the right to quality health services and the right to health itself has been effectively discussed by Wolff (2012). Goodhart (2007) agreed with the position taken here that the right to health itself is a step to far, stating "the ICESCR's 'highest attainable standard' of health criterion seems problematic for numerous reasons" (p. 101n).
14. World Health Organization (1978).
15. The approach therefore has connections to the decent minimum approach of Buchanan (1984), the needs approach of Doyal (2001), and the threshold approach of Alvarez (2007) as applied to his notion of "resources."

16. http://www.who.int/publications/almaata_declaration_en.pdf.

17. United Nations High Commissioner for Human Rights (2000)

18. In a widely cited editorial, Easterly (2009) criticized the human right to health on the grounds that "It is impossible for everyone immediately to attain the 'highest attainable standard' of health." This is in accordance with the basic goods approach and was pointed out by Buchanan (1984). Easterly also argued that "The pragmatic approach—directing public resources to where they have the most health benefits for a given cost—historically achieved far more than the moral approach." The basic goods approach is consistent with pragmatism in healthcare delivery in the face of limited resources. In particular, directing resources to the services that are most essential in saving lives is fully consistent with the approach. However, acknowledging the right to health services is helpful when budgets are set at a *higher level*, say between health services and pet projects for the military or, less starkly, between esoteric, high-end services in urban hospitals and primary services in rural clinics.

19. Wolff (2012), p. xiv.

20. Perehudoff, Laing, and Hogerzeil (2010) also noted that about half of national constitutions recognize some sort of right to access health facilities, goods, and services.

21. http://www.who.int/mediacentre/factsheets/fs310/en/index2.html.

22. As far as is discernable, the notion of epidemiological transition was first introduced by Omran (1971).

23. The notion of the epidemiological backlog was first introduced in the Latin American context by Londoño and Frenk (1997).

24. United Nations Inter-Agency Groups for Child Mortality Estimation (2013, 2015).

25. The original Millennium Development Goal was to reduce the rate to thirty deaths per 1,000 live births by 2015. This goal was not met.

26. See, for example, United Nations (2008) and UNICEF (2013).

27. See Luby et al. (2005) for the case of Pakistan. These authors found that handwashing with soap reduces diarrhea and pneumonia infections by 50 percent.

28. UNICEF (2013), p. 29.

29. UNICEF (2013), p. 29.

30. UNICEF (2013), p. 29.

31. UNICEF (2013), p. 27.

32. It is important to keep in mind there that infants receive *immune support* via breastfeeding along with nutrition.

33. On some controversies concerning the relative effectiveness of water and sanitation improvements, see Waddington and Snilstveit (2009).

34. UNICEF (2013), p. 11.

35. See, for example, the discussion of and references cited in O'Donnell (2007).

36. O'Donnell (2007) reported that "In most cases, there is a prorich bias in the distribution of public primary care even though this is exactly the type of health care that is supposed to best meet the health needs of the poor" (p. 2823). The primary reason for this is the focus of public health expenditures on hospital-based systems.

37. O'Donnell (2007), p. 2820.

38. See Pechansky and Thomas (1981).

39. As reported by Filmer, Hammer, and Pritchett (2000), "in many developing countries the public budget for health is principally absorbed by public hospitals staffed by doctors expensively trained at public expense who use costly medical technologies to treat conditions of the urban elite, while in those same countries children die from diseases that could have been treated for a few cents or avoided altogether with basic hygienic practices" (p. 199).

40. Quality issues were emphasized by Filmer, Hammer, and Pritchett (2000) and O'Donnell (2007). In her book *Beyond the Beautiful Forevers* on life in a Mumbai slum, Katherine Boo (2012) documented a number of instances of doctors demanding bribes for treatment and even the falsification of medical records.

41. O'Donnell (2007), p. 2826. Note that this author provides references for each of these quality issues.

42. See, for example, Chapter 3 of Banerjee and Duflo (2011) and the references therein.
43. Citing increasing numbers of measles cases in the United States, Banerjee and Duflo (2011) commented, "If people in the West, with all of the insights of the best scientists in the world at their disposal, find it hard to base their choices on hard evidence, how hard must it be for the poor, who have much less information? People make their choices based on what makes sense to them, but given that most of them have not had rudimentary high school biology and have no reason . . . to trust the competence and professionalism of their doctors, their decision is essentially a shot in the dark" (p. 59).
44. See, for example, Ekman et al. (2008). The authors' concluded that "Vietnam has attained considerable achievements in developing a coherent and potentially comprehensive health insurance system that contributes to a sustainable, efficient and equitable heath care sector" (p. 261).
45. See, for example, del Rocío Sáenz, Bermúdez, and Acosta (2010).
46. See Lomelí (2008) and Fiszbein and Schady (2009).
47. http://www.who.int/medicines/services/essmedicines_def/en/. The first WHO list of essential medicines was set out in 1977, a year before the previously discussed 1978 Alma Ata Declaration.
48. Hogerzeil (2006), pp. 371–372.
49. Notable exceptions are Bukhari et al. (2010) on Pakistan; Tumwine et al. (2010) on Uganda; and Vledder et al. (2015) on Zambia. The rural supply of essential medicines problem can be considered in terms of mathematical programming tools designed to ensure adequate supply of a number of essential medicines at a number of demand points across a network of particular qualities and given expiration durations. This is a fairly standard framework that is not difficult to address.
50. Kollar and Buyx (2013), p. 1. See also Goldin, Reinert, and Beverinotti (2012).
51. *The Economist* (2017c) reported, "Before the Ebola outbreak of 2014, nearly half of Liberians could not afford primary care and the deadly virus spread quickly. In parts of west Africa with better primary care, it was more easily contained" (p. 10).
52. See, for example, Dovlo (2004); Mullan and Frehywot (2007); and Eyal and Hurst (2008). Eyal and Hurst advocated a specific type of two-tier training that they term "locally-relevant training." The authors gave a flavor of what they had in mind here: "Students in locally relevant medical school learn . . . how to prescribe drugs that are more affordable for poor patients than the western standard of care (often generic equivalents) and that are safer to prescribe when supply or refrigeration are erratic. They gain true mastery in gleaning information using inexpensive tools like the physical exam. For example, they develop advanced expertise in stethoscope diagnosis, to a degree that Western physicians with access to expensive lab tests, x-ray and magnetic resonance imaging (MRI) usually do not require. These students become fluent at strategies and decision algorithms that might be irrelevant or grossly suboptimal in well-equipped western settings, but remain highly recommended for scarcity conditions" (pp. 182–183). *The Economist* (2017c) also reported, "Some medical bodies would like to see care-providers without formal medical qualifications banned, but the evidence is that even short training courses can greatly improve their diagnoses" (pp. 10–11).
53. Barry (2005), p. 5.
54. See, for example, WHO (2014).
55. To address AMR in the case of TB, there needs to be continued commitment to the WHO's Directly Observed Treatment Short-Course (DOTS) (http://www.who.int/tb/dots/whatis-dots/en/). The DOTS is crucial because it ensures that there is no incomplete treatment that contributes to AMR. An increased commitment to DOTS and an increased awareness of these other evolving AMR risks is important to ensuring that poor people can maintain recent-gained improvements in health and avoid future pandemics. The DOTS involves the elements of government commitment, case detection, standardized treatment of six to eight months, an uninterrupted supply of TB drugs, and a standardized recording and reporting system.

8

Education Services

As in the case of health services discussed in Chapter 7, the growth perspective and the capabilities perspective diverge significantly in their approaches to basic goods provision in the form of education services. Recall from Chapter 2 that one growth economist claimed that "education is worth little more than hula-hoops to a society" due to a lack of evidence that it contributed to growth.[1] Researchers and practitioners working in the capabilities or human development perspective would never make such a statement. For them, education matters *in and of itself* because it directly contributes to human capabilities such as literacy and numeracy. It is for this reason that education forms one of the three elements of the HDI and is a central part of the capabilities approach.

The basic goods approach views education differently from both the growth and capabilities approaches, namely from the perspective of human need. Whether education contributes to growth (and as you will see it probably does), primary and secondary education meet the human need to be able to operate at a minimal level in the myriad societies that make up the world. Without at least a minimal level of education, it is difficult to be healthy and to have healthy children, to effectively participate in institutional structures, to successfully run a business enterprise of any size, or to exercise any basic political rights to which one is entitled. And in contrast to the capabilities approach, the basic goods approach puts more emphasis on the *provision process* in education services. It does not assume that educational aspirations easily translate into educational achievements. Indeed, as we will see, there is ample evidence that this is often *not* the case.

As I discussed in Chapter 3, education services are a way of increasing *human capital*. As with all types of capital, there is an inherent "capital goods problem" in that time horizons are very long (even reaching across generations) and returns uncertain. This often makes the optimal consumption of education services unknown. On top of this, there are positive interpersonal and intertemporal externalities present in the consumption of education services. For these reasons, there is no guarantee that the private consumption decisions with respect to education will be *either* individually *or* socially optimal. Efforts to nudge primary and secondary education provision in the right direction can therefore often be appropriate, and most societies do this on one way or another.

Evidence suggests that, despite significant progress in expanding education provision (since approximately 1960), education is still an underprovided basic good in many countries.[2] With regard to school *enrollment*, for example, World Bank data indicate that, globally, approximately 10 percent of primary-aged children are not enrolled in primary education and approximately 35 percent of secondary-aged children are not enrolled in secondary education.[3] Over time, substantial progress has been made in boosting participation of children in primary school, but much remains to be done with regard to actual *achievement*. This has been pointed out in a recent UNESCO report, for example.[4] This study estimates that approximately 250 million of the 650 primary school age children (nearly 40 percent) have not mastered basic literacy and numeracy. Of these, 170 million cannot read a single sentence and over 100 million spend little or no time in school. And *The Economist* has reported that "half of children in South Asia and a third of those in Africa who complete four years of schooling cannot read properly."[5] As will be demonstrated, issues of education service *quality* are central to the effective provision of these basic goods.

Turning to *literacy* measures, data from a few sources suggest that there are more than 750 million illiterate adults.[6] This has been, roughly speaking, constant since 1990. Figure 8.1 gives a sense of where most of these individuals reside by presenting the total number of illiterate adults for the year 2015 for the top 25 countries. These countries account for approximately 600 million of the over 750 million illiterate individuals. As can be seen, India is vastly over-represented here, with approximately 260 million illiterate adults. Recall from Chapter 6 that India also has nearly 500 million individuals practicing open defecation. As mentioned in Chapter 2, it is difficult to imagine that these characteristics of the Indian economy do not hold back its growth prospects. China, with a population on par with India's, only has about fifty million illiterate adults, and two other South Asian countries, Pakistan and Bangladesh, also appear at the top of the list. In the African case, it is Nigeria and Ethiopia with the most illiterate adults. Together, these six countries represent about 470 million of the world's illiterate adults.

These educational shortfalls have detrimental impacts on the individuals, families, and societies involved. The effects show up in fewer job prospects, lower wages, and poorer health. More generally, the shortfalls prevent the individuals involved from effectively participating in the economic, political, and social systems in which they reside. It is for these reasons that early childhood, primary, and secondary education are considered by some observers to be basic subsistence rights.

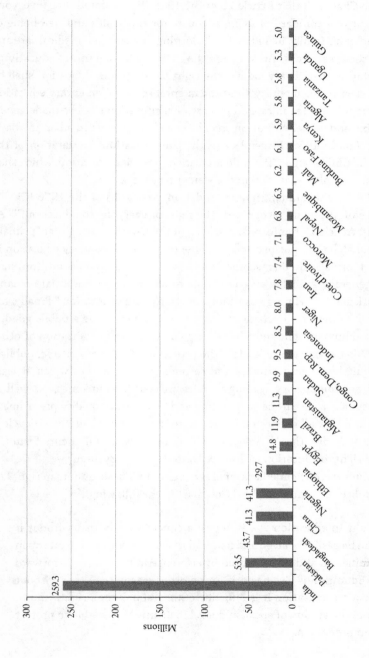

Figure 8.1 Number of illiterate adults by country, 2015 (millions ages 15 and above). Source: World Bank, World Development Indicators

The Right to Education

Recall from Chapter 3 that Article 25 of the 1948 UDHR stated that "Everyone has the right to a standard of living adequate for the health and well-being of himself and of his family, including food, clothing, housing and medical care and necessary social services."[7] Article 26 of the UDHR extended this to educational services, stating that "Everyone has the right to education. Education shall be free, at least in the elementary and fundamental stages. Elementary education shall be compulsory. Technical and professional education shall be made generally available and higher education shall be equally accessible to all on the basis of merit."[8] And in 1959, Principle 7 of the United Nations Declaration of the Rights of the Child stated, "The child is entitled to receive education, which shall be free and compulsory, at least in the elementary stage."[9]

Following on this human rights foundation, Article 13 of the 1976 ICESCR addressed education and recognized "the right of everyone to education."[10] As part of this, Article 13 reinforced Article 26 of the UDHR, stating that "primary education shall be compulsory and available free to all. Secondary education in its different forms, including technical and vocational secondary education, shall be made generally available and accessible to all by every appropriate means, and in particular by the progressive introduction of free education." Finally, the 2015 UNESCO Incheon Declaration stated that "education is a public good, a fundamental human right and a basis for guaranteeing the realization of other rights."[11] This Declaration called for "the provision of 12 years of free, publicly funded, equitable quality primary and secondary education, of which at least nine years are compulsory, leading to relevant learning outcomes," as well as "the provision of at least one year of free and compulsory quality pre-primary education and that all children have access to quality early childhood development, care and education."[12] Taken together, all of these statements form the core of the right to education within the United Nations system.[13]

Why would we consider educational services to be a basic or human right? As noted by political scientist Michael Goodhart in the following:[14]

> The right to education . . . is key to emancipation in that without it one can be easily deceived and manipulated by others, leaving one open to domination and unwarranted interference in fairly straightforward ways. Education is also basic, if for no other reason than that without an adequate education it is difficult to understand one's rights and to navigate the system of social and legal institutions available to protect and promote them.

It is the latter observation that makes education a basic or subsistence right in the sense of political philosopher Henry Shue as being a right that must be fulfilled so that other rights can be enjoyed.[15] Or to put it in other words, education can be the "ultimate sanction and guarantee" of other rights.[16]

If we agree that educational services are a basic subsistence right, we still need to decide at what *level* of education the right applies. In the Latin American context, for example, it is not unusual for students to protest (sometimes violently), demanding the "right" to free tertiary or university education. Free university education, however, does not look like an *authentic basic* right, whereas primary education certainly does. Another consideration takes place much earlier in the age spectrum. Education policy largely addresses primary, secondary, and tertiary education, but the empirical evidence suggests that education (and life) outcomes are greatly affected by experiences *before* primary school.[17] Therefore, preschool and other early-childhood interventions matter. For the purposes of this chapter, and in accordance with the previously mentioned Incheon Declaration, I consider only preschool, primary, and secondary education to have basic rights associated with them, with the strength of the right being higher the earlier the education level. For this reason, I largely ignore higher education.[18]

Education and Growth

I discussed growth in Chapter 2, noting that the role of education in growth processes has at times been something of a mystery. From a simple observational viewpoint, countries that grow have invested in education. For example, the economic historian Angus Maddison noted that "a significant characteristic of advanced capitalist counties is the effort they have made over the long run to raise the level of education of their population. . . . The higher the average level of education, the easier it is for a working population to understand and apply the fruits of technical progress."[19] But he also noted that "the specific identification of the role of education in economic performance is very difficult."[20] This latter observation proved to be prescient: the identification of the role of education in growth processes *has* turned out to be difficult.

Early attempts to address the potential contribution of education to growth suggested that education was indeed a statistically significant factor.[21] Subsequent work, however, questioned education's empirical relevance. For example, the development economist William Easterly (of the above-mentioned hula hoops analogy) noted in 2001 that "the growth response to the dramatic educational expansion of the last four decades has been distinctly disappointing. If the incentives to invest in the future are not there, expanding education is worth little. . . . Creating skills where there exists no technology to use them is not going to foster economic growth."[22] Other researchers expressed similar concerns.[23]

Why did the seeming importance of human capital as education not show up as significant in empirical investigations? Evidence began to build that it was due to *measurement errors*.[24] Subsequent work correcting for these measurement errors suggested that *education does indeed support growth processes*.[25] The caveat is that the *quality* of education matters, as well as the extent to which education attainment (years of schooling) actually translates into educational *achievement*, particularly in the form of cognitive skills.[26] Growth depends on what students actually learn, and as we will see, there is evidence of poor education quality where it is most needed. There also seems to be evidence of education achievement in the form of cognitive skills interacting positively with quality institutions in growth processes.[27] As I suggested in Chapter 3, it can be difficult for poorly educated individuals to make effective use of available institutions in ways that support growth.

There is another strand of research relevant to the role of education in growth, namely that of the *rate of return to education* (RORE).[28] These studies measured the private rates of return to education across many countries and time periods. They revealed that education generally has significant rates of return, often higher than that of physical capital. They also revealed that primary education tends to have a higher rate of return than secondary education, and that secondary education tends to have a higher rate of return than tertiary education. More recent, work on early childhood education revealed that this can have an even higher rate of return.[29] This evidence suggested that, in setting educational priorities, earlier stages are more important than later ones.[30] When researchers were doubtful of the role of education in growth, it was something of a mystery why education was privately but not collectively beneficial. With the data issues resolved in the education-and-growth field, this mystery has been resolved. It is also notable that the RORE results map directly on to the just-discussed human rights framework, both emphasizing earlier levels of education over latter levels.

Overall, evidence now suggests that basic goods provision in the form of education can support positive growth processes. So, for example, in the iconic case of East Asian growth, advances in both primary and secondary education seem to have played a significant role.[31] There is also the broader historical pattern that advances in education universally *precede* periods of sustained growth and development.[32] If there is a modicum of quality to primary and secondary education (a big "if" in some cases), the cost of providing these types of education (and no doubt early childhood education as well) can have payoffs in higher future incomes. For this reason, as suggested in Chapter 3, the growth perspective, the basic goods perspective, and even the capabilities perspective can work together in the education policy realm.

Girls' Education

One profound result from numerous development policy studies has been the transformational impact of girls' and therefore women's education. Indeed, one early review concluded that "there are few instances in international quantitative social science research where the application of common statistical methods has yielded more consistent findings than in the area of gender returns to schooling."[33] And the positive benefits seem to be broad, including higher birthweights, increased infant and child survival, increased ability to be nourished, higher levels of school enrollment and attainment, lower fertility rates, and productivity and earnings.[34] There is even evidence that girls' education or the reduction of gender inequality in education can contribute to growth.[35] The potential growth effects of girls' and women's education are not perhaps surprising, because they seem to have played a role in the East Asia case.[36] From a number of perspectives, girls' education is a particularly good investment.

When initial assessments of the impacts of girls' education were made, the evidence suggested that girls were disadvantaged in their access to educational services. A recent assessment by the World Bank suggested that, in many locations, this was no longer the case.[37] Gender parity has been achieved in *primary* education in most countries, with some African countries being the exception. At low overall levels of *secondary* education, girls are disadvantaged, but at high overall levels of secondary education, boys are actually disadvantaged. So this World Bank report concluded, "There are many reasons to feel optimistic about the state of women's education around the world. Progress has been remarkable, and many of the gaps salient in the 20th century have closed. Today, girls and boys around the world participate equally in primary and secondary education."[38] This is cause for optimism.

The reasons for this positive change cited by the World Bank are increases in the RORE to education for girls and women, lower school fees in some countries, higher and more predictable sources of household income, and CCTs discussed in Chapter 3. That said, there are still countries (e.g., Afghanistan and Pakistan) in which girls are significantly disadvantaged in their access to education. The World Bank concluded that this reflects geographical isolation, linguistic fragmentation, and lack of safety. Rather than gender discrimination, it is often poverty itself that holds back girls' education.[39] It is interesting to note, however, that even in the traditionally conservative Federally Administered Tribal Areas of Pakistan along the Afghan border, survey evidence suggests that nine out of every ten people identified lack of education and schools as their most important problem and that building new schools for girls as well as boys was identified as a high priority.[40] So even where girls are most disadvantaged in their access to educational services, there appears to be unfulfilled demand for these education services for girls. Meeting this demand is the difficulty.

Education Quality

In Chapter 3, I considered the question of the effective delivery of basic services and noted that deprived individuals and households are often poorly served by the systems that are supposed to deliver these services to them. I stated that, even if the right to the basic service is recognized and there is an available delivery technology, success is not necessarily assured. This problem reflects the fact that there can be interests opposed to the effective delivery of the service, with basic service provision thereby becoming a political issue. More simply, it also can just reflect negligence and disorganization. In the case of education services, poor service delivery is regrettable because, as I have demonstrated, educational achievements matter a great deal. It is unfortunate that there is substantial evidence of a *lack of quality* in educational service provision and a consequent shortfall in educational achievement. These shortfalls hold back both capability expansion and growth prospects for the countries involved.

One recognized quality issue relates to instructional time and teacher absence. For example, in a widely cited study of six developing countries, researchers found an average primary school teacher absence rate of about 20 percent and that even teacher presence did not always imply actual teaching.[41] As the authors of this study noted, "in low-income countries, substitutes rarely replace absent teachers, and so students simply mill around, go home or join another class, often of a different grade."[42] Compounding this, absence rates perversely increase with lower incomes, so the students who most need quality primary education are less likely to get it. Other studies concur that teacher absence is a significant problem and can differentially impact girls' education.[43] And teacher absence is not the only source of the larger instructional time loss problem. Schools can simply be closed, have delayed openings and early departures, or poorly utilize the available classrooms. One study of four developing countries found the number of school days devoted to learning ranged from approximately seventy five to approximately 150. It concluded that "in many lower income countries or socioeconomic groups the time and opportunity to learn are limited, and this limitation is linked to student achievement."[44]

Educational systems also suffer from what is politely called "leakage" of public funds. This can reflect ineffective accounting and finance systems but, more seriously, can stem from corruption and theft. Preliminary evidence suggests that such leakage is fairly widespread, can amount to a substantial portion of total fund flows, and holds back positive educational outcomes.[45] In countries characterized by histories of racial and ethnic discrimination, instructional time and leakage problems can adversely affect communities suffering from past or current discrimination, reinforcing differential life outcomes.[46]

Earlier, I considered the reasons that early-childhood, primary, and secondary education are basic rights and noted the ways that these rights were part of the United Nations system. If there is a right to education within this system, the assumption is that the right applies to a minimum threshold of *quality* in that education. For example, the educational quality issue was effectively summarized by education researcher Angeline Barrett:[47]

> As the world moves closer to the United Nations goal of primary education for all, the importance of the "quality imperative" is increasingly recognized. With rapid expansion of enrollments in many countries, the reality for many learners experience is overcrowded classrooms, poorly motivated and often unqualified teachers, delivering increasingly complex curricula sometimes through a medium of instruction in which neither learner nor teacher is fluent. Yet, if education is to contribute towards national development, sustainable livelihoods and individual capabilities, it needs to be of a good quality. . . . This is especially true when the quality of education for disadvantaged learners is in question.

So it is not just that the child has a right to a desk in a classroom, but rather a right to an educational service of minimal quality. For this reason, poor educational quality is an issue of basic rights and social justice. Researchers working on the link between education quality and rights disagree on the specific ways that the right to educational quality should be cast, but it is clear that the right itself exists.[48] Making progress to address this right involves attention being paid to education accountability.

Education Accountability

The widespread and ongoing issues of education quality and funding leakages reflects the fact that the education sector often suffers from poor provisioning or *service delivery failure*. There seems to be a consensus emerging in the education policy community that this poor provisioning can, at least in part, be addressed through increased accountability measures. Education accountability involves a rather large agenda, but its elements include the better use of information to evaluate impacts, appropriately devolving authority to more local levels, and providing incentives to teachers.[49] Let us consider these three elements in turn and the ways that increased involvement of parents can contribute to each.

The better use of information can provide a feedback loop to school systems on education outcomes than can positively affect service delivery. The feedback can be achieved via both impact evaluation through student testing (test-based accountability) and increase participation by families (client empowerment). Of course, as many parents and teachers will confirm, test-based accountability has its limits, because it increases incentives to just "teach to the test." However, having no information at all about outcomes makes improvement all but impossible. Likewise, increased participation by families also has limits. In the United States, parent teacher associations (PTAs) are sometimes humorously referred to as "Parents who Talk A lot." But to expect quality education without some significant empowerment of families is clearly a mistake. So, for example, providing public information to parents has been shown to help with service delivery and to reduce educational funding leakage.[50] It seems that, in both cases, a balance must be sought that provides enough information to school systems and enough parent involvement to make improved service delivery possible.

The role of testing in information-based accountability is expanding significantly but is also contested. Concerns with educational accountability, along with the recognition that educational attainment is not the same as educational achievement, have prompted an increased dependence on standardized educational testing. As a result, there are many types of standardized tests, some would say, too many.[51] One test that is gaining a great deal of attention is the Program for International Student Assessment (PISA) developed by the Organization for Economic Cooperation and Development (OECD). The PISA tests the "skills and knowledge" of 15-year-olds in the three areas of mathematics, reading and science and has become a touchstone in international education policy debates. For illustration purposes, Table 8.1 presents the ten countries with the lowest 2015 PISA scores, with high-scoring Japan included as a comparison. It is important to note that the 2015 PISA only covered 72 countries of the world. So it is far from a complete picture, and Table 8.1 gives only a suggestive sense of educational deprivations from the point of view of test-based evidence of achievement.

Within the OECD, PISA is conceived of as a measure of the human capital flow within the countries to which it is applied.[52] Recent work by the OECD has emphasized flexibility with regard to the geographical level of its testing. For example, it is now developing a PISA-like Test for Schools that can be implemented at the school level. With this project, the OECD is positioning itself as a center for educational assessment within an emerging system of global education governance for accountability.[53] Not everyone is pleased with this development, but it is a developing reality.

The second area for educational accountability is the devolution of authority. This involves allowing schools or school districts to make a specified set of decisions for themselves rather than centrally. In the terminology of the field, this is often called school-based management (SBM), but this term should not obscure the fact that devolution policies can take many forms. SBM is an active area of educational policy reform in many developing countries.[54] In principle, SBM can

Table 8.1 **Ten Countries with the Lowest 2015 PISA Test Scores Compared to Japan**

Mathematics		Reading		Science	
Country	*Score*	*Country*	*Score*	*Country*	*Score*
Japan	532	Japan	516	Japan	538
Lebanon	396	Qatar	402	Jordan	409
Peru	387	Georgia	401	Indonesia	403
Indonesia	386	Peru	398	Brazil	401
Jordan	380	Indonesia	397	Peru	397
Brazil	377	Tunisia	361	Lebanon	386
Macedonia	371	Dominican Republic	358	Tunisia	386
Tunisia	367	Macedonia	352	Macedonia	384
Kosovo	362	Algeria	350	Kosovo	378
Algeria	360	Lebanon	347	Algeria	376
Dominican Republic	328	Kosovo	347	Dominican Republic	332

Source: http://www.oecd.org/pisa/

have a number of positive effects by tailoring educational services to local conditions and preferences, potentially providing more accountability to local clients (parents and students), and increase participation by families (client empowerment again). SBM advocates Barbara Bruns, Deone Filmer, and Harry Patrinos made significant claims for the approach:[55]

> SBM is used to increase school autonomy and accountability, which can help solve some of the most fundamental problems in schools. Accordingly, while increasing resource flows and other support to the education sector is necessary to give the poor greater access to quality education, it is by no means sufficient. It is also necessary to translate these resources into basic services that are accessible to the poor. Therefore, under SBM, schools are given some autonomy over the use of their inputs and are held accountable for using these inputs efficiently.

On the negative side, however, it is possible for SBM to result in capture by local elites or to be confounded by low administrative capacities, obviating potential improvements. Further, assessments of SBM tend to fall short of the claims made for it. One study of SBM in Central America found mixed results but suggested that there could be some positive outcomes with regard to use of school resources and student learning outcomes.[56] A study of the Philippines found positive but very small impacts, and a study of Gambia found that a lack of local capacity held back positive results.[57] It is interesting that in the Gambian study, the illiteracy of parents proved to be an obstacle to their effective involvement. As the authors of this study concluded,[58]

> A structural feature that matters for an effective local management program . . . is local baseline basic human capital such as literacy in the communities. The gap between local capacity at the central level and the local level is a key determinant of the success of this kind of policies. In countries where this gap is small, regardless of the levels, a decentralized policy would be superior because of the added value of localized information. However, if the gap is sufficiently high in favor of the central government, then the localized information plays less of a role because the communities are not well equipped to act on them.

I mentioned client empowerment both in terms of the better use of information and in terms of devolution of authority. Evidence seems to suggest that there is a positive relationship between devolution of authority and client empowerment. Indeed, one study in Argentina found that, although decentralization led to higher test scores overall, this was not the case in poorer municipalities.[59] Further, a second study in Argentina found that there was a mutually supportive relationship between school autonomy and parental participation as evidenced by higher test scores. More important, this result appears to be stronger for disadvantaged families.[60] So decentralization may not be usable as an aspect of accountability without client empowerment as well, but effective client empowerment also depends on client capacity.

As seen from these results, SBM is not a policy switch that can be turned on and off to ensure education accountability. Its effectiveness varies and depends on a number of supporting factors. For this reason, some of the claims for SBM may be exaggerated. SBM also is not an all-or-nothing proposition. Rather, it is a matter of deciding which functions should be devolved and which kept centralized. [61] Nevertheless, SBM is an active area of experimentation for attempting to achieve greater educational accountability and effectiveness.

The third area for education accountability is providing incentives to teachers to be actually present in the classroom and to teach well. Education accountability advocates Barbara Bruns, Deone Filmer, and Harry Patrinos noted that: "The clear implication of available research is that most school systems are recruiting and rewarding teachers for the wrong things, failing to encourage the capacities and behaviors that contribute most directly to student learning results, and unable to sanction ineffective performance."[62] Incentives for education accountability therefore involve taking hold of the full range of incentives affecting teacher performance to improve child learning outcomes. Given the widespread lack of education quality, innovations in incentives need to be taken seriously.

Some recommendations on teacher incentives are system wide. For example, there have been calls for wholesale moves to short-term, nontenure contracts. Indeed, Bruns, Filmer, and Patrinos called for "the creation of a parallel teacher cadre hired on short-term contracts, typically covering a single school year and renewable based on performance."[63] This advice has been taken up in recent decades, particularly where there have been persistent teacher shortages. However, it is important to recognize that the incentive structure here can work in *both directions*. The short-term contracts with lower remuneration and job security might be an incentive to teach better to achieve contract renewal, but it might also be a disincentive given secondary status to more standard teacher contracts and therefore result in increased turnover. It is also important to recognize that the one-year renewable structure is just one of many possibilities. Alternatively, school systems could put *effective limits* on longer-term, tenured contracts where effective teaching has not been achieved or consider three- and five-year renewable contracts to allow teachers time to develop and maintain the skills they need to be continually effective in the classroom.

Shorter-term contracts are a reality of the global educational landscape and are being assessed. There is some evidence that, in particular African countries, contract teachers can help, particularly for poor students, but the effects can differ among countries and even be negative in some cases.[64] There is also positive evidence on contract teachers in India.[65] There is evidence from Kenya that locally hired contract teachers can improve test scores when there is the incentive for these teachers to eventually be hired on a regular, tenure contract.[66] In this education policy arena, continued experimentation and assessment are necessary.

Less system-wide incentive efforts are also possible. One possible means to improve teacher incentives is the use of monitoring systems to help to alleviate the problem of absence. For example, in one study, monitoring teacher attendance using cameras and making salaries dependent on attendance significantly reduced teacher absence.[67] It is also possible to simply provide additional rewards to teachers related to student test scores, and in some instances, this can have a positive effect.[68] Again, innovation and assessment on creative incentives needs to be an ongoing effort.

There is a final issue that needs to be recognized in the realm of education accountability: helping poorly performing students from disadvantaged families. It is possible to design interventions to supplement the instruction and resources for these students, and there is some evidence that this can work.[69] Language of instruction can also matter here. One well-cited study of new text-books in Kenya found that they did not help with test scores because they were written in English (the language of instruction) and many students spoke a dif-ferent language.[70] Being sensitive to the languages spoken in homes can matter.

Schools as Basic Goods Provision Centers

It is possible for schools to serve as more than just locations for quality edu-cation. The children who attend schools are at developmentally critical stages in their lives and can be deprived of more than just education. For this reason, there has been consideration of ways in which schools can be used to provide a number of basic goods and services. I mentioned one example of this already. In Chapter 4, I considered the difficulties in the provision of nutritious food, and I mentioned that there is some evidence that school feeding programs con-tribute to nutritional outcomes, school enrollment, and potentially to cognitive development.[71] School feeding programs have a relatively long history, are quite common, and are supported by various development agencies. Some school feeding programs go so far as to provide food cooked on the premises, and this requires that the appropriate facilities be available.[72] As mentioned in Chapter 4, it is also possible to use local smallholder farmers as suppliers for school feeding programs, an approach known as HGSF.[73]

It is also possible to go one step further to envision schools as multipurpose facilities that can serve as what environmental designer Ola Uduku called *devel-opment hubs* or what in the context of this book can be called *basic goods provision centers*.[74] These hubs or centers can help to deliver education services for children and adults, nutrition and primary healthcare services, and agricultural exten-sion services potentially using school farms. Using schools as provision centers also could have benefits in helping to foster family and community involvement in education and support client empowerment. As noted by Ola Uduku:[75]

> Greater community use of school facilities is likely to enhance a sense of ownership of the physical infrastructure of the school amongst com-munity members, who very often have contributed towards construct-ing the buildings. It offers an alternative to the extractive relationship that often exists between schools and community, whereby community participation is interpreted in practice only as community contribution of finance, building materials or labor to the school. Opening up school buildings for use by community members may contribute towards eroding the barriers of mistrust that too often exist between schools and communities, leading to greater transparency and accountability.

It also offers community members the possibility of taking a leadership role in negotiating their preferred uses of the school space during or after school hours.

In this way, the use of schools as basic goods provision centers can help to support some aspects of education accountability and, hopefully, the improvement of education quality.

Demand Side Issues and Provisioning

As previously discussed, education is a central form human capital investment and is therefore subject to both interpersonal and intertemporal considerations. For example, development economists Abhijit Benerjee and Esther Duflo wryly noted that "the obvious problem with thinking of education as an investment is that parents do the investing and children get the benefits, sometimes much later."[76] And there are other wrinkles as well. First, Banerjee and Duflo presented evidence that some parents overinvest in the "smartest" kid in the family, neglecting "less smart" children. Second, there is no guarantee that the children will "repay" the investment to their parents in later years. So from the parent's point of view, educating their children is part investment and part gift.[77] Third, there is also the problem that the ability to make education investments and bestow education gifts depends on the income and wealth of the parents, and children from poor families receive less education investment and smaller education gifts. Consequently, significant inequities are present along with interpersonal and intertemporal effects.

Given all of these considerations, it is highly unlikely that purely private decisions with regard to the provision of education services will either be socially optimal or ensure that subsistence rights to primary and secondary education will be met. It is for this reason, that Article 13 of the UDHR states that "primary education shall be compulsory and available free to all."[78] It is also for this reason, that most national governments consider primary education to be compulsory. Although much is made of the manufacturing export success of East Asia, for example, the education policies of these countries are less often discussed. After World War II, compulsory primary education was the norm in these countries, and compulsory secondary education is the modern norm. Such norms help to shape the consumption of basic education services in ways that are beneficial to entire societies.

One obvious focus in the educational provisioning process is educational spending. It is clear that to provide basic educational services spending on these services needs to take place. But the relationship between educational spending and educational outcomes is not direct. This is in part due to the previously discussed quality issues. The World Bank has pointed out that, on average, low- and middle-income countries spend about the same percent of GDP on education as high-income countries (about 5 percent). Further, the correlations between spending and educational outcomes in terms of enrollment, attainment, or achievement are not always as high as wished or expected. [79] But such figures are largely focused on averages, and educational spending is often inequitable, benefitting high-income households more than low-income households. This reflects the political power of high-income households and their consequent ability to lobby on behalf of their children's education. Indeed, by all accounts, inequalities in household income and household education opportunities are self-reinforcing.

One means of helping to provide education emerged in the 1990s in the form of something I mentioned in Chapter 3, namely CCTs. As previously mentioned, CCTs involve governments placing a balance on a smartcard for a family if their children are enrolled in school and have the required primary healthcare visits. Since the introduction of these programs in Mexico and Brazil, CCTs have expanded throughout the world, and as they have expanded, they have been evaluated. By and large, the evaluations suggest that CCTs help to increase school enrollments and attainment, although the evidence on educational achievement is more mixed.[80] It seems that, from the point of view of enrollments at least, the conditional nature of CCTs helps.[81] There is also evidence that CCTs can help support girls' education attainment.[82] Overall, there appears to be strong support for CCTs as a way of supporting the consumption of basic education services.

Another provisioning mode that has received a lot of attention lately is *private* provisioning. The reality is that in many countries, the public education system is of very low quality, and this has prompted many parents to choose to place their children in the many types of private schools available. *The Economist* estimates that there are approximately one million private schools in low- and middle-income countries.[83] Figures 8.2 and 8.3 provide a more temporal view in terms of private schooling as a percentage of primary and secondary school enrollment, respectively. In both low- and middle-income countries, primary school enrollment is approximately 14 percent of the total.[84] For secondary school enrollment the figures are approximately 20 and 26 percent, respectively. So private schooling does account for a significant amount of enrollment at both primary and secondary levels.

There is opposition to the private education trend. For example, the United Nations Special Rapporteur on Education, Kishore Singh, publically came out against private education on human rights and equity grounds:[85]

Education is not a privilege of the rich and well-to-do; it is the inalienable right of every child. The state must discharge its responsibility as

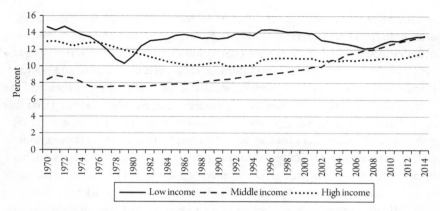

Figure 8.2 Private primary school provisioning (percentage of primary school enrollment). Source: World Bank, World Development Indicators

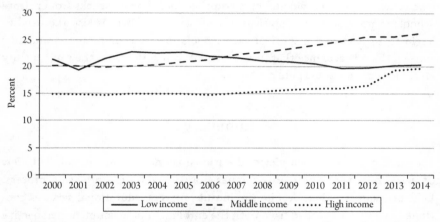

Figure 8.3 Private secondary school provisioning (percentage of secondary school enrollment). Source: World Bank, World Development Indicators

guarantor and regulator of education as a fundamental human entitlement and as a public cause. The provision of basic education, free of cost, is not only a core obligation of states but also a moral imperative.

Privatization cripples the notion of education as a universal human right and—by aggravating marginalization and exclusion—runs counter to the fundamental principles of human rights law. It creates social inequity.

The admission policy in private schools is based on the ability to pay, and on the socio-economic background of parents. As a result, private schools lack the diversified system of learning and cultural plurality that is so necessary today. They promote market economy values rather than the humanist mission of education.

Others argue in the opposite direction, making the case for national governments to support private education, including through the use of vouchers, often citing the case of Chile's voucher system without carefully assessing the evidence.[86] It would seem that an intermediate position is possible and relevant. Robust systems of universal primary education are the first-best option, and the historical evidence from Europe, North America, and East Asia suggests that this approach can have significant payoffs. However, it is clear that, in many cases, public school systems are inadequate. If parents chose to forgo these systems, that is their choice. Of course, reforming the public school systems remains a priority, but there are often political forces opposing the necessary reforms. It makes no sense to "resist" private schools, as suggested the Kishore Singh, in these circumstances because they can be an effective BoP function on the part of the private sector. Whether the government should support these enterprises through vouchers is another matter, particularly where they are religious in nature or where there is evidence of corruption, including kickbacks from private schools to political representatives or civil servants. There is also the need to begin to register and inspect private schools to ensure minimum standards. Indeed, there is evidence that private schools can suffer from the same quality issues that plague some public schools.[87]

Summary

The basic goods approach views educational services from the point of view of needs fulfilment and places emphasis on the education provision process. Evidence suggests that, despite significant progress, educational services continue to be underprovided from both the enrollment or attainment perspective and the achievement perspective. This is evidenced by over 750 million illiterate adults. Early childhood, primary, and secondary education services are basic rights, and these rights are widely recognized within the UN system. Education also appears to positively support growth processes despite some past controversy on this issue, and girls' education is particularly important from both growth and human development perspectives.

Education quality is a pervasive issue, and there is an evolving program of education accountability that attempts to address quality shortfalls through better use of information, the devolution of authority, and teacher incentives. An honest assessment of these efforts suggests that they still need continued experimentation and evaluation. Even then, what works in one context may not work in another. CCTs seem to support the delivery of education services and, although public education is the first-best approach, private education also can play an important role in some circumstances. Overall, providing basic goods in the form of education services remains a significant challenge.

Notes

1. Easterly (2001), p. 82.
2. See, for example, Morrisson and Murtin (2009) and Patrinos and Psacharopoulos (2011).
3. The most recent year for which these data were available at the time of this writing is 2012.
4. UNESCO (2014).
5. *The Economist* (2015c), p. 9.
6. The World Bank's World Development Indicators show 780 million in 2010, the most recent year available at the time of writing. UNESCO (2013a) puts the figure at 770 million in 2011. The United Nations (2015b) puts the figure at 780 million in 2015.
7. United Nations General Assembly (1948).
8. United Nations General Assembly (1948).
9. United Nations General Assembly (1959).
10. United Nations General Assembly (1966b), p. 8.
11. United Nations Educational, Scientific and Cultural Organization (2015).
12. See https://en.unesco.org/world-education-forum-2015/incheon-declaration.
13. Human rights language related to education is also contained in the UNESCO charter.
14. Goodhart (2007), p. 101.
15. Shue (1996).
16. Ray and Tarrow (1987), p. 3.
17. In the context of the United States, for example, see Heckman (2008). In an evocative statement, Heckman noted that "children in affluent homes are bathed in financial and cognitive resources" (p. 305). However, "a substantial body of evidence suggests that a major determinant of child disadvantage is the quality of the nurturing environment rather than just financial resources available or the presence or absence of parents" (p. 306).
18. To be clear, it is not that I consider higher education to be unimportant. It is important. It is just that it largely falls outside of the basic goods considerations of this book.
19. Maddison (1991), pp. 63–64.
20. Maddison (1991), p. 23.
21. For example, Mankiw, Romer, and Weil (1992) and Hall and Jones (1999) showed that including human capital in growth models can contribute to their ability to explain the variation of per capita incomes among the countries of the world.
22. Easterly (2001), p. 73.
23. See Pritchett (2001), for example.
24. See, for example, Krueger and Lindahl (2001) and Wößmann (2004).
25. See de la Fuente and Doménech (2006); Cohen and Soto (2007); Hanuschek and Woessmann (2008, 2012); and Glewwe, Maïga, and Zheng (2014).
26. For example, Hanuschek and Woessmann (2008) stated that: "Models that include direct measures of cognitive skills can account for about three times the variation in economic growth than models that include only years of schooling; including the cognitive skills measures makes the coefficient on years of schooling go to zero; and the estimates of such more inclusive models are far more robust to variations in the overall model specification" (p. 609). The authors also demonstrated that the distribution of cognitive skills in a population also affected the distribution of income.
27. For example, see again Hanuschek and Woessmann (2008).
28. For two reviews, see Psacharopoulos (1994, 2006).
29. For a review, see Heckman (2008).
30. The Commission on Growth and Development (2008) stated, "It seems reasonable to us to focus first on preschool and early childhood education, then on elementary education and literacy, and then increase the numbers in secondary school. Nor should governments forget the importance of a small tertiary sector that should grow as incomes rise and the demand for human capital sharpens" (p. 38).
31. For the East Asian case, see Stiglitz (1996) and McMahon (1998). Weaver, Rock, and Kusterer (1997) noted that "in each of the East Asian (newly industrializing countries), the

earliest emphasis was on expanding primary enrollment. This was followed with timed expansion of the secondary and then the tertiary systems" (p. 166).

32. Weaver, Rock, and Kusterer (1997) noted that "no country since 1850 has achieved self-sustaining growth without first achieving universal primary education (p. 166). The Commission on Growth and Development (2008) concluded that "Every country that sustained high growth for long periods put substantial effort into schooling its citizens and deepening its human capital" (p. 37). In an extensive review, Szirmai (2015) concluded that "there is not a single case of successful catch-up in the world economy since the last quarter of the nineteenth century, where *advances in educational levels did not precede subsequent economic growth*. Education is indeed one of the necessary conditions for economic development" (p. 249, emphasis in original).

33. Schultz (2002), p. 207. Schultz went on to say "The conclusion of many empirical studies of child development is that increased schooling of the mother is associated with larger improvements in child quality outcomes than is the increased schooling of the father. This has been studied with birth outcomes (e.g., birth weight), child survival, good nutrition, earlier entry into school, increases school enrollment adjusted for age, and more years of schooling completed on reaching adulthood" (p. 212).

34. See Schultz (2002) and Tembon and Fort (2008).

35. See Klasen (2002) and Klasen and Lamanna (2009).

36. See Stiglitz (1996).

37. World Bank (2011a).

38. World Bank (2011a), p. 106. See Figure 3.1 in this report on p. 107. In tertiary education, women are actually *advantaged* relative to men except in sub-Saharan Africa.

39. One issue that often escapes attention in development policy communities when it comes to girls' education is that of menstrual hygiene. This neglect is changing, and the evidence suggests that basic goods provision in the form of menstrual hygiene products can have a positive impact on girls' education by reducing missed days of school. See, for example, Sommer (2010) and Dolan et al. (2014).

40. New America Foundation (2010).

41. Chaudhury et al. (2006). These authors reported that "only 50 percent of teachers in Indian public schools who should be teaching at a given point in time are in fact doing so" (p. 96). And "the absence rate of Indian private-school teachers is only slightly lower than that of public-school teachers" (p. 106).

42. Chaudhury et al. (2006), p. 96.

43. In the case of Pakistan, Andrabi et al. (2007) found that "a teacher in public school is absent one-fifth of the time and has students that perform very poorly but still earns 5 times more than a teacher in a private school who is present nearly every day and has students that perform very well" (p. 58). Even if this is overstating the issue somewhat, the issue clearly exists. In the case of Kenya, Glewwe, Ilias, and Kremer (2010) also reported teacher absence of out 20 percent. *The Economist* (2015d) reported that teacher absence rates in some African countries reach 15 to 20 percent. On the differential impact on girls in Pakistan, see Ghuman and Lloyd (2010).

44. Abadzi (2009), p. 285.

45. See, for example, Canagarajah and Ye (2001) for the case of Ghana; Reinikka and Svensson (2004, 2005) for the case of Uganda; and Ferraz, Finan, and Moreira (2012) for the case of Brazil.

46. On the case of black individuals in South Africa, see Murtin (2013), for example.

47. Barrett (2011), p. 1.

48. For one discussion on alternative conceptions of the right to education quality, see Tikly and Barrett (2011).

49. See, for example, Bruns, Filmer, and Patrinos (2011).

50. On service delivery, see for example Pandey, Goyal, and Sundararaman (2009) for the case of India. On the impact of funding leakage, see for example, Reinikka and Svensson (2011) for the case of Uganda.

51. Here is a partial list: the International Association for the Evaluation of Educational Achievement's (IEA) International Evaluation of Educational Achievement (IEA); the IEA's Progress in International Reading Literacy (PIRLS); the IEA's First International Mathematics Study (FIMS); the IEA's Second International Mathematics Study (SIMS); Statistics Canada's International Adult Literacy Survey (IALS); the OECD's PISA; the OECD's Program for the International Assessment of Adult Competencies (PIAAC); the OECD's Teaching and Learning International Survey (TALIS); UNESCO's Global Monitoring Report (GMR); and the U.S. Center for Education Statistics' Trends in International Mathematics and Science Study (TIMSS).

52. Sellar and Lingard (2014).

53. Again see Sellar and Lingard (2014).

54. See, for example, Chapter 3 of Bruns, Filmer, and Patrinos (2011).

55. Bruns, Filmer, and Patrinos (2011), p. 90.

56. Di Gropello (2006).

57. For the Philippines case, see Khattri, Ling and Jha (2012); for the Gambian case, see Blimpo and Evans (2011). In the later study, positive effects were only found in the form of reduced student and teacher absence, not in the form of improved test scores.

58. Blimpo and Evans (2011), pp. 28–29.

59. Galiani, Gertler, and Schargrodsky (2008).

60. Eskeland and Filmer (2007).

61. See, for example, Fuchs and Wößmann (2007). The authors reported: "Consistent with theory as well as previous evidence, superior student performance is associated with school autonomy in personnel-management and process decisions such as deciding budget allocations within schools, textbook choice and hiring of teachers (the latter only in math). By contrast, superior performance is associated with centralized decision-making in areas with scope for decentralized opportunistic behavior, such as formulating the overall school budget" (p. 461).

62. Bruns, Filmer, and Patrinos (2011), p. 143.

63. Bruns, Filmer, and Patrinos (2011), p. 146.

64. See, for example, Bourdon, Frölich, and Michaelowa (2010) for the African case.

65. See Muralidharan and Sundararaman (2013) for the Indian case.

66. See Duflo, Dupas, and Kremer (2015) for the Kenyan case.

67. Duflo, Hanna, and Ryan (2012).

68. For the Kenyan case, see Glewwe, Ilias, and Kremer (2010).

69. See, for example, Banerjee et al. (2007) for the case of India.

70. Glewwe, Kremer, and Moulin (2009).

71. See Adelman, Gilligan, and Lehrer (2008); Bundy et al. (2009); and Jomaa, McDonnell, and Probart (2011).

72. See Uduku (2011) for the Ghana and South Africa cases.

73. Home-grown school feeding programs are currently being explored by the World Food Program, the Gates Foundation, and the New Partnership for Africa's Development.

74. Uduku (2011).

75. Uduku (2011), p. 65.

76. Banerjee and Duflo (2011), p. 77.

77. Banerjee and Duflo (2011), p. 78.

78. United Nations General Assembly (1948).

79. Bruns, Filmer, and Patrinos (2011), p. 5.

80. There are now a multitude of studies on the effects of CCTs on education outcomes. Schultz (2004) provided an early assessment of the Mexican Progressa program and found a positive impact on enrollment. The same was true for de Janvry et al. (2006). Rawlings and Rubio (2005) reported positive enrollment effects of CCTs in Colombia, Mexico, and Nicaragua. Positive enrollment effects for Brazil's Bolsa Escola/Familia program have been demonstrated by Glewwe and Kassouf (2012). Heinrich (2007) demonstrates similar results for Argentina, and Baird, McIntosh, and Özler (2011) do the same for Malawi. Handa and Davis (2006) offered a more critical view, largely due to concerns over whether demand side

interventions such as CCTs are the right instrument when supply side, school quality issues can be paramount.

81. See de Brauw and Hoddinott (2011) for the Mexican case and Baird, McIntosh, and Özler (2011) for the Malawian case.

82. See Schultz (2004) for the Mexican case and Baird, McIntosh, and Özler (2011) for the Malawian case.

83. *The Economist* (2015d).

84. *The Economist* (2015d) stated that one-fifth of primary school students in low-income countries are enrolled in private schools. As can be seen in Figure 8.2, however, World Bank data suggest that it is less than that approximately 14 percent in 2014 rather than 20 percent.

85. Singh (2015).

86. The Chilean voucher system was instituted under the Pinochet military dictatorship in 1981 (not an auspicious beginning). Wolff and de Moura Castro (2003) concluded that "after controlling for social class, secular private schools in Chile do no better than public schools in achievement tests. There has been increased social stratification with middle-class families moving to private subsidized schools while poor families remain in public municipal schools" (p. 202). Contreras, Sepúlveda, and Bustos (2010) noted that "The Chilean experience is the most significant international example of a competition- and incentive-based educational system. It is one of the few nationwide systems of this type in the world and has proper data for statistical analysis" (p. 1349–1350). Their assessment was that "the results show that the impact of attending a private school with low socioeconomic levels is negative and statistically significant in all estimates. The results suggest that public schools are neither uniformly worse nor better than private schools; rather, public schools are relatively more effective for students from disadvantaged family backgrounds. Thus, a basic belief of the voucher system in Chile that competition will lead to better quality of all schools is not being met" (p. 1351). Even *The Economist* (2015d), supportive of Chilean vouchers, admitted that "once the relatively privileged background of private-school pupils is taken into account . . ., state schools do better, especially since they serve the hardest-to-teach children" (p. 20).

87. For example, Banerjee and Duflo (2011) reported that "we know that in India a full one-third of fifth-graders in private schools cannot read at the first-grade level" (p. 86).

9

Housing

In 2005, the UN Special Rapporteur on Adequate Housing announced an estimate of the under provision of housing, namely that one billion individuals lacked adequate housing and that 100 million were homeless. Although it was never clear what the empirical basis for these estimates was, they have been widely cited to this day. However, actual research considerations suggest that it may not even be *possible* to make such estimates with any sort of certainty.[1] Although it is frustrating to admit, we *don't really know* the extent of housing deprivation, but it seems safe to assume that the problem is very large. The UN figures are probably *underestimates*. For example, given that in 2015 there were approximately sixty-five million refugees (to be discussed further later), the estimate of 100 million homeless individuals might actually be low. By some measures, there are twenty-five million homeless people in India alone.[2] Even where housing is present, it can be characterized by inadequate structures and unacceptably high room densities that result from poverty. However, all that can be said with any accuracy is that the extent of basic goods deprivation in housing is *extensive*. Exactly how extensive, is not exactly known.[3]

Although the quantitative extent of homelessness is not known, what is known, is that both homelessness and poor housing quality have severe, negative implications for human well-being. Recall from Chapter 3 that a minimal level of housing quality is important to protect individuals against the elements and to provide space for food preparation and hygiene. Further, basic housing is generally essential for effective participation in human life. I emphasized that basic goods tend to work together, and this is definitely the case with housing. The household is the locus where much of the basic goods provision takes place: food preparation, hygiene, and taking care of the sick, for example. When the housing component is missing, much can and does go wrong. Where it is present, much can be improved. As one set of researchers observed, "provision of housing for the poor not only has social benefits but also improves human capital and lifts . . . economic capacity."[4] When it is not provided, there are consequent social costs.

An editorial in the *British Medical Journal* stated that "It has been known for centuries that housing and health are inextricably linked."[5] This link actually consists of multiple connections. At the most extreme, being homeless increases the risk of a number of different types of infections and thereby contributes to ill health. These include cutaneous (skin) infections, blood-borne infections, pulmonary infections, urogenital infections, and sexually transmitted diseases.[6] The same is true for mosquito-borne diseases such as malaria, dengue, and yellow fever. Being homeless increases the risks of adverse effects of disasters, both manmade and natural.[7] Finally, and more important, homelessness compromises access to basic goods and services of all types, but particularly water, sanitation, health services, and education services.[8] Even searching for a safe place to sleep with minimal shelter from the elements puts the homeless at the mercy of providers that can range from legitimate, BoP entrepreneurs to quasi-mafia operations.[9] The latter negatively affect human security discussed in Chapter 11.

Far short of the catastrophe of homelessness, poor housing quality also has adverse impacts on health, even in high-income countries. These include asthma, other respiratory illnesses, and lead poisoning.[10] Poor housing conditions tend to be agglomerated in particular geographical areas leading to poor neighborhoods. These negative agglomeration effects provide environments for crime and drug use that have further negative impacts on health and human security. Neighborhoods with poor housing quality are often characterized by limited property rights that dampen the ability of the poor to invest in housing upgrades, as well a physical and human capital in general.[11] For these reasons, housing specialists Xing Quan Zhang and Michael Ball concluded that "adverse housing experiences can have considerable knock-on effects on overall life chances and well-being."[12]

So what does housing deprivation look like? Here are the housing aspirations of one woman in a slum in Mumbai, India as described by Katherine Boo in her book *Behind the Beautiful Forevers*:[13]

> She wanted a more hygienic home . . ., in the name of her children's vitality. She wanted a shelf on which to cook without rat intrusions— a stone shelf, not some cast-off piece of plywood. She wanted a small window to vent the cooking smoke that caused the little ones to cough like their father. On the floor she wanted ceramic tiles . . . that could be scrubbed clean, instead of broken concrete that harbored filth in each striation.

Such aspirations are the stuff of housing deprivation, and they affect a large proportion of people on the planet. The framework of basic goods as basic rights suggests that these aspirations deserve the utmost attention.

The Right to Housing

Along with other subsistence rights, the right to housing is a *basic right* as identified by political philosopher Henry Shue.[14] Recall from Chapter 3 that both Article 25 of the UDHR[15] and Article 11 of the ICESCR[16] recognized the right to housing as part of a larger right to a standard of living. In 1991, the UN Committee of Economic, Social and Cultural Rights further recognized the right to adequate housing in General Comment 4 on the Right to Adequate Housing and extended it beyond mere shelter to "the right to live somewhere in security, peace and dignity."[17] General Comment 4 identified seven elements of the right to housing: security of tenure, access to services and infrastructure, affordability, habitability, physical accessibility, location, and cultural adequacy. With regard to security of tenure, General Comment 4 drew attention to forced eviction.[18] It also linked the right to housing to the provision of other basic goods, including water, sanitation, energy, and emergency services. This is important because, as we have seen, deprivations in housing exacerbate deprivations in these other basic goods and services. The language of General Comment 4 also employs the logic of "basic needs" and "physical safety."

The UN CESCR followed in 1998 with General Comment 7[19] on the Right to Adequate Housing that drew attention to the issue of forced evictions. Finally, with reference to the discussion of health in Chapter 7, General Comment 14 on the Right to the Highest Attainable Standard of Health explicitly draws a link between subsistence rights in housing and subsistence rights to health services.

All of these statements within the United Nations system of human rights carry obligations. Legal scholar Padraic Kenna explained some of these in the following:[20]

> Firstly, all countries must recognize the human rights dimensions of housing, and ensure that no measures of any kind are taken with the intention of eroding the legal status of this right. Second, legislative measures, coupled with appropriate policies geared towards the progressive realization of housing rights, form part of the obligation. . . . Thirdly, a genuine attempt must be made by States to determine the degree to which this right is not in place, and to target housing policies and laws towards attaining this right for everyone in the shortest possible time.

Kenna also noted that the right to housing is closely aligned with the minimum thresholds advocated in the basic goods approach in the form of a "guarantee that everyone (enjoys) a right to adequate shelter and a minimum level of housing services, without discrimination."[21] And that "If a State claims that it is unable to meet even its minimum obligations because of a lack of resources, it must at least be able to demonstrate that every effort has been made to use all resources at its disposal to satisfy, as a matter of priority, those minimum obligations."[22] But there is substantial evidence that governments do not meet these obligations. Indeed, as often noted, the right to housing can be easily lost due to a host of exigencies, including poverty, debt, and increased land values leading to eviction and expropriation. Such possibilities were emphasized by human rights lawyers Cathy Albisa, Brittany Scott, and Kate Tissington, who noted the following:[23]

> Although poor communities may in fact highly value their right to remain in their homes and occupy certain land, they do not have economic power to express that value in monetary terms. Therefore, land-use decisions based solely on market valuations do not take into account their interests. . . . These particular inhabitants . . . do not have an equal say in land-use decisions, nor do they equitably benefit from development, and, as a result are subject to greater instability.

Although this chapter embraces this rights-based approach to the provision of housing, as I emphasized in Chapter 3, there is also room for provision activities from the private sector. So although the provisioning *responsibility* ultimately rests with governments at the appropriate levels, the provisioning *process* could be undertaken by firms, including BoP enterprises, provided that these are legitimate and not simply exploiting the deprivations of their customers.

Refugees and Displaced People

The deprivation of basic goods provision, and in particular housing, becomes most acute in the case of refugees. The 1951 Refugee Convention defined the notion of "refugee" as someone who "owing to a well-founded fear of being persecuted for reasons of race, religion, nationality, membership of a particular social group or political opinion, is outside the country of his nationality, and is unable to, or owing to such fear, is unwilling to avail himself of the protection of that country." As can be seen from this definition, this conception is a political one and is used to distinguish refugees from other types of migrants. But there is also the possibility of including individuals who are forced to leave their country of origin due nonpolitical factors such as famine, civil war, and environmental collapse because such individuals could in no way be considered just economic migrants in the usual sense of the term.[24] Some of these more expansive considerations arise in the international legal definition of "internally displaced persons," namely "persons or groups of persons who have been forced or obliged to flee or to leave their homes or places of habitual residence, in particular as a result of or in order to avoid the effects of armed conflict, situations of generalized violence, violations of human rights or natural or human-made disasters, and who have not crossed an internationally recognized State border." From the point of view of basic goods deprivation, if not from asylum law, a more expansive definition of both refugees and internally displaced persons for a total of "displaced people" makes sense.

As can be seen in Figure 9.1, the number of displaced people in the world is rising. The data reported in this figure are those of the United Nation High Commissioner for Refugees (UNHCR). They show that deteriorating security conditions in the Middle East, North Africa, and East Africa have pushed refugee flows above where they were during the Second World War to approximately sixty-six million in 2016. In 2015, for example, Germany alone took in one million refugees from these regions, and the European Union subsequently confronted a political crisis as a result of increased refugee flows, calling into question the EU's Schengen Agreement[25] for the free movement of persons. In 2016 and in response to these developments, the United Nations General Assembly held the first-ever Summit on Large Movements of Migrants and Refugees. Given current political and climatic developments, there does not seem to be too much chance for these increased numbers of displaced people to be dramatically reversed.

In an ideal world, refugees will eventually return to their home country or become integrated into a host country. It is unfortunate that we do not live in such a world. Take for example the Somalian refugee camp Dadaab in Kenya. This camp was established in 1992 to assist refugees fleeing civil war and resulting

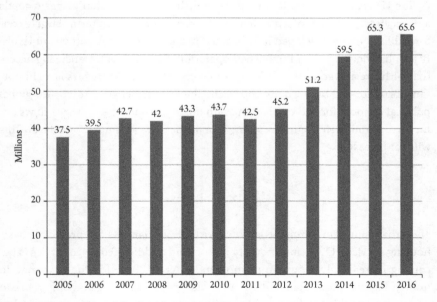

Figure 9.1 Number of displaced people (millions). Source: UNHCR (2014 to 2017)

famine in Somalia. It still exists today, one of the world's largest refugee camps. Refugees still arrive in Dadaab, which has become a small city of half a million people waiting for resettlement. It contains schools and hospitals, police stations, and even grave yards. Although the standard shelter consists of tents provided by the UNHCR, many families need to wait a long time to receive this basic good. Consequently, Doctors without Borders reported that "families build makeshift shelters out of whatever materials they can find or borrow—sticks, cardboard, polythene—to provide some shelter from the sun, the wind, the choking dust and . . . rains."[26] Late arrivals have the most difficulty establishing suitable shelter, and these often prove to be unsatisfactory in the face of rains. As one Somali refugee stated, "my only hopes are for shelter, water and safety."[27] Given poor shelter options, water and sanitation services are often very poor.[28] Examples such as this suggest that refugee crises are not short-term in nature. Rather, they can result in semipermanent displacement that can last for decades.

As I mentioned in Chapter 2, the case of refugees is one where difficult choices need to be made in the provision of basic goods and services. The United Nations Convention and Protocol Relating to the Status of Refugees outlined refugee rights in the areas of housing, public education, and social security.[29] But in practice, these are not guaranteed. Housing, even temporary housing, obviously rises to the top of the list basic goods list for refugees. So does water, sanitation, and primary health. It is unfortunate that in this context, other basic goods and services become lower priorities. Available evidence suggests widespread inability to meet even the restricted list of housing, water, sanitation, and primary healthcare.[30] So difficult choices cannot be avoided.

The UNHCR considers its mandate to include the provision of basic goods and services. Indeed, it often articulates its responsibilities in terms largely conformable to those developed in this book, including minimum provision levels. It also has developed and published operational guidelines for ensuring access to healthcare and education.[31] So the problem of homeless refugees is an important locus for the basic goods approach. The key challenge is to ensure global political support for the UNHCR mission during a time when refugee flows are increasing and their plight becoming a political issue at the national level. This will not be easy.

Urban Slums

The urban slum environment is an important special case for providing basic housing services. Over time, poverty in low- and middle-income countries is becoming increasingly an urban phenomenon. As of 2007, for the first time in human history, more than half of the world's population began living in urban areas, and one third of those urban residents live in slums.[32] This suggests that about 17 percent of the world's population lives in urban slums. And although most of the world's poor people still live in rural areas, this will not be the case much longer. Most poor people will soon be living in urban areas.[33] Indeed, whereas in the past, urban slums were seen as temporary phenomenon that aided in the transitions taking place as a result of rural–urban migration, it is now apparent that they are often becoming *permanent* features of many national and regional economies. They need to be taken seriously.

Urban slums can be very difficult environments. As Katherine Boo noted in her book on an urban slum in Mumbai, India, "The city was rough on migrants, terrible sometimes, and also better than anywhere else."[34] Because they are "better than anywhere else," urban slums persist and grow. Residents of urban slums risk displacement, however, when economic winds change. In the case of Mumbai, the urban development plan *Vision Mumbai* displaced hundreds of thousands of slum dwellers.[35] A similar process of slum clearance has taken place in Delhi, India.[36] The pursuit of slum clearance or elimination as a goal can be misdirected.

One characteristic of housing in urban slums is *informality*. Urban slum housing does not generally conform to our preexisting notions. But it is important to recognize that the informal nature of urban slum housing has its own functionality. Consider this from housing researchers Xing Quan Zhang and Michael Ball:[37]

> Informal housing has many flaws (e.g., land tenure insecurity, inadequate services, hazardous locations), but also advantages over formal housing, besides lower costs. It is often located near employment centers and offers opportunities for home-based income generation. Informality permits a wide range of tenure forms and housing types to meet the wide variety of housing needs of the poor. It is flexible and adaptable to different and changing needs, and provides temporary alternative shelter for the poor.

In the context of urban slums, housing can sometimes be *multipurpose*. Along with the standard function of "putting a roof over their heads," a single room in an urban house can also provide a space for a microenterprise or a rental property. One researcher noted that "extra space if often viewed as an insurance policy or a guarantee of retirement income."[38] Microenterprise and informal renting are a part of a wider set of informal economic activities that characterize urban slums.[39] Despite the lack of formal contracts, informal renting appears to work relatively well and plays a significant role in the provision of housing.[40]

As mass informality rose in urban slums, so did mass home ownership, albeit often of a fragile nature. Owned informal housing is often located in unstable physical environments that can be prone to natural disasters and lack basic services. And as land in urban areas becomes more expensive, the cost of informal housing increases, sometimes reflecting the need to pay off officials not to confiscate the land on which informal settlements have developed. Despite these problems, it is safe to say that informal housing will remain a widespread feature of housing poor people in urban slums. It needs to be recognized as such.

Providing Housing

As previously noted, while housing represents a basic good in and of itself, it is also central to the provision of other basic goods. To be more specific, in a quote given earlier, legal scholar Padraic Kenna stated that country governments were obliged to pursue "appropriate policies geared towards the progressive realization of housing rights."[41] It is somewhat ironic then that the provision of housing often receives less policy attention than do other basic goods and services. For example, as noted by one set of human rights lawyers, "unlike in education and health care, . . . there are few if any publicly designed or regulated comprehensive national systems for housing that ensure decent access and stability for all."[42] This mismatch between basic needs and policy is notable. As a consequence, the first step in addressing the provision of housing is to recognize its centrality. With this established, there are a number of policy areas concerning housing that are worth examining in some detail.

There is a *traditional approach* to providing housing that consists of *slum clearance* and *public housing projects*. In many cases, this approach has not worked. It proves to be expensive and can often ignore the preference of the basic-goods-deprived individuals involved. For example, families might have their own reasons for locating in a slum and do not want to be moved to another location.[43] There is also a tendency for public housing to provide units that many poor families cannot afford.[44] Finally, the public housing approach has proven to be too costly for the governments involved.[45] These realities have shifted the emphasis in housing policy to finding ways that the public and private sectors can complement one another and do so in locally relevant ways.[46] These approaches must also pay attention to the provision of water and sanitation, while seeking local solutions to the provision of housing.

As in many areas of public policy, top-down approaches have significant limits. Another tradition is a *sites-and-services approach* that provides basic services (water, sanitation) to building sites and allows individuals and families to attend to their own housing construction. This proves to be less expensive but is confined to "green-field" situations. The equivalent "brown-field" approach is that of *slum upgrading*. Where successful, the sites-and-services and slum-upgrading approaches employ what is perhaps an over-used concept in development, namely *participation*.[47] Participation is also key when people in urban slums are being relocated due to slum clearing and redevelopment.[48] As housing researcher Marie Huchzermeyer put it in the Kenyan slum context:[49]

People living in slums, and whose economic stakes are linked to the housing and service delivery situation in the slums, are able to predict the impact that a public intervention may have on their economic standing. These predictions usually manifest themselves in fear. NGO staff working close to the ground, thus in conversations with residents about their fears, may also articulate accurate predictions.

Making use of this type of local information via various kinds of participatory processes is a prerequisite for any successful slum upgrading.

Examples of success in pursuing the slum upgrading approach do exist. One often-mentioned case is the Sri Lankan Million Houses Program that was in existence for the decade of 1983 to 1994. It followed a Hundred Thousand Houses Program in existence from 1971 to 1977. The main thrust of the program was to shift from the government building houses itself to assisting families in doing so. By a number of accounts, the Million Houses Program effectively combined the elements of community participation, a large number of beneficiaries, recognition of a diversity of housing needs, and access to housing finance via microloans.[50] Despite some subsequent criticisms, the program offers a model for future endeavors. Another example with mixed reviews, the Kibera slum of Nairobi Kenya, is considered in Box 9.1.[51]

In recent decades, the issue of housing policy has often been cast in the simple terms of land titling. This has reflected the impact of a famous book by Hernando de Soto, *The Mystery of Capital*, claiming that land titling would have significant knock-on effects in promoting capitalist development through a process of unlocking wealth. This argument was probably overstated.[52] Although no doubt useful in many instances, land titling is not necessarily a panacea. Like all institutional development, land titling can be expensive, and the land that is to be titled can have been taken from previous owners through a process of squatting. In some instances, holding a land title does not even provide security of tenure, and sorting through such conflicting claims is not always straightforward. So although titling processes will continue to be important, they are not *the* solution to the provision of housing.[53]

With regard to the public–private divide, there does seem to be some evidence that the private sector has responded to *some* housing needs. For example, evidence suggests that this sector has moved to providing smaller units in Asian countries.[54] That said, there is often an incentive problem for providing housing to the most deprived individuals and families. There have been suggestions that public–private partnerships can help to overcome this incentive problem. So, for example, some of the profits made in an urban slum redevelopment project could be required to be used to provide low-income housing to the affected families. Although there are some examples of successes with this approach, there are also examples of failure.[55]

Box 9.1 **Upgrading the Kibera Slum of Nairobi, Kenya**

The Kibera slum in Nairobi, Kenya is home to approximately one million people residing on 550 acres, approximately 1,800 people per acre. By some measurements, it is the world's third-largest slum. Kibara began in 1912 as an informal settlement and continued to grow after World War I with the settlement of Kenyan soldiers. Despite this early origin, as of the mid 1960s, the Kibera slum only housed about 6,000 people. So its growth since then has been dramatic. The multiethnic and multilingual nature of Kibera gives it a complex social character, and the slum is composed of fourteen different villages. An average household in Kibera consists of seven members living in a 12 foot by 12 foot structure made of mud, thatch (wattle and daub), and corrugated iron. Most Kibera residents rent from illegal structure owners.

The land on which Kibera has developed is owned by the Kenyan government. But government policy toward Kibera has largely been one of benign neglect, with the government offering few basic services. As a consequence, most basic services are provided by the informal sector itself, with largely inadequate results. Researchers Emmanuel Mutisya and Masaru Yarime listed the challenges faced by Kibera residents in terms of basic goods deprivation: "Access to clean water, improved sanitation, good housing, solid waste management, proper health care, security and energy are some of the most fundamental challenges faced by slum dwellers. Together with this is the lack of enough schools and educational centers and a huge deficiency of other urban infrastructure." To the extent that basic services are provided, this provision process is largely private, including NGOs and CBOs. In many instances, private provision of basic goods (e.g., water) is at inflated prices relative to the rest of Nairobi.

In 2000, UN-Habitat and the government of Kenya initiated the Kenyan Slum Upgrading Program (KENSUP). Fairly early in this process, there was a decision to target the Kibera slum as part of KENSUP and set up a pilot project in the Kibera village of Soweto. The resultant Kibera–Soweto pilot project was announced on World Habitat Day in 2004 with the objective of providing one-, two-, and three-bedroom units to be constructed with the temporary relocation of affected residents. The question raised by some observers is whether these units will actually be affordable or will just end up benefitting individuals and families that are better off than the average Kibera–Soweto resident or even of the Nairobi lower-middle class. Indeed, there is evidence that the jump from traditional wattle and daub housing to government-mandated apartment standards could be too ambitious.

As the Kibera–Soweto project got underway, the emerging multistory units became known by the local residents as The Promised Land. Relocated residents were issued identification cards. However, a 2009 assessment of the Kibera–Soweto project suggested a lack of collaboration and communication with affected residents. In particular, residents were concerned with the sustainability of their informal livelihoods during temporary relocation, as was as with the affordability of the new units. There also was concern that too little attention had been paid to rental options rather than ownership. More recent assessments note that some owners of the new units simply rented them to higher income families and moved back to the slum. Nonetheless, as of 2016 nearly 1,000 new units were available, and the UN has handed the project to the Kenyan government.

One policy area in housing provision that needs continued investigation is that of housing *finance*. Standard housing finance in the form of mortgages has appeared in many developing countries and is tied in to global financial markets. As noted some years ago in one World Bank publication, "Since about 2000, the world changed from one in which most of the world's population did not have access to mortgage finance to one in which most of the world's population now lives in countries with a market-based mortgage finance system with generally affordable terms."[56] But the basic goods deprived are not always able to make use of these financial services. As the same report noted, "While market-based housing finance is now available to most middle-income people in the world, it is still not available in most countries or for the poorest people."[57] A more recent World Bank report on housing finance in South Asia reaffirmed this view:[58]

Financial markets, dominated by large banking sectors in South Asia, have seen a gradual liberalization in recent decades, and have been exhibiting remarkable growth as a result. Yet outreach remains limited, in view of extensive rural populations and predominating informality of finances for lower-income groups. Financial services have been limited to basic products, and have extended in a very modest manner into housing or related insurance products. Most banks avoid lending for housing, which typically involves long-term commitments to clients. Among the main reasons for this are the lack of an adequate supporting legal framework, including poor foreclosure and eviction procedures and land titling regimes; absence of reliable property valuation; lack of a well-functioning collateral system; a missing yield curve; and absence of long-term treasury instruments in some countries. Further complications include weak competition in the financial sector, poor transparency, underdeveloped market structural features such as second-tier lenders, and the lack of a level playing field for financial institutions.

Given these realities, many basic goods deprived individuals need to rely on informal financial systems for housing finance, namely family, friends, and traditional lending circles of various kinds. When these sources are absent, then these individuals remain in rental markets. But one additional possibility for providing housing finance to poor people is the lending activities of *microfinance* institutions. The evidence suggests that, to some significant extent at least, housing microfinance (HMF) is beginning to help, although it is often targeted to home improvement rather than to the purchase of new homes.

Microfinance began with the now-famous Grameen Bank in Bangladesh. Grameen began to include housing microfinance in its portfolio in 1987. It now has a sizable mortgage portfolio and has financed hundreds of thousands of homes with a respectable repayment rate. In many cases, HMF goes to very incremental improvements to housing that take place over time as conditions allow. For example, in the Angolan case, a researcher reported,[59]

> The house construction process and speed can be adapted according to family finances and available labor. In practice, because most people are very poor houses are built slowly and in phases. Many start with cardboard and plastic; the more fortunate use adobe or cement blocks and mortar immediately. First, they build the two-room core house but expand this later if they obtain further resources. Many families take 10 years or more to complete their houses. Most are constantly upgrading and expanding them as their families grow, then either sub-dividing for grown children or renting out extra rooms to provide eventual retirement income.

We can gain some idea of the role of microfinance in housing using Figure 9.2. This figure begins with the arrival of an individual (or family) in a new location, perhaps a city or even a refugee camp. If there is a relative or friend in this location, the newly arrived individual can seek shelter with them. Otherwise, they or homeless or seeking some housing services from potential providers in a refugee camp. In most instances, the individual will begin to work in some part of the informal labor market, perhaps as a day laborer or attempting to supply some type of petty service.

The individual can move from the informal labor market by borrowing money from a friend or relative to attempt to set up some kind of microenterprise. This could be something as simple as procuring storage containers for a recycling business. Absent or in addition to this relational loan, the individual could benefit from a standard microfinance loan. At some point, the individual's income may become large enough to begin to rent some kind of housing and no longer rely on a relative or friend.

Housing microfinance can move the individual from renter to owner. It can also help an owner upgrade his or her property, usually in incremental small ways as in the just-mentioned Angolan case. Sometimes, upgrades consist of an additional room used to rent, so HMF can provide rental properties to those who do not own. So as shown in Figure 9.2, microfinance affects individuals in both microenterprise finance and housing finance.

Housing finance is a focus on house *ownership*. Although this has its place, there also needs to be a focus on *rental* opportunities.[60] Renting offers a number of advantages, including flexibility of relocating in response to changing job opportunities, particularly when those jobs are in the informal sector. Renting

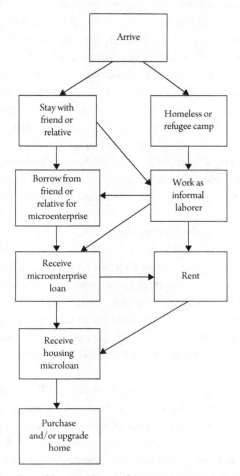

Figure 9.2 New arrivals and housing microfinance. Source: Adapted from Cain (2007).

is an area where both formal and informal private sector provision can help to supply a variety of housing options.

For individuals in these rental markets, a key issue is the appropriate role of *rent control*. Traditionally, economists have been disdainful of this policy. Rent control is a type of price ceiling and it inevitably leads to excess demand for housing and a cascade of less-than-optimal effects that arise to address this excess demand.[61] That said, there are still discussions among housing economists as to whether "second-generation" rent control policies might play some useful role in the provision of housing. These second-generation programs contain a number of elements that make them different from the previous generation of policies. These include: inflation adjustment, cost pass-through, hardship provisions, and rate of return provisions.[62] These provisions, as well as recognizing imperfect competition in rental markets, suggest that the standard "free-market" opposition to rent control is less strong than previously thought.[63]

Another policy approach to housing provision is the use of *vouchers*. Vouchers are seen as a way to avoid the downsides of large-scale public housing and to engage private market transactions. Nonetheless, this approach seems to present a number of its own problems.[64] As with many poverty-based policies, vouchers can often be taken away when individuals obtain employment and thus act as a disincentive to employment. Vouchers can also be an incentive for landlords to increase rents. Finally, vouchers put an additional strain on government budgets.

If we were to summarize the evolving role of the public sector in providing housing it would be a move to facilitating and regulating the private provision of housing rather than attempting to control housing markets for the poor. This is sometimes referred to as an *enabling approach* or *enabling strategy*.[65] Former UN official and housing specialist Kioe Sheng Yap described the enabling strategy as follows:[66]

> The strategy contends that markets should be the primary housing delivery mechanism and that the public sector's role is to introduce incentives and facilitate housing actions by other actors, through partnerships of local government, the private sector and non-governmental and community-based organizations (NGOs and CBOs). The strategy accepts the limitations of the market for housing the poor and stresses the need for government to recognize and upgrade informal settlements and to develop innovative approaches to low-income housing.

The enabling strategy is not without its critics. Housing researchers Xing Quan Zhang and Michael Ball argued that the approach "works better in economically advanced countries and for the relatively well-off population in the developing countries." More specifically, they argued that it "is not very effective in addressing the most targeted poor population in most countries."[67] One reason for this is that it is difficult to target the *very poor* in the face of rising land values, particularly in urban areas. This remains an ongoing challenge.

Regulatory Frameworks

Regardless of the position one takes on the extent of the market in housing provision, there will be the need for some basic *regulatory frameworks* for the provision process to be successful. Housing researcher Geoffrey Payne identified three broad elements of regulatory frameworks: planning regulations, planning standards, and administrative procedures.[68] At a minimum, *planning regulations* ensure that land use does not pose a threat to the health and safety of residents. *Planning standards* go one step further and impose minimum requirements for the buildings themselves. *Administrative procedures* involve the required governmental steps that accompany aspects of housing development. Each of these is necessary, but can be overdone relative to their optimal levels.

Payne noted that, in some instances, these regulatory frameworks have been *imported* from elsewhere.[69] They also can be onerous and inappropriate. These facts can suppress housing sector development because inappropriate or too stringent regulatory frameworks place the bottom rung of what Payne called the "legal housing ladder" at too high a level, putting it out of reach for poor people.[70] An example of this was shown earlier in the case of the Kibera slum in Nairobi, Kenya, where the jump from wattle and daub housing to unit types seemed to be leap too far.[71] This can have the effect of placing informal housing (particularly informal urban housing) beyond the legal realm. The relevant question posed by Payne was, "what aspects of the land and housing development process should be regulated and how should this be achieved?"[72] The objective to be kept in mind in answering this question is "to minimize initial entry costs to *legal* shelter—to lower the bottom rung of the housing ladder."[73]

But the rung should not be removed completely. For example, if planning regulations are to too lax, residents can be living too close to polluting factories, and as a result of too loose planning standards, earthquakes and other natural disasters can inflict much more damage than they need to. On the other hand, preventing a poor household from using their dwelling to operate some sort of microenterprise or renting rooms is not appropriate. At present, there is enough applied research in this area to make wise decisions.[74]

Summary

Housing is a basic good that satisfies a basic right. Minimal levels of housing are important in themselves and also in the provision of a locational and familial context where other basic goods can be provided. For these reasons, the basic goods approach is central to housing policy formation.[75] It is unfortunate that available data do not allow us to assess the extent to which housing is underprovided. It seems clear from some available data, however, that deprivation in housing is extensive. The extreme case of housing deprivation is that of displaced people, the number of which is increasing rapidly due to political conflict and climate change. Ensuring basic goods provision for these individuals will be an increasingly important challenge.

Despite international recognition of housing as a basic right, in many cases, little is done to ensure that housing provision is successfully achieved within the exigencies of market-based rental and property markets. Bare minimum thresholds of basic goods provision are therefore of great relevance in this case. The provision of housing is complicated, with both formal and informal sectors, rental and ownership possibilities, and potentially inappropriate regulatory systems.

As policy approaches to housing provision evolve, it is clear that well-thought-out enabling approaches are a good starting point but that these need to target the severely housing deprived and recognize their special needs. But the enabling approach should not be an excuse to forget the potential role of governments of various levels and the potential use of public–private partnerships. Although there are many examples of failed housing policies, there are also examples of successes. The central point is to make housing provision a real priority.

Notes

1. Busch-Geertsema, Culhane, and Fitzpatrick (2015) questioned the empirical basic for these estimates. They also reported that: "it is the firm conviction of the authors—after an intensive search for existing data on homelessness at the national, regional and local levels in various world regions—that it is not possible at this stage to generate a defensible estimate of the extent of homelessness" (p. 17). Although these authors propose a means of estimating global homelessness, they emphasize that it would take "many years" to complete (p. 28).
2. Nenova (2010), p. xiii.
3. The World Bank's World Development Indicators do not contain any series on housing.
4. Zhang and Ball (2016), p. 161.
5. Thomson and Petticrew (2007), p. 434.
6. See, for example, Rimawi, Mirdamani, and John (2014).
7. See Walters and Gaillard (2014) for the case of Delhi, India.
8. In the case of Delhi, India, Walters and Gaillard (2014) noted that "The homeless are also vulnerable to many everyday hazards that arise from a lack of basic services such safe water sources and sanitation facilities. The public water utility, the Delhi Jal Board, supplies drinking water to temporary and semi-permanent shelters throughout the city every two-to-three days but there are either poor or no sanitation facilities provided. For those who do not stay in shelters and who lack access to a safe drinking water source they have to buy water from vendors at exorbitant prices, use un-safe and un-potable water, limit their daily water intake, or collect water from public taps. Sanitation facilities are seldom provided at shelters, and when they are they can be in very poor condition. In the Nigambodh Ghat where Ajay stays there is chronic shortage of clean water for bathing and washing clothes. The Yamuna River is highly polluted and the water cannot even be used for washing clothes" (p. 215).
9. For the example of homeless in Delhi, India, see Barry (2016).
10. See Jacobs et al. (2009), for example.
11. In the Argentine context, see for example, Galiani and Schargrodsky (2010). For the Peruvian context, see for example Fields (2005).

12. Zhang and Ball (2016), p. 164.
13. Boo (2012), p. 83.
14. Shue (1996).
15. United Nations High Commissioner for Human Rights (1991).
16. United Nations General Assembly (1966b), p. 7.
17. United Nations High Commissioner for Human Rights (1991).
18. UN-HABITAT (2011) noted that forced evictions, particularly those in urban areas, are on the rise across the globe. See also Albisa, Scott, and Tissington (2013).
19. United Nations High Commissioner for Human Rights (1991).
20. Kenna (2005), p. 2.
21. Kenna (2005), p. 3. In keeping with the approach of this book, but in the specific context of housing, Kenna also stated that "the minimum core obligation has narrowed the problem of distributive justice to that of assessing the evenness of the distribution of the socially guaranteed minimum levels of certain goods and benefits among individual groups within a country" (p. 2).
22. Kenna (2005), p. 3.
23. Albisa, Scott, and Tissington (2013), p. 105.
24. See, for example, Beath, Goldin, and Reinert (2009).
25. http://eur-lex.europa.eu/legal-content/EN/ALL/?uri=CELEX:42000A0922(01).
26. Doctors without Borders (2011), p. 2.
27. Doctors without Borders (2011), p. 2.
28. Sa'Da and Bianchi (2014).
29. See United Nations High Commissioner for Refugees (2010).
30. For the example of primary healthcare and refugees in Southern Africa, Zihindula, Meyer-Weitz, and Akintola (2015) concluded, "Ultimately, the importance of access to health care for all form of refugees is acknowledged widely, but limitations in the availability of resources prevent the full realization of this right. The state is therefore required to commit to the delivery of a set of services while also providing the fall-back that it meets its obligation in the context of available resources. . . . Challenges of availability and affordability of drugs as well as the acceptability of the refugee individual by the health care workers and the community were the dominant barriers identified. Some other barriers specific to each country that were identified included but were not limited to language and cultural barriers, discrimination, policy and its implementation, health care workers xenophobia, and refugee documentation" (p. 29).
31. See UNHCR (2011a,b).
32. See Zhang and Ball (2016).
33. See Buckley and Kalarickal (2005).
34. Boo (2012), p. 41.
35. See Albisa, Scott, and Tissington (2013).
36. See Yap (2016).
37. Zhang and Ball (2016), p. 162.
38. Cain (2007), p. 377.
39. See, for example, Werbach (2011).
40. See, for example, Gilbert (2016).
41. Kenna (2005), p. 2.
42. Albisa, Scott, and Tissington (2013), p. 87. These authors further noted that "There are many government programs to create access to housing for the poor, from government housing to subsidies. However, these tend to be patchwork programs to address gaps left by the market, rather than a systematic approach" (p. 87n).
43. This point was made by Rondinelli (1990) among others.
44. See Buckley and Kalarickal (2005).
45. See, for example, Gilbert (2016) as well at *The Economist* (2017e) on the case of Ethiopia.
46. Buckley and Kalarickal (2005) stated that "many countries now adopt a community-based perspective—rather than the engineering, technocratic approach embodied in earlier

shelter projects—that focuses on providing what might be termed the local public goods involved" (p. 240).

47. Although participation became somewhat of a contemporary development fad, it does have roots in development thought. See, for example, Mishra and Sharma (1982).

48. This point was made by Albisa, Scott, and Tissington (2013). They stated, "Why should communities accept alternative accommodation, even if well-defined, when without their participation it has been determined that their use of the land upon which they live is not of the highest value?" (p. 108) and "At a minimum, a more serious right to participation and engagement should take effect prior to any decision to change land use" (p. 109).

49. Huchzermeyer (2008), p. 22.

50. See, for example, Yap (2016) and Joshi and Khan (2010).

51. This box draws on Huchzermeyer (2008); Amnesty International (2009); and Mutisya and Yarime (2011).

52. See, for example, Woodruff (2001) and Buckley and Kalarickal (2005).

53. Because so much has been claimed in policy circles for land titling, it is worthwhile to quote an alternative view. Based on a review of research, for example, Payne, Alain and Rakodi (2009) concluded, "land titling has not been shown to achieve the social and economic benefits claimed for it; in fact, many of the advantages for which titles are promoted, such as stimulating investment in property improvement, have been realized for less formal increases in tenure status. Moreover, these less formal means may be much cheaper and easier to implement given limited institutional and human resources. This suggests that before launching land titling programmes in urban or peri-urban areas, land administration agencies should explore a wide range of alternative tenure options for achieving social and economic policy objectives" (p. 459).

54. See Yap (2016).

55. See, for example, Yap (2016).

56. Buckley and Kalarickal (2006), p. xii.

57. Buckley and Kalarickal (2006), p. xii.

58. Nenova (2010), p. 19.

59. Cain (2007), p. 371.

60. This point was made by Gilbert (2016) and Yap (2016).

61. As Arnott (1995) noted, "There has been widespread agreement that rent controls discourage new construction, cause abandonment, retard maintenance, reduce mobility, generate mismatch between housing units and tenants, exacerbate discrimination in rental housing, create black markets, encourage the conversion of rental to owner-occupied housing, and generally short-circuit the market mechanism for housing" (p. 99).

62. See Arnott (1995).

63. See Arnott (1995) and Buckley and Kalarickal (2006).

64. See Peppercorn and Taffin (2013) and Gilbert (2016).

65. See, for example, Zhang and Ball (2016).

66. Yap (2016), p. 166.

67. Zhang and Ball (2016), p. 163.

68. Payne (2001). See also Payne and Majale (2004).

69. "For example, building regulations in the Southern African kingdom of Lesotho are based on those of Sweden, and those of the highlands of Papua New Guinea on Australian category 'A' regulations derived from coastal conditions" (Payne, 2001, p. 309).

70. For evidence of this in the context of Nairobi, Kenya, see Huchzermeyer (2008).

71. Huchzermeyer (2008) explicitly recognized this, stating, "In Nairobi's housing market, slum rooms are at the bottom of the housing ladder. The next rung, rooms in multistory tenements, are out of their reach" (p. 35).

72. Payne, 2001, p. 314.

73. Payne, 2001, p. 315, emphasis added.

74. See, for example, Payne and Majale (2004).

75. See, for example, Muñoz Conde (2011).

10

Electricity

Electricity has long been thought of as something that meets basic human needs and promotes human development.[1] Nevertheless, it is worth reconsidering why I included electricity as a basic good. Recall from Chapter 3 that electricity contributes to refrigeration. This can improve food storage to prevent illness and preserve medicines to address any existing illness. With regard to food storage, refrigerating animal products is particularly important for children when fortified cereals are unavailable.[2] Electricity also makes air conditioning possible, and this has been shown to improve health and increase productivity in hot environments.[3] In these ways, electricity helps support health. Electricity also makes possible radio and television, potentially providing access to critical information. These and other critical roles played by electricity were summarized by international law scholar Stephen Tully as follows:[4]

> Electricity access in particular has become virtually essential to contemporary human survival. Electricity cooks food, powers household appliances, supports a healthy temperature (heating or air conditioning), provides clean water (by powering pumps or desalination treatment), and enables proper health care (refrigerated vaccines, operating theatres, life support systems, . . ., emergency treatment, or intensive care). Electricity enables agricultural production, processing, and marketing (thereby ensuring food security), provides educational aids (computers, printers and photocopiers), encourages social cohesion (participation in cultural production, entertainment, or recreation) and generates income earning opportunities.

So electricity is important. Recognizing this importance, one set of researchers wrote that "Electricity is in fact an integral component of socio-economic development. . . . Lacking access is therefore a major impediment to development."[5] Exploring ways to remove this impediment is a main objective of this chapter. As will be seen, in the case of electricity, technological changes are proving to play a role in mitigating electricity deprivation.

Deprivation in electricity is fairly extensive, with approximately 1.1 billion people living without access.[6] Approximately 85 percent of those without electricity live in rural areas or at the edge of cities, and current trends suggest that the number of people without electricity will not fall any time soon.[7] A regional breakdown of this lack of access is available for the year 2012 and is presented in Figure 10.1. As shown in Figure 10.1, the bulk of the deprivation in electricity (approximately one billion individuals in 2012) is concentrated in sub-Saharan Africa and South Asia. This is in keeping with the deprivations of other basic goods and services concentrated in these regions, namely clean water and sanitation services. There is evidence that electricity provision is increasing somewhat faster in India but not in sub-Saharan Africa.[8]

The lack of electricity supply in sub-Saharan Africa is particularly notable. This situation was summarized by *The Economist* as follows: "South of the Sahara there are only seven countries . . . in which more than 50% of people have access to electricity. In a typical year, the whole region generates less electricity than Canada, and half of that supply is in South Africa."[9] The International Energy Agency (IEA) forecasts suggested that, by 2040, nearly all the deprivation in electricity access will be in sub-Saharan Africa with a total of about 500 million lacking access.[10] So the picture is one of improvements in provision in South Asia but persistent deprivation in sub-Saharan Africa.

Figure 10.2 gives a country-based view of the number of people without access to electricity. Here we see that the vast bulk of people without electricity are found in India. This is in keeping with the deprivations of other basic goods in India seen in previous chapters. Most of the other countries in Figure 10.2 are

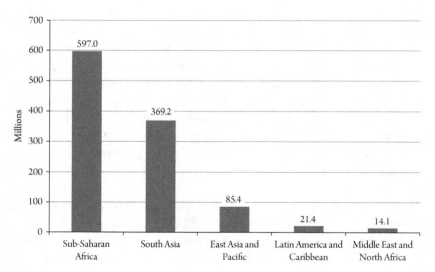

Figure 10.1 Number of people without access to electricity by region, 2012.
Source: World Bank, World Development Indicators

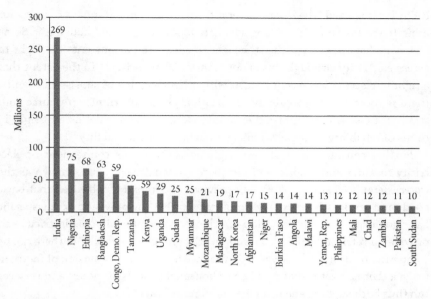

Figure 10.2 Number of people without access to electricity by country, 2012.
Source: World Bank, World Development Indicators

sub-Saharan African countries, but also a few other South Asian and Southeast Asian countries, such as Bangladesh, Myanmar and Pakistan are found on the list as well. In the case of North Korea, famous satellite images attest that this country is largely dark at night. The main point here is that electricity deprivations are highly concentrated among the countries of the world.

The Right to Electricity

For each of the other basic goods and services, I could point to language within the United Nations system supporting a right to minimum provision levels. This is much less the case with electricity. Nevertheless, there are considerations and emerging traditions that do suggest a right to electricity. For example, Article 14(2) of the 1979 United Nations Convention on the Elimination of all Forms of Discrimination Against Women (CEDAW) obligates parties to "take all appropriate measures to eliminate discrimination against women in rural areas . . . and, in particular, shall ensure to such women the right . . . to enjoy adequate living conditions, particularly in relation to . . . electricity."[11] This is the one explicit recognition of a right to electricity within the UN system.

Recall from Chapter 3 that the 1976 ICESCR reiterated what was stated in Article 25 of the UDHR with regard to standard of living.[12] Article 11 of the

ICESCR recognized "the right of everyone to an adequate standard of living for himself and his family, including adequate food, clothing and housing."[13] Some observers have suggested that the right to adequate housing entails a right to access electricity although this is not mentioned explicitly.[14] To the extent that a right to electricity is recognized, as with other elements of subsistence rights, there is room for its progressive realization given government resource constraints. Those who recognize the right to electricity access define that right in terms of reliability, adequacy, sufficient quality, and affordability.[15]

Further considerations of basic rights arise from the connections of electricity to water and food, a reality explored in what has become known as the *water-energy-food nexus* (WEF).[16] In previous chapters, I emphasized that basic goods and services are mutually supporting in that the provision of any specific basic good supports the provision of others. As the provision of electricity can provide for refrigeration that can support the provision of food. But there can be competing relationships as well as in the case in which the provision of food can make a claim to water that could go to household use. Basic goods and services can thus both support and compete with one another.

An analytical recognition of these relationships is what is emphasized in the WEF nexus. According to the Food and Agricultural Organization, "The water, energy and food (WEF) nexus means that the three sectors—water security, energy security and food security—are inextricably linked and that actions in one area more often than not have impacts in one or both of the others."[17] Water, energy, and food can be linked as a final provision to households but also can depend on each other as intermediate inputs. As shown in Chapter 4, agriculture accounts for 70 percent of the demand for water and is also energy intensive. And as shown in Chapter 5, water production in the form of desalination can be very energy intensive. The same can be true of water pumps and irrigation systems at a local level. Further, energy demand in the form of biofuels can compete with the provision of food, but energy production via agricultural waste does not have to compete.

Although the WEF nexus considers the broad issue of *energy* rather than only *electricity*, in practice, much (not all) of the analysis of this nexus does turn out to be focused on electricity itself. It begins with the recognition of the lack of access to electricity but then moves on to a number of specific issues. These include the use of electricity in water pumps and irrigation, the subsidization of water pumping via subsidized electricity, the use of water as a coolant in coal and nuclear electricity generation, the use of water to generate electricity via hydropower, and the use of electricity in desalination. So in some important instances, we need to consider electricity as being intimately connected to water and food, as well as how the rights to these three basic goods are connected to each other.

Whether there is a firmly established right to electricity access within the UN system, such access is very important from a subsistence standpoint, and this makes electricity a basic good. Doubtless, human rights considerations with regard to electricity will continue to evolve, and the basic goods quality of electricity will be an important part of that evolution.[18] But given electricity's importance and evolving role in subsistence rights frameworks, the question to address is *how* to effectively lessen levels of deprivations of this basic good.

Provision Paradigms

Some observers divide provision systems for electricity into standard "top-down" approaches and emerging "bottom-up" approaches. Top-down approaches involve centralized, utility-based systems with large generation and distribution facilities. These still have their place. But flexible, bottom-up approaches are gradually gaining increased attention particularly for poor communities without access to electricity.[19] One can make an analogy to telephone services. Not long ago, the expectation was that people without telephone service would need to wait for centralized landline systems to slowly grow and finally provide service to them or to their children. Then mobile telephone service arrived in what can accurately be described as a technological revolution that provided unforeseen access to communication. Something similar is happening with electricity provision.

Another term for bottom-up approaches is *distributed generation* (DG), and this approach is gaining increased attention from researchers and policy analysts. The change in paradigm has been described by one set of researchers as follows:[20]

> The paradigm for how to provide affordable electricity for the world's poor—power for development—has changed over the past two decades. Historically, highly centralized (and often authoritarian) governments built largescale hydroelectric dams and power plants, as well as lengthy distribution and transmission lines, with the ultimate goal of providing electricity to all of a nation's citizens. Today, however, a wide range of actors quietly contests this centralized and top-down approach to electrification. Donors, nongovernmental organizations (NGOs), private-sector firms, and communities are collaborating with governments to develop small-scale localized energy generation systems known as distributed generation (DG). . . . DG is an increasingly common alternative or complement to large-scale grid electrification because of its promise to enhance local decision making, facilitate energy access for the poor, and protect the environment.

There are many types of distributed generation systems. They include solar, wind, biomass, and hydropower systems that range from the very small up to three megawatts. Distributed generation overlaps greatly with the notion of off-grid electricity generation. Within the distributed generation paradigm, a central transition is from diesel and kerosene power to off-grid electricity.[21] This transition can be potentially widespread and address electricity deprivation long before centralized systems become available. This is not to say that households and businesses that make this transition will be forever restricted from joining a grid, but rather that they may well remain off-grid for some significant time, benefiting from distributed generation while grids are slowly developed.

One specific class of distributed generation that involves potential off-grid applications is that of renewable-based systems, including solar and wind. These systems have the added benefit of not involving increased fossil fuels and therefore offset additional greenhouse gas emissions that contribute to climate change. Given the impacts of global warming on food security and water availability, these renewable-based systems are worth considering in some more detail.[22]

Renewable Technology

As discussed in Chapter 3, this book takes a sober view of what I termed "technological optimism." Technological change is real and can have significant impacts, but it is unlikely to be able to solve all basic goods provision problems on the scale that is often claimed. Nonetheless, there are cases where technological change can indeed solve problems on a broad scale, and electricity generation and use appears to be one such case. There are some important technological changes taking place in the realm of electricity that will have some significant impacts. These changes concern light-emitting diode (LED) lighting, solar power electricity generation, and battery-based electricity storage.

LED lighting originated in the early 1960s and was initially applied to calculator displays. More recently, advances in white LEDs have led to a near-revolution in indoor lighting with the old incandescent bulb becoming a thing of the past. This new LED technology is much more efficient that the old incandescent bulb, using about 20 percent of the energy of traditional light. They also have a much longer life, and their cost has fallen substantially. As discussed later, LED lights are helpful to the electricity deprived because they require less electricity to generate effective lighting.

As with LED lighting, solar or photovoltaic panels made an appearance in the 1960s. A single panel consists of many individual solar cells, with the standard cell being composed of crystalline-silicon (c-Si). The economics of solar panels also have improved substantially. In 2008, the cost of photovoltaics was at about

$4.00/watt. By 2011, this had fallen to $1.00/watt, a threshold commonly associated with what is known as "grid parity."[23] All evidence suggests that the cost has continued to fall significantly since then, with one source reporting that the cost declined by 80 percent between 2010 and 2016.[24] It now seems safe to assume that solar panels are indeed economical, and as we will see, evolving market conditions in a number of regions of the world support this view. The combination of solar panels and LED lighting makes providing lighting to those deprived of it much easier than it has been in the past.

In situations where electricity supply is unreliable, including where households rely on renewable sources of electricity, battery storage becomes critical. Fortunately, advances in battery storage have taken place along with LED lighting and solar panels. The standard technology for battery storage is lead-acid batteries, but there are many other battery types, including lithium-ion, sodium-sulfur, and nickel-cadmium. A common denominator across all of these battery types is that significant advancements are taking place. Quality battery technologies are appearing as solar panels are becoming economical. For example, California is beginning to install large numbers of lithium-ion batteries as a storage solution for its solar panels.[25] Indeed, lithium-ion batteries are now taking center stage in most applications.[26]

In some instances, appliances are coming on market with their own battery backup. For example, the Korean firm LG is beginning to supply refrigerators with their own backup batteries that can continue to refrigerate for up to seven hours without power supply. The British company Sure Chill has a refrigerator that only needs a few hours of power a day. These advances help to make refrigeration possible in the face of the inherent intermittency of solar power. Therefore, it also makes possible two fundamental basic goods roles of refrigeration: food safety and medicine storage.

There is a great deal of emerging evidence that the combination of LED lighting, solar panels, batteries, and new appliances coming on market via frugal innovation can help to address (if not to solve) deprivations in electricity. These technological changes are combining to support the provision of electricity in DG systems. Let us look at these trends in some more detail.

Renewable Applications

Evidence suggests that the economics of home-based solar systems are beginning to undercut that of kerosene lamps and generators. For example, a *New York Times* article considered Mr. Ali in rural Bangladesh and stated the following:[27]

> Solar energy is reliable, clean and cheaper in the long run than kerosene and the village's generator. It costs about 3,000 taka ($38) a month

for the diesel generator to light a three-room house. But for the solar equipment, Mr. Ali pays 1,355 taka ($17) in monthly installments after a down payment of 6,500 taka ($83) on a loan he expects to pay off within two years.

In the case of Bangladesh, the diffusion of this technology is helped by the government-backed Infrastructure Development Company Limited (Idcol), which has succeeded in helping to install solar panels on four million homes housing eighteen million people. The work of Idcol has been supported by the World Bank. Part of its success seems to reside in its ability to partner with local, grass-roots development organizations and microfinance institutions. The same *New York Times* article reported that the majority of installations are for the smallest solar panel that provides only twenty watts of power. So this is clearly a case of successful BoP provision of a basic good. One study of the program suggested that "adoption of a solar home system improves children's evening study time, lowers kerosene consumption, and provides health benefits for household members, in particular for women."[28] More generally, climate investigations suggest that Bangladesh is suitable for significantly more solar and wind electricity generation.[29]

As shown, the country with the largest number of individuals deprived of electricity is India. India is a large importer of fossil fuels in the form of coal, but it is also a country with a significant amount of solar potential. Given that a number of observers have suggested that coal imports are not sustainable in the long run, attention in India is turning to solar. Solar power does seem to be making a difference in India, but perhaps in a somewhat different manner than in Bangladesh. India is noted for having built the world's largest solar electric power plant, the 650 MW Kamuthi facility in Tamil Nadu.[30] Nonetheless, a significant number of the electricity deprived individuals in India are rural residents, and for this reason, distributed solar systems are also important.[31] The Indian government is moving to support this provision paradigm in the form of rooftop solar and is providing a subsidy for them.[32] India is a location of many innovative firms, and at least one firm, Basil Energetics, is developing solar systems and appliances for households and enterprises that run in an integrated mini-grid.[33] The company is focusing on air conditioners, refrigerators, fans, and LED lights. This is a case of a relatively high-tech, BoP provision strategy.

One of India's leading industrial group, Tata, is beginning to push for an increased role for solar power in India's energy future with its Bridge to India initiative.[34] Because Bridge to India is a consultancy, Tata's initiative here is profit making. However, the company clearly sees India's current coal-based electricity generation system as growth constraining for the country and sees renewables, including solar power, as removing a roadblock to future growth prospects. It is interesting that for a large conglomerate, Tata's Bridge to India initiative sees DG in the form of rooftop solar as an important part of India's energy future.[35]

It appears that the same significant change in off-grid solar power can take place on the African continent. In a few short years up to 2016, the number of households in Africa receiving electricity from off-grid solar increased from nearly zero to 600,000, and the rate of growth in this process has been estimated to be between 60 and 100 percent. Customers taking part in this process include hospitals and enterprises as well as households.[36] Earlier I suggested that it could be possible for DG to follow the path of mobile telephones and bypass centralized grid systems. This seems to be an emerging pattern in Africa. For example, *The Economist* stated that the "fast pace of growth suggests that, if sustained, off-grid connections will within a few years outstrip the rate at which people are being connected to the grid, leapfrogging power lines in much the same way that mobile phones bypassed fixed-line telephone networks."[37] This is good news in a severely electricity-deprived continent.

Distributed solar power is not just about residential and small business uses. For example the We Care Solar Suitcase is a specially designed solar system for off-grid health clinics.[38] I once spoke to an Ethiopian doctor who related his experiences trying to deliver babies by flashlight in a rural area. The Solar Suitcase remedies this problem. Indeed, its primary application is in obstetric care. Such innovations will support the positive interaction between the basic goods electricity and health services. With maternal mortality rates occurring at about 300,000 per year, this is good news. In addition, the Solar Electric Light Fund (SELF) has developed projects to provide electricity to health clinics and surgical facilities, including in the Brazilian Amazon region. SELF reported: "The solar-powered clinic now has a Sunfrost refrigerator that reliably preserves fragile vaccines and snake bite serums. Solar lights allow for emergency surgical operations to be performed at night."[39] Distributed renewables can indeed have profound health implications.

Part of the reason for this rapid uptake of off-grid solar is the combination of LED lighting, solar panels, batteries, and new appliances mentioned earlier. Another part is the rapid reduction in the cost of providing these systems relative to past and to on-grid connections. A third element is the increase in BoP businesses providing the solar systems. Technology, economics and enterprise seem to be coming together to help ameliorate electricity deprivation in support of the right to electricity. The case of electricity provision in the Kibera slum of Kenya is considered in Box 10.1.[40]

Box 10.1 Electricity Provision in the Kibera Slum of Nairobi, Kenya

In Box 9.1, I discussed the housing challenges of the Kibera slum of Nairobi, Kenya. Recall that the Kibera slum is home to approximately one million people, mostly living in inadequate housing. Much of the lighting in Kibera is provided through kerosene, but electricity is also an important source. Electricity provision in Kibera has been a distinct challenge with electricity being provided via illegal connections maintained by cartels or, more politely, informal power distributors (IPDs). Although this has proved economical for Kibera's residents, there have been cases of electricity fires and electrocutions due to faulty connections. For example, one Kibera resident reported:

"I was in one of the neighborhoods here that I was not really familiar with. I had no shoes on, and my feet were wet," she said. "I saw a flower and I wanted to go get the flower. By bad luck, I stepped on a live wire. I could not move. My sister ran to rescue me. She also got stuck with me. We started pulling ourselves away from the point. We managed to escape, but for some minutes my brain could not process what was going on."

This kind of danger adds to the many challenges faced by Kibera residents, including housing, sanitation, clean water supply, education, healthcare, and security.

Kenya's sole, legal power company is Kenya Power. Kenya Power spent a number of years trying to displace the IPDs with legal power connections with very little success. Research has suggested that connection fees were a major sticking point for Kibera residents. The lack of success changed when Kenya Power shifted its strategy to a community-based approach that explained to Kibera residents the benefits of legal connections, including safety. Subsidies for connections, including those from the World Bank, appear to be helping with the number of legal connections and they are finally beginning to increase rapidly.

As a result, a Kenya Power Company director stated, "The solution is not to stop illegal connections. The solution is to offer alternative cheaper and safe connections to Kibera people. We have given Kibera people electricity at the cost of $10 per month. There is no motivation whatsoever for anyone in Kibera to want to steal an illegal connection, because that illegal connection will be much higher in cost than the formal one that we are giving them. So what we are seeing in Kibera is the slowing down of those illegal connections." This is the way in which Kenya Power and the World Bank are working together to promote legal household connections.

Along with a focus on electricity connections, the Kenyan government has begun to focus on installing LED street lamps in Kibera. Private contributions also have helped with the Philips Corporation installing solar-powered LED lighting at community centers. As discussed in the case of off-the-grid residential applications, the Philips program combines LEDs, long lasting batteries, and solar panels. Progress in electricity access is slowly taking place in Africa's largest slum.

The Case of Wind Power

Wind energy is another emerging technology with the potential to address electricity deprivation in some locations. As with solar photovoltaics, there have been a number of significant technological innovations affecting wind energy conversion systems. The "capacity factors" of these systems have increased substantially through larger rotors, improved blade design (aerodynamics), blade materials, gearbox advances, overall size (measured by hub height), and reduced weight-size ratios. Evidence seems to suggest that these advances are still ongoing and will continue to positively affect the economics of wind energy. At present, wind energy is competitive with fossil fuels in an increasing number of sites.[41]

As with solar, wind power has the property of being intermittent and therefore often needs battery-based storage as part of the system to move beyond merely contributing to grid systems that receive most of their power from fossil fuels.[42] A number of technical issues (such as optimal location of battery storage systems and optimal control strategies) need to be addressed to put wind power on par with fossil fuels, but the available evidence suggests that this is indeed possible given current battery-storage advances.[43]

As a result of these changes, wind energy capacity is increasing rapidly, from less than 20,000 MW in 2000 to over 430,000 MW in 2015. By some estimates, wind energy is becoming increasingly important with increases in installed capacity accounting for half of the *growth* in total capacity. A great deal of this increase is taking place in Asia, with China and India leading the way. Indeed, China now has the largest installed wind capacity of any country in the world, twice that of the United States as of 2015.[44]

There are a number of low- and middle-income countries where wind energy *potential* is quite large. In the case of Africa, these include Somalia, Sudan, Libya, Mauritania, Egypt, Madagascar, Kenya, and Chad for onshore sources and Mozambique, Tanzania, Angola, South Africa, and Namibia for offshore sources.[45] There are some positive developments in wind power projects in Africa such as movements away from concessional finance and greater amounts of private sector funding. There are also signs of increasing installed capacity in Egypt and South Africa. However, generally speaking, the market entry of firms to make use of the potential is insufficient for wind power to play a substantial role in the near term.[46] To date, there is not much of an increase in installed wind power capacity in Africa.[47] This is one reason why distributed solar panels are all the more important in this case.

Renewable versus Nonrenewable Energy Sources and Climate Change

At a couple of junctures in this book, it has been relevant and even necessary to talk about climate change. Climate change (global warming) has been implicated in an increased amount of conflict in certain parts of the world, as well as an increased number of refugees.[48] Although there is a significant amount of uncertainty regarding the impacts of climate change on agriculture, in some key regions at least, these impacts are going to be negative.[49] And as discussed in some detail in Chapter 5, climate change is going to have a significant impact on the ability to provide water as a basic good. According to the IEA, just under half of global carbon emissions can be attributed to electricity and heat production, and a similar figure for the United States is about 30 percent.[50] Although we can quibble about what the exact figures are, electricity generation is a significant contributor to greenhouse gas emissions and therefore to climate change. To the extent that electricity generation shifts to renewable sources, some amount of climate change is prevented, along with its negative impacts on the provision of other basic goods.

That said, despite the advantages of renewable energy sources, there is no question that nonrenewable sources will continue to be part of the energy mix. As can be seen in Figure 10.3, according to the projections of the United States Energy Information Agency, the contribution of renewable energy sources is projected to increase from a current 10 percent to about 30 percent in 2040. That said, some large countries, notably China and India, seem to have begun a move away from coal as a default source of electricity generation. This reflects oversupply, climate concerns, and simple economics.[51] South Africa is very dependent on coal for more than 90 percent of its electricity generation. This is a legacy of its coal industry and, indeed, a significant share of the electricity generated goes to the mining sector itself, while one third of households lack access to the electricity.[52] Despite emerging limitations to coal-powered electricity production in South Africa, the path dependency of this sector is strong.

Nonrenewable energy sources are the recipients of a significant amount of subsidies, estimated to be approximately US$500 billion.[53] These subsidies tilt

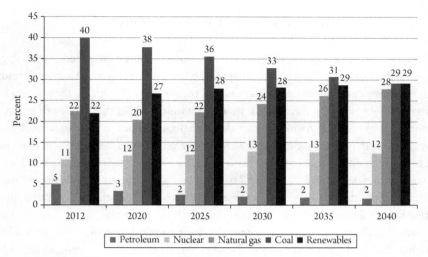

Figure 10.3 World net electricity generation by fuel (percentage), 2012 to 2040.
Source: United States Energy Information Agency.

the global energy supply system sharply in favor of nonrenewable energy sources while doing relatively little to address basic goods deprivation. *The Economist* described this as follows:[54]

> The proceeds flow overwhelmingly to the car-driving urban elite. In the typical emerging economy the richest fifth of households hoover up 40% of the benefits of fuel subsidies; the poorest fifth get only 7%. But the poorest suffer disproportionately from the distortions that such intervention creates. Egypt spends seven times more on fuel subsidies than on health. Cheap fuel encourages the development of heavy industry rather than the job-rich light manufacturing that offers far more people a route out of poverty. For all these reasons the benefits of scrapping subsidies are immense. Emerging economies could easily compensate every poor person with a handout that was bigger than the benefits they got from cheap fuel and still save money.

Given the presence of such subsidies, we need to keep in mind that, in many countries, renewable energy sources are operating at a *disadvantage* vis-à-vis nonrenewable energy sources. Given the set of negative environmental externalities associated with nonrenewable energy sources, this is *exactly backward* from what basic economic theory would suggest is appropriate. As a consequence, one appropriate policy step would be to begin to level the economic playing field between renewable and nonrenewable energy sources by reducing subsidies for the latter.

Technological Optimism Revisited

Chapter 3 expressed some critical opinions about what I have called "technological optimism." The basic opinion expressed in that chapter was that we cannot simply invoke technological advances and their rapid diffusion as *the solution* to the problem of basic goods provision. Any yet much of this chapter seems to have done just this in the form of new solar, lighting, and battery technologies. Are we contradicting ourselves? No, we are not. What Chapter 3 was critical of is the tendency to cite technological advances (and potentially entrepreneurship) as a *quick and reliable cure* for nearly *all* basic goods provision problems. Sometimes technologies do diffuse quickly, such as the case of mobile telephones, but sometimes they do not, such as the case of modern toilets. Solar systems are at the moment diffusing quickly, but we need to keep in mind that these systems, LED lights, and battery storage are all decades old. So the diffusion process was not actually quick. It took a confluence of incremental technological changes, relative energy price changes, supportive institutional environments, and BoP entrepreneurship development to bring us to where we are today. Rapid diffusion of basic goods and services innovations do sometimes occur, but we cannot invoke such processes as a general rule. The changes currently taking place in renewable energy are an exception that helps to illustrate this principle.

Electricity and Growth

Another argument from Chapter 3 is that basic goods provision and growth processes are mutually reinforcing. This claim has statistical evidence behind it in the case of education and health services. Given the role of health in growth processes, this statistical evidence would seem to apply to water, sanitation, and housing as well, although this has not been formally tested. In the case of electricity, however, there has long been an observed direct relationship between electricity consumption and growth.[55] In fact, the relationship between growth and electricity consumption is so direct that electricity use is sometimes used as a *proxy* for economic activity or to measure hidden economic activity in statistical analyses.[56] However, the direction of causality between electricity consumption and growth is always a question. Some statistical analyses find that the causality runs from growth to electricity use.[57] Other studies find causality running the opposite direction.[58] It may be that the direction of causality varies by time and place or that it runs in both directions simultaneously.

Common business sense suggests that reliable electricity supply is a prerequisite for sustained economic activity. And there is evidence that unreliable electricity supply has a negative impact on firm-level capital accumulation.[59] Even where firms respond creatively to unreliable electricity supplies (via the factor substitution of microeconomic theory), the unreliability is costly to the firms.[60] Such costs can fall most heavily on small enterprises. One study of small enterprises in Ghana found that electricity blackouts had detrimental impacts on machinery, inhibited the ability of entrepreneurs to satisfy contracts, and substantially increased costs.[61] Similar issues affect small enterprises in South Africa.[62] Given the extent to which development strategies have pinned their hopes on small enterprises for employment and income generation, electricity unreliability does indeed seem to be a significant issue. Basic goods provision in the form of electricity and growth strategies are mutually dependent on each other.

Solar power technologies can be and have been applied to support business development and thereby facilitate growth. For example, SELF has developed a solar-powered microenterprise center in Benin. In the same country, SELF also developed a solar application to support drip irrigation. Assessments suggest that the latter has contributed to food security, a key issue discussed in Chapter 4.[63] More broad research suggests that solar power can help small businesses, particularly those in rural areas, extend their hours of operation.[64] In these cases, solar-sourced electricity is supporting economic activity and therefore growth.

Summary

As is the case with the other basic goods considered in this book, electricity is underprovided, with over one billion individuals lacking access. This deprivation has a number of important and negative implications in the realm of food safety, health, water supply, communications, and opportunities for income generation. Human rights language is not as developed in the case of electricity as with the cases of other basic goods and services. However, whether there currently is an established right to electricity access, such access is very important from a subsistence standpoint, and this is what makes electricity a basic good. As with other basic goods and services, deprivations are concentrated in South Asia and sub-Saharan Africa, with projections suggesting that sub-Saharan Africa is the major long-term challenge.

With regard to provision paradigm, flexible, bottom-up approaches are gaining increasing attention with the notion of *distributed generation* having a great deal of traction. Advances in solar photovoltaics, battery storage, LED lighting, and appliances have combined to make distributed generation a growing reality for many electricity-deprived households. The world seems to be finally crossing over into an era where renewable energy sources are economically viable even for poor households. This is an importance case in which technological innovations are having a significant, positive impact on basic goods provision.

One major claim of this book is that basic goods provision and economic growth are mutually reinforcing. A number of different types of evidence suggest that this is indeed the case with electricity provision. Although some evidence suggests that electricity consumption is driven by growth, there is also evidence that electricity provision is pro-growth. Finally, to the extent that renewable sources of electricity mitigate the climate change effects of growth, that impact is an additional benefit for food and water security.

Notes

1. See, for example, Goldemberg et al. (1985) and Alstone, Gershenson, and Kammen (2015). Alstone, Gershenson, and Kammen (2015) stated that "Although it is difficult to determine causality, there is a strong case that electricity access is a necessary, but not sufficient, condition for improving human development (p. 306).
2. *The Economist* (2014f) reported that: "In places where fortified cereals are unavailable, the World Health Organization recommends that toddlers eat food from animal sources daily. Many poor mothers could afford to by meat relatively often, but cannot find cuts small enough: with fridges they can store larger portions and use only a bit at a time" (p. 54).
3. See *The Economist* (2013a).
4. Tully (2006), p. 34.
5. Samar et al. (2013), p. 2.
6. UNDP (2009) and Sustainable Energy for All (2015).
7. *The Economist* (2010).
8. See Sustainable Energy for All (2015).
9. *The Economist* (2016a), p. 42.
10. www.worldenergyoutlook.org.
11. http://www.un.org/womenwatch/daw/cedaw/text/econvention.htm.
12. United Nations General Assembly (1948).
13. United Nations General Assembly (1966b), p. 7.
14. See, for example, Office of the United Nations High Commissioner for Human Rights (n.d.); Bradbrook and Gardham (2006); and Tully (2006).
15. See Tully (2006).
16. See Brazilian et al. (2011); Flammini et al. (2014); and http://www.fao.org/energy/water-food-energy-nexus/en/.
17. http://www.fao.org/energy/water-food-energy-nexus/en/.
18. So, for example, Tully (2006) stated that "poverty can be defined as the inability to meet one's basic needs such as lack of access to essential social services including electricity" (p. 33).
19. See, for example, *The Economist* (2010).
20. Brass et al. (2012), pp. 108–109.
21. See, for example, Alstone, Gershenson, and Kammen (2015).
22. Again see Alstone, Gershenson, and Kammen (2015).
23. See Brazilian et al. (2013).
24. *The Economist* (2016e).
25. See Cardwell and Krauss (2017).
26. *The Economist* (2017b) reported, "Other battery technologies that sound as if, in principle, they might have advantages are often touted—but none of them enjoys the decades of development that have turned lithium-ion devices from an intriguing idea into a dominant technology" (p. 17).
27. Yee (2016).

28. Samar et al. (2013), abstract.
29. See, for example, Nandi et al. (2012).
30. Ostroff (2016).
31. See, for example, Palit, Sarangi, and Krithica (2014).
32. See, for example, Kenning (2015).
33. http://basilenergetics.com/.
34. See http://bridgetoindia.com.
35. See Bridge to India (2014).
36. *The Economist* (2016e).
37. *The Economist* (2016e), p. 39.
38. For more information on this important innovation, see http://wecaresolar.org/solutions/we-care-solar-suitcase/.
39. http://self.org/archive-brazil/.
40. This box draws on Karekezi, Kimani, and Onguru (2008); Ombuor (2016); and World Bank (2015). Quotes are from Ombuor (2016).
41. See Islam, Mekhilef, and Saidur (2013); Martino (2014).
42. See, for example, Reinert (1983) and Díaz-González et al. (2012).
43. See Díaz-González et al. (2012) who concluded that it is possible to achieve a nearly continuous power supply from wind power systems combined with storage technologies.
44. Global Wind Energy Council at http://gwec.net.
45. Buys et al. (2007) and Mukasa et al. (2013).
46. Mukasa et al. (2013).
47. Global Wind Energy Council at http://gwec.net.
48. For example, Gemenne (2015) stated that "The difficulty of isolating environmental factors from other drivers of migration still exists but no-one now seems to deny their importance as a driving force of displacement" (p. 70). There are legal arguments over whether the term "climate migrant" is appropriate, but the phenomenon of forced migration due to climate change is real.
49. In a review for *Science*, Wheeler and von Braun (2013) stated, "Climate change could potentially interrupt progress toward a world without hunger. A robust and coherent global pattern is discernible of the impacts of climate change on crop productivity that could have consequences for food availability. The stability of whole food systems may be at risk under climate change because of short-term variability in supply. However, the potential impact is less clear at regional scales, but it is likely that climate variability and change will exacerbate food insecurity in areas currently vulnerable to hunger and undernutrition" (p. 508).
50. See http://www.iea.org/statistics/ and https://19january2017snapshot.epa.gov/ghgemissions_.html.
51. Doyle (2016).
52. These figures are from Baker, Newell, and Phillips (2014).
53. *The Economist* (2014f).
54. *The Economist* (2014f).
55. See, for example, Ferguson, Wilkinson, and Hill (2000).
56. See, for example, Henderson, Storeygard, and Weil (2012).
57. See, for example, Ghosh (2002) for the case of India.
58. See, for example, Odhiambo (2009) for the case of Tanzania.
59. See Reinikka and Svensson (2002) for the case of Uganda.
60. See Fisher, Mansur, and Wang (2012) for the case of China.
61. Braimah and Amponsah (2012).
62. See Von Ketelhodt and Wöcke (2008).
63. See Burney et al. (2010).
64. See Obeng and Evers (2010) for the case of Ghana.

11

Human Security

When we read or hear the term *security*, we usually think of "national security" and its many military connotations. *Human security* shifts this focus and is usually defined as having two main components: *freedom from fear* (security rights) and *freedom from want* (subsistence rights).[1] In its later aspect, freedom from want, the human security notion emphasizes the provision (or under-provision) of basic goods. In this way, the human security and basic goods notions overlap and are largely consistent with each other. The reason for this is that the human security concept, along with the basic goods approach, recognizes the role of human needs. In the words of one set of proponents, human security "has to do with human need at moments of extreme vulnerability" due to violence or natural disasters.[2] The need concept brings the human security and basic goods approaches close together.

The overlap between the human security and basic goods approaches is not always seen as positive. As noted by a number of observers, the inclusion of both freedom from fear and freedom from want makes the human security concept *expansive*, and this is a central issue in ongoing arguments over the usefulness of the concept.[3] For the purposes of this chapter, I am going to emphasize the *freedom from fear* aspect of human security. This is not to downplay the role of freedom from want in the concept, but this aspect of human security has been largely addressed in previous chapters. I will avoid criticisms of overexpansiveness by focusing on freedom from fear or physical safety. What I add to the discussion in this chapter is that achieving human security in its physical security aspect necessarily requires *security service inputs*. Conceptual language alone and even the establishment of recognized rights are not sufficient.

To make the issue of human security more tangible, it is helpful to focus on its absence, human *insecurity*. Human insecurity reflects vulnerability to violence, either directly or indirectly from wars, other types of conflicts, and crime.[4] Nonconflict violence (crime) is often more important than conflict violence, and it is often the *indirect* effects of both conflict and nonconflict violence that are the most profound. Human insecurity is also related to the deprivations of other basic goods and services caused by wars, conflicts, and crime, as well as by natural disasters of various kinds. Human insecurity compromises human life in potentially extreme ways by ensuring that needs of various types remain unmet, sometimes with deadly impact.

As I discuss later, human security is the *most basic* of basic goods. Failure to provide human security services has knock-on effects in the realms of most other basic goods. Consider for example Northeast Nigeria. As of 2016, the effects of the Boko Haram insurgency in that region resulted in over four million individuals being in need of food aid, with a quarter million children in the Borno State alone suffering from severe malnutrition and over 100 of them dying a day.[5] In this way, lack of human security directly impacts the provision of other basic goods. I consider a similar case, Yemen, in Box 11.1 later in the chapter. These examples illustrate how the provision of food, water, sanitation, health services, education services, housing, and electricity can be and often are dependent on the provision of human security services.

There is one ironic and tragic aspect to basic goods deprivation. No matter how severe the deprivation, no matter how little water, food, and basic services, there is often more than enough weaponry. This reflects the complex nature of humans and the greed of arms traffickers. But it also is a signal that, even where poverty and deprivation are at their most extreme, there are still resources present. The problem is that these resources have been deployed to undermine human security rather than to support it.

As with other basic goods and services, the lack of human security services is significant in a number of geographic areas. This results in the deaths of approximately half a million people each year by armed violence. These include direct conflict deaths, intentional homicides, unintentional homicides, legal intervention deaths (as a result of police activity), and victims of terrorism. These deaths are highly concentrated among the countries of the world, with eighteen countries accounting for one quarter of all the deaths but comprising only 4 percent of the world's population.[6] As of 2015, the top ten countries for deaths by armed violence as a percentage of the population were Syria, Honduras, Venezuela, Swaziland, Afghanistan, El Salvador, Belize, Jamaica, Lesotho, and Colombia. The degree to which Latin American countries feature on this list may be surprising to some. Further, these violent deaths are a good proxy for other types of violence, including those wounded or otherwise assaulted.[7]

The roots of violence are many. The World Bank groups these into local intergroup conflict (e.g., militias, ethnic groups), conventional political conflict, gang-related violence, organized crime and trafficking, and conflicts that are part of transnational political struggles.[8] These sources of violence can become interlinked, such as when violent gangs become part of electoral politics or when armed groups involved in political struggles move into trafficking. Once begun, ongoing cycles of violence are often quite difficult to stop.

Violent deaths are not just concentrated in certain countries. They are geographically concentrated in subnational geographic areas: regions, cities, and even neighborhoods. For example, analysis by the Geneva Declaration on Armed Violence and Development reveals that "When plotted on a map, lethal incidents tend to appear as clusters. Many armed conflicts are concentrated in spaces that do not correspond to that of national territories; indeed, these spaces can be smaller than the states themselves or extend beyond the national borders."[9] This is what the Geneva Declaration referred to as "hubs of violence." This clustering can apply to both conflict-driven deaths and those outside of conflicts (homicides). It demonstrates that the requisite increased provision of human security services must have a geographical focus.

More important, however, lack of human security goes beyond the estimated half a million deaths. The World Bank estimated that 1.5 billion people "live in areas affected by fragility, conflict, or large-scale, organized criminal violence." For this reason, the World Bank calls insecurity "a primary development challenge of our time" with negative implications for both growth processes and human development outcomes.[10] For example, the World Bank noted that "People in fragile and conflict-affected states are more than twice as likely to be undernourished as those in other developing countries, more than three times as likely to be unable to send their children to school, twice as likely to see their children die before age five, and more than twice as likely to lack clean water."[11] This chapter considers a number of aspects of this development challenge.

The Right to Human Security

The rights to basic goods I discussed in previous chapters fall under what is known as economic and social rights. Human security in the way I am using the term in this chapter falls under civil and political rights that compose the original core of human rights considerations and language. There has been a tendency to view civil and political rights as "negative rights" and economic and social rights as "positive rights."[12] However, as demonstrated by the political philosopher Henry Shue, even negative, political rights (e.g., freedom from violence or freedom of political participation) require positive action in the form of the provision of basic human security services, legal services, and judicial services.[13] In this chapter, I focus on basic human security services because, as previously stated, there are no functioning political rights for the prematurely dead. For this reason, basic human security services are *basic rights* that must be fulfilled so that other rights can be enjoyed.

Shue made a strong argument in favor of security rights as the *most funda-mental* of all rights, the rights on which all others are predicated. It is worth presenting his argument in full:[14]

> In the absence of physical security people are unable to use any other rights that society may be said to be protecting without being liable to encounter many of the worst dangers they would encounter if society were not protecting the rights. A right to physical security belongs, then, among the basic rights—not because the enjoyment of it would be more satisfying to someone who was also enjoying a full range of other rights, but because its absence would leave available extremely effecting means for others . . . to interfere with or prevent the actual exercise of any other rights that were supposedly protected. Regardless of whether the enjoyment of physical security is also desirable for its own sake, it is desirable as part of the enjoyment of every other right. No rights other than a right to physical security can in fact be enjoyed if a right to physical security is not protected. *Being physically secure is a necessary condition for the exercise of any other right*, and guaranteeing physical security must be part of guaranteeing anything else as a right. (emphasis added)

The implication of Shue's argument is that, if we accept that human beings have any rights at all (and this book does), then we must recognize the basic right to physical security (freedom from fear). The contention of Shue whole-heartedly adopted by this book is that security rights and subsistence rights (to basic goods and services) are both basic rights on which any other rights and aspirations rest.

Within the United Nations system, the cornerstone of human security is the 1948 Universal Declaration of Human Rights.[15] The Preamble of this Declaration established human security rights in the following manner:

> Whereas disregard and contempt for human rights have resulted in barbarous acts which have outraged the conscience of mankind, and the advent of a world in which human beings shall enjoy freedom of speech and belief and freedom from fear and want has been proclaimed as the highest aspiration of the common people.

The mention of "barbarous acts" is clearly a reference to violations of human security in its physical safety aspect, as is the mention of "freedom from fear." Article 3 of the Universal Declaration states that "Everyone has the right to life, liberty and *security of person*" (emphasis added). Security of person is the very aspect of human security I emphasize in this chapter. The right to physical security is further reiterated in the 1966 International Covenant on Civil and Political Rights[16] and the 1989 Convention on the Rights of the Child[17]. As reflected in these statements, physical safety is at the core of traditional conceptions of human rights.

More recent, a 2005 United Nations World Summit adopted a definition of human security (more expansive than the one used in this chapter) as follows: [18]

> We stress the right of people to live in freedom and dignity, free from poverty and despair. We recognize that all individuals, in particular, vulnerable people, are entitled to freedom from fear and freedom from want, with an equal opportunity to enjoy all their rights and fully develop their human potential.

One legal scholar called this statement "probably the most important step yet, on the UN level, toward institutionalizing human security by finding common ground for a definition of the concept."[19] It clearly shows a centerpiece for the human security concept in the UN system. If we were to identify one central aspect of the human rights impact of the human security concept, it is the elevation of the rights of individuals relative to those of states and state sovereignty. It is not that the human security principle has overturned state sovereignty, but that it has circumscribed or conditioned it on states' ability to protect and provide for its citizens.[20] This is an important development.

More recent still, the 2006 Geneva Declaration on Armed Violence and Development[21] signed by more than 100 countries stated that "Living free from the threat of armed violence is a basic human need. It is a precondition for human development, dignity and well-being. Providing for the human security of its citizens is a core responsibility of governments." The 2006 Geneva Declaration cites the 2005 World Summit and commits its signatories to a set of actions toward reducing armed violence and its negative development impacts.

As I discussed in Chapter 3, the basic goods approach is part of a minimalist approach to ethics. Recall from that chapter that this approach to ethics was described by philosopher Henry Shue as the "morality of the depths" or "the line beneath which no one is allowed to sink" and by philosopher David Braybrooke as the "rock bottom" of ethics.[22] Something similar applies to the human security notion. For example, it has been described as an approach to security whose purpose is to establish a "floor of decency" below which individuals will not be allowed to fall.[23] This brings us back to the work of political philosopher Joshua Cohen, as well as the author Michael Ignatieff, both of whom emphasized moral minimalism in traditional human rights, namely the assurance of bodily security. Cohen was the source of the title of this book with his statement that "The world that the minimalist imagines . . . is no small hope." Likewise, Ignatieff stated that moral minimalism is "the most we can hope for."[24] The goal of human security through the provision of appropriate services is therefore at the core of the minimalist ethical system that the basic goods approach advocates.

Despite the presence of the right to human security, the past and present human condition is one where these rights are violated *on a vast scale*. This reality was alluded to by Henry Shue when he stated that "A proclamation may or may not be an initial step toward the fulfillment of the rights listed. It is frequently the substitute of the promise in the place of the fulfillment."[25] This has indeed been the case with the right to human security. As previously mentioned, currently, half a million people die each year as a result of armed violence, and crimes against humanity are continually taking place.[26] These ongoing events (with no end in sight) represent vast violations of the right to human security. They are the result of a failure to provide *human security services* that can ensure the outcome of human security. These services include an effective military force, an effective policing system, and an effective judicial system, as well as effective peacekeeping forces where conflict has already broken out. To be effective, each of these services needs to be directed toward the "responsibility to protect."

Responsibility to Protect and Humanitarian Space

One cannot get too far in investigating the concept of human security without encountering the notions of "responsibility to protect" and "humanitarian space." Together, these two concepts provide the impetus to ensure human security in its freedom from fear aspect and hint at a set of potential means for pursuing this end. As we will see, these concepts are not just aspirational, nor have they been implemented nearly as effectively as one would hope. They are rather part of an imperfect struggle to respond to ongoing violations of human security.

The idea of a responsibility to protect (R2P) grew out of the 2005 United Nations World Summit.[27] Formally, R2P is the "responsibility to protect populations from genocide, war crimes, ethnic cleansing and crimes against humanity." The responsibility rests on both individual states and the international community, the latter being able to take collective action to pursue R2P. The World Summit document identified "peaceful means" to address genocide, war crimes, ethnic cleansing, and crimes against humanity, including "appropriate diplomatic, humanitarian and other peaceful means."[28] Should these peaceful means prove to be ineffective, the document calls for unspecified, coercive means to meet R2P obligations. To date, almost 200 countries have committed themselves to the responsibility to protect principle, and the United Nations has established a Joint Office for the Prevention of Genocide and the Responsibility to Protect. That said, the ability to make R2P real within the UN system always depends on the political deliberations of the UN Security Council.[29]

Although the idea of "humanitarian space" is seemingly quaint, it is a potentially powerful concept that is at the heart of the human security paradigm. Human security advocates Mary Kaldor, Mary Martin, and Sabine Selchow described humanitarian space as follows:[30]

> Human security . . . is not about war-fighting; it is about protection of individuals and communities, and it is about expanding the rule of law, while squeezing the arena of war. In contemporary wars, where civilians are targets, humanitarian space is disappearing. In a human security operation, the job of the military is to protect and preserve that space rather than to fight an enemy. Thus human security is not just about developing a culture of military–civil cooperation; it is about an entirely new way of functioning in crises that is best described by a new language of human security.

What does this mean in practice? First, it requires a rethinking of the *ends* of military operations. As stated by Kaldor, Martin, and Selchow, "For the military, it means the primary goal is protecting civilians rather than defeating an adversary. Of course, sometimes it is necessary to try to capture or even defeat insurgents, but this has to be seen as a means to an end, civilian protection, rather than the other way round."[31] Second, it is a call to rethink the general tolerance for "collateral damage" in standard military operations. In many cases, this collateral damage actually involves significant human rights violations. Third, it requires thinking very carefully about what happens *after* military operations, including developing the institutions and infrastructure to ensure the continued safety of individuals and the provision of basic goods.[32]

A fourth and final point is about war fighting itself. Although military strategy is far beyond the scope of this chapter, it is clear that war fighting (in particular counterinsurgency operations) fought on human security lines would look very different than contemporary practices. The tendency of military forces to push operations into completely destructive realms (in Chechnya, Syria, and Yemen to name just a few) is a gross violation of human security principles.[33] The humanitarian space concept sheds light on these violations and provides a potentially workable alternative.

The case of Syria is a dramatic example of the failure of both R2P and the establishment of humanitarian spaces. The UN Security Council was able to act on the issue of the Syrian government's use of chemical weapons, but was not able to effectively go much further than that. This led to the unusual step of the UN General Assembly issuing a public criticism of the Security Council for its failure to act. This failure resulted in at least 300,000 deaths through 2016 and the displacement of millions, a gross failure of R2P. It also has substantially contributed to the increase in displaced persons reported in Figure 9.1.[34] The repeated use of chemical weapons by the Syrian government in 2017 was further proof of the failure of R2P.

The case of Libya is in some respects the opposite of Syria. Military intervention took place through the invocation of R2P, and this resulted in the fall of the Gaddafi regime. The issue here is whether military means were used too soon, without peaceful means being fully explored. A second issue is whether it is responsible to intervene militarily without being prepared for the eventual outcomes of that intervention, including the potential need to rebuild the country.[35] This failure to prepare for eventual outcomes was also dramatically and catastrophically evidenced in the previous case of Iraq.[36]

Part of the failures in Syria and Libya (as well as Iraq) was conflation of R2P with regime change. Pursuing regime change in these cases (however desirable it appeared to be at the time) had the unfortunate effect of undermining the ability to protect. It is unfortunate that the right to intervene for human security ends often morphs into the impulse to intervene for more standard, national security ends.[37] Although difficult, it is imperative to shield human security operations from traditional military and geopolitical goals. Old military habits die hard.

As previously mentioned, violent deaths tend to be clustered in geographic areas, a process known as geolocalization.[38] Transforming these "hubs of violence" into humanitarian spaces is *very difficult*, but this is the challenge that the pattern of human violence presents. Although clusters of violence can be rural, cities are emerging as a common location.[39] The Geneva Declaration on Armed Violence and Development has described this process as follows:[40]

> The urban environment, while offering attractive socio-economic opportunities, also seems to provide a context in which violence can grow. Urbanization brings its own development challenges, because some countries are unable to respond to the demands of rapid urban growth. Migration from the countryside to cities can overstretch infrastructure, social services, and security providers. Meanwhile, informal arrangements can exacerbate inequalities in terms of access to social services and opportunities, while allowing for the emergence of parallel social, economic, and political orders. Such informal communities . . . function as hotbeds for gangs, armed groups, radical religious movements, and criminal organizations.

The case of urban violence shifts human security needs in the form of R2P and humanitarian space from the national level to the local government level. This can be very challenging, and I discuss some of these challenges later.

Causes of Human Insecurity

Human insecurity in its fear aspect is caused by both conflict and crime (non-conflict violence). It is important to recognize the role of *both* of these, although traditionally the focus of research and policy has been on conflict. A further complication is that conflict and crime can feed off of each other in complicated ways, so separating one from the other is difficult.

What causes conflict? There is an ongoing and vigorous debate on this question, a debate too vast to fully describe here. One way of summarizing the research and discussion on the causes of conflict is through the following four factors:[41]

- Basic needs or grievances.
- Identities or rights.
- Resources or greed.
- Government fragility or failure.

Each of these factors can help to cause conflict independently but also in consort with the others. Empirically sorting out their relative roles and the way they interact with each other is not easy, and there are disagreements among researchers on what the evidence shows. Material deprivation, including basic goods deprivation does seem to be a relevant factor, particularly when expectations and aspirations have been thwarted.[42] As stated by international relations scholar I. William Zartman, "grievances come from unmet needs, unwarranted deprivation, felt hurts, and resentment against the withholding of just deserts, and thus they relate to other dimensions such as distribution and justice."[43] So unmet basic needs, and the grievances they generate, can contribute to conflict.[44] But grievances take on particular salience when there is ascribed, identity-based discrimination that violates basic rights. Stark violations of basic rights, based on ascribed identities, significantly heighten tensions that can lead to outright conflict.[45]

Although a *lack* of resources in the form of needs deprivation can cause conflict, the very *presence* of certain types of resources also can cause conflict. This is the form of conflict that reflects greed. The resources in question are primary commodities and the economic rents they can generate. Criminal or identity-based groups attempt to control the rents associated with a particular primary commodity (e.g., minerals, drug cultivation areas) and stand ready to use force to maintain this control. Greed-based conflict may be dependent on initial grievance- and identity-based mobilization.[46] If conflict does break out and is protracted, access to the rents can become more important over time, increasing the willingness to use more extreme forms of violence.[47] It is often the case that, at this stage of greed-based conflict, some type of military intervention focused on reestablishing minimal levels of human security is necessary.

Finally, levels of government fragility and even outright government failure can prevent conflict mediation and compromise the ability to meet basic needs. The case of Yemen is considered in Box 11.1. As stated by I. William Zartman, "weak states unable to meet the demands of their citizens in general or in groups with appropriately balanced provisions and with judicious controls when necessary are both inviting conflict and ill prepared to handle it. . . . (W)eak states are conflicts waiting to happen."[48] To say the least, strengthening states has turned out be a very difficult enterprise, but waiting until conflict becomes severe does not make the enterprise any easier.[49]

As I stated, however, conflict-based violence is not the only source of human insecurity. Criminal violence, or what some refer to as "large-scale predatory criminal violence," is as important.[50] The causes of criminal violence are similar but not exactly the same as conflict. They include the following:[51]

- Previous exposure to violence, particularly on the part of young males.
- Socioeconomic exclusion.
- Rapid and unregulated urbanization.
- Deprivation of basic goods and services.
- Poor policing and justice systems.

Criminal violence can include the same primary commodities as greed-based conflict. Indeed the two can morph into one another. Once it is entrenched, criminal violence also can be very difficult to address. Together, conflict-based and criminal violence undermine the right to freedom from fear. I next consider two related factors, the drug and arms trade.

Drug Trade and Human Security

One particular type of primary resource that can cause conflict- and criminal-based violence is illegal drugs and associated organized crime. Political scientist Desmond Arias described this as follows:[52]

> The production, trafficking, and consumption of illegal narcotics pose substantial challenges in a range of countries across the Global South. Coca- and opium-growing have contributed greatly to civil conflict in Colombia, Peru, Afghanistan and Myanmar by providing a source of funding to armed actors. Similarly the movement of drugs has generated intense conflict in a range of rural and urban locales across an extremely diverse array of countries including Mali, Mexico, the Dominican Republic and Turkey. Finally, the consumption of drugs also creates significant challenges for security in Brazil, Argentina and Mexico.

Arias went on to emphasize that the traditional national security approach is not appropriate for addressing the drug trade, stating that the shift in perspective from national security to human security "is tremendously helpful in specifying the material security challenges posed by the illegal narcotics without laying the intellectual grounding for states waging war on their own citizens. This approach shifts security debates on drugs away from the needs of states to those of human beings."[53] This is one example of the shift from the national security perspective to the human security perspective that reflects the R2P and humanitarian space concepts.

According to Arias, the drug trade undermines human security in a number of ways. The most important way is through increased levels of violence directed at both individuals and communities, distributed across the entire drug value chain, from production through commercialization, shipment, and consumption. At each stage, violence can coalesce in a particular geographic area ("hubs of violence" again). The drug trade also undermines human health outside of the realm of violence through addiction, overdoses, compromised mental health, and increased disease transmission. The violence caused by drug production and trade often results in the destruction of economic assets, including in the health, education, and economic sectors. In this way, the human insecurity caused by the drug trade undermines growth prospects both directly via destruction of human and physical capital and indirectly via degradation of institutional quality (e.g., diminished rule of law, increased corruption).[54]

What is to be done? There is much evidence that the national-security-based "war on drugs" has *not* been a success.[55] A shift of focus to protecting affected communities and attempting to improve their security is more promising. To again quote Arias, "On the whole, the national security implications of the drug trade are limited for most countries. Instead the problems generated by the drug trade connect most distinctly to the risks faced by individuals and communities in their neighborhoods, their economies, and their health. Focusing state responses in these areas will do much more for augmenting popular security than will policies that focus on the broad gauged repression of the drug trade in an effort to secure territory."[56] It is unfortunate that this broad shift of focus has not yet taken place.

Arms Trade

In most types of international trade, there are good reasons to expect that the outcome will be the standard *gains from trade* of international economic theory. This is decidedly not the case for the global arms trade.[57] First, the arms trade is characterized by large, government interventions rather than simply reflecting the activities of households and firms. Second, the goods involved in the trade

are decidedly *harmful*, being designed to destroy human beings and thereby compromise human security. Third, some components of the arms trade are undertaken in the realm of illicit trade, often conducted by criminal organizations,
including drug gangs.[58] Recognizing these issues, the United Nations Office for
Disarmament Affairs stated,[59]

> Those suffering most from the adverse effects of the poorly regulated
> arms trade are the men, women, girls and boys trapped in situations
> of armed violence and conflict, often in conditions of poverty, depri-
> vation and extreme inequality, where they are all too frequently on
> the receiving end of the misuse of arms by State armed and security
> forces, non-State armed groups and criminal gangs. The human cost of
> the consequences of the poorly regulated global trade in conventional
> arms are manifested in several ways: in the killing, wounding and rape
> of civilians—including children, the most vulnerable of all—and the
> perpetration of other serious violations of international humanitarian
> law and human rights law; in the displacement of people within and
> across borders; and in the endurance of extreme insecurity and eco-
> nomic hardships by those affected by armed violence and conflict.

Most of the global arms trade is directed toward low- and middle-income
countries where basic goods deprivation is the most concentrated. Indeed, the
imports of low- and middle-income countries account for approximately 70 percent of the global arms trade, a value of over US$30 billion in 2015. The export-
ers of such arms, in order of importance in 2015, are the United States, Russia,
France, the United Kingdom, China, Germany, and Italy.[60] Large importers of
arms include the basic-goods deprived South Asian countries India, Pakistan,
and Bangladesh.

There is broad recognition that large imports of arms into low- and middle-
income countries have negative development impacts (including on human security) and compete with basic goods provision. For these reasons, the United
Nations has sponsored an Arms Trade Treaty (ATT) that came into force in
2014 and covers all types of conventional weapons with an aim of "reducing
human suffering." The purpose of the ATT is to enforce common standards for
the arms trade, particularly in the area of illicit trade in arms through national
control systems that are meant to limit arms diversion through recordkeeping
and international cooperation. It also calls for limits to arms sales where there
is an "overriding risk" that the sales will result in human rights violations. This
is to be achieved via risk assessment processes. Unfortunately, two major arms
exporters, Russia and China, have not signed the ATT, limiting its effectiveness.
Further, there are no effective sanctions for failure to abide by the ATT, nor real
incentives to abide by it.[61]

The case of South Sudan is illustrative of the impacts of arms trade on basic goods deprived countries. After approximately twenty years of violent struggle for independence, and perhaps two million deaths, South Sudan gained independence from Sudan in 2011. In 2013, however, the country entered into a tragically new conflict, this time in the form of civil war. Despite a short-lived peace agreement in 2015, the civil war has continued to the time of this writing.

There are many causal factors in the current South Sudan civil war, but it is clear that arms flows are one of these factors.[62] The arms involved originate from a few sources. First, in keeping with the independence struggle period, there are arms imports from Eastern Europe, particularly Bulgaria. Second, the Sudanese government has supplied Chinese-made arms and ammunition to factions in South Sudan to help to foment the civil war. There are also Sudanese-manufactured arms (made with support from Iran) that help to fuel the conflict.[63] Chinese, Russian, and Iranian landmines also have been deployed, a very worrisome trend given the difficulty of removing landmines even if the conflict is resolved.

By early 2017, famine was affecting perhaps 100,000 South Sudanese citizens, and perhaps five million were suffering from significant food insecurity. The United Nations issued a confidential report on this issue, noting that a significant amount of South Sudan's oil revenues were being spent on arms imports rather than on efforts to address food insecurity and famine. While the South Sudan government rejected this argument, mounting evidence is not in its favor: substantial arms imports are often a critical factor in basic goods deprivation.

Mikhail T. Kalashnikov, inventor of the Avtomat Kalashnikova 47 or AK-47, is reported to have stated that "my spiritual torment is unbearable" given the human suffering caused by his invention.[64] Limiting the proliferations of arms is a necessary part of beginning to restrict the multiple torments caused by largely unregulated arms trade, to protect human security, and to ensure the provision of the full range of basic goods.

The Costs of Human Insecurity

Violations of human security impose significant costs, both direct and indirect. We can begin to consider these costs by first addressing the impacts of human insecurity on growth prospects. One widely cited rule of thumb is that the average civil war reduces growth rates by 2 to 3 percent. [65] Another is that the average civil war can cost up to thirty years (a generation) of growth.[66] These large growth impacts reflect the way that violence suppresses both economic activity and investment levels. Consider the growth comparison between Burundi and

Burkina Faso in Figure 11.1. Real (inflation adjusted) GDP per capita for these two countries track each other very closely between 1960 and 1990, displaying steady, if low, growth. During this time, there were a number of cases of political violence in Burundi, including mass killings in 1972. But 1988 marked a period in Burundi characterized by a significant number of battle deaths, a political assassination, more mass killings, and mass forced displacement. These aspects of political violence continued through 2001, but even then, Burundi entered into a period of time that was politically described as "no war, no peace."[67] As can be seen in Figure 11.1, this set into motion a period of negative growth in real GDP per capita followed by long-term stagnation.[68] Although real GDP per capita in Burkina Faso increased by 170 percent between 1960 and 2015, in Burundi it fell by 3 percent. As can be seen in this example, human insecurity is bad for growth.

Beyond negative growth impacts, human insecurity has a multitude of other negative impacts as well. These include the following:

- Lost lives and injuries.
- Opportunity costs of private and public spending on weaponry.
- The costs of institutional degradation.
- Costs of increased corruption and organized crime as previous institutions and social norms break down in the face of violence.

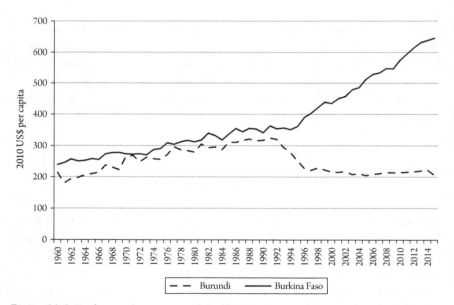

Figure 11.1 Real gross domestic product (GDP) per capita in Burundi and Burkina Faso, 1960 to 2015. Source: World Bank, World Development Indicators.

- Psychic costs of violence, particularly on children, and their cognitive impacts.
- Peacekeeping costs, including those of the United Nations.
- Costs of disarming, demobilizing, and reintegrating (DDR) former combatants.
- Rebuilding infrastructure (including in health and education).
- Significantly decreased health and nutrition of those affected by violence.
- Reduced mobility and, thereby, reduced economic opportunities.
- Reduced agricultural productivity.
- Impeded ability to reduce poverty over time.
- Direct and opportunity costs of forced internal displacement, forced international migration, and the increased number of refugees.
- Cross-border, spillover effects on neighboring countries.
- Reduced domestic investment, international trade, and foreign direct investment.
- Increased maritime piracy for coastal countries.

This list is both long and incomplete, and the example of Yemen is given in Box 11.1.[69] A full accounting of the costs of human insecurity is probably not possible, but we know that such an accounting would show that human insecurity imposes highly significant costs that are, in all cases, antidevelopment. And for most of these types of costs, there is a persistence factor that lingers even after the conflict ends. Injuries need to heal, arms stay in circulation, DDR takes a long time, criminal organizations do not disappear, displaced persons and refugees take a long time to return to their original homes (if the homes still exist), infrastructure is only rebuilt slowly, and trade and foreign direct investment take a long time to recover.[70]

Even when DDR and reconstruction takes place relatively quickly, there is accumulating evidence that the *experience* of violence has lasting, lifelong effects on the health profiles of those involved either as perpetrators or as victims. These impacts even include effects on brain structure and function and on genetic predispositions, no less on standard measures of health. The causal factor that has been identified in these processes is prolonged "toxic stress."[71] Although these effects can occur in adults, they are most prominent in children. This is the means by which prolonged human insecurity robs a country, region, or community of a fully functioning future generation. For example, these effects were considered by Save the Children for the case of Syria. The report found that the experience of the Syrian civil war has resulted in children displaying increased aggressive behavior, involuntary urination, the loss of the ability to speak, head and chest pains, temporary loss of the ability to move limbs, and drug use. It is likely that this generation of children will be severely compromised both behaviorally and cognitively, passing these "invisible wounds" to their own children.

Box 11.1 Human Insecurity in Yemen

Yemen is the poorest country in the Middle East, and its citizens are enduring multiple basic goods deprivations that are extreme in nature. Lacking fresh water supplies, Yemen has always been characterized by water shortages. At the current time, the country is literally running out of water. Things took a significant turn for the worse beginning in 2014 when Houthi rebels took over the capital Sana'a. This led to an intervention on the part of Saudi Arabia beginning in 2015 that included air strikes (with US- and UK-manufactured weapons, including cluster bombs) and an intermittent naval blockade. All but one of Yemen's twenty-two governorates have seen fighting. The airstrikes have caused deaths and the destruction of physical capital. The latter includes approximately one quarter of the country's health facilities and the largest port, Hodeida. As a result of the bombings, approximately 2.5 million Yemenis have been displaced from their homes.

The blockade and port damage have resulted in shortages of food, fuel, and medical supplies. As of 2017, approximately two million Yemenis, including about one million children, have suffered from acute malnutrition. Another five to eight million are simply hungry. The blockade has even negatively affected humanitarian efforts with allegations by the Saudis that aid agencies might be unloading weapons. Drugs are now in short supply, and vaccination efforts have been undermined due to the inability to maintain cold chains in the face of fuel shortages. As of 2017, more than 15 million Yemenis lacked access to basic healthcare.

The war has significantly damaged Yemen's water and sanitation systems. These impacts, along with fuel shortages, have exacerbated the water shortage, with approximately twenty million of Yemen's total population of twenty-eight million (70 percent) lacking access to potable water (and sanitation services) and 2.5 million Yemeni children being at risk of diarrheal diseases. The year 2017 brought a widespread cholera epidemic.

The case of Yemen dramatically demonstrates the ways that threats to physical security due to a breakdown in the provision of security services spill over into the full range of basic goods and services. Such negative spillovers are evidence of the importance of preventing human security breakdowns in the first place. It is also worth noting that shortages in basic goods can exacerbate pre-existing conflicts. There is evidence that, even prior to the Saudi intervention in Yemen, water scarcity was a significant driver of increasing amounts of conflict.

Providing Human Security

Discussions of human security inevitably need to move from rights to *provision processes*, but this latter step is a difficult one. In its report on conflict and security, the World Bank stated that "When facing the risks of conflict and violence, citizen security, justice and jobs are the key elements of protection to achieve human security."[72] The report went on to say that "Security operations can facilitate safe trade and transit, and the economic activity that creates jobs. Services delivered to marginalized groups can support perceptions of justice."[73] It is worth translating these statement a bit into the language of the basic goods approach. First, in the face of risks of violence, there must be increased provision of *human security services*. It is important to keep in mind that, at some level, human security is a good like any other and that human security needs have to be provided for through a service provision process. The type of service can vary, from the level of local police forces to that of national armies. Second, the delivery of services to marginalized groups is another way of emphasizing the importance of basic goods and services provision to those most deprived of them. The perception of justice that this causes reflects the fact that there has been a real movement toward just provision that can lessen grievance-based conflict.

Human security services are delivered at a number of different levels, from the national to the local. Policing services are essential at all of these levels and are linked to the justice and corrections systems. The doctrinal and practical training of these forces is no small matter even under the best of circumstances. In situations of severely compromised human security, they are as difficult as they are critical. One thing that has become clear is that relying only on top-down approaches to security service provision has its limits. As noted by the World Bank:[74]

If services and public works are delivered only through top-down national programs, there will be few incentives for communities to take responsibility for violence prevention or for national institutions to undertake responsibility to protect all vulnerable citizens, men and women. A mixture of state and nonstate, bottom-up and top-down approaches is a better underpinning for longer-term institutional transformation.

That said, when both local and national institutions have been completely overwhelmed by a human insecurity crisis, countries will need to draw on international humanitarian aid, preventative diplomacy, and outside peacekeeping forces. Preventative diplomacy and other conflict prevention tools are provided by the United Nations Department of Political Affairs (UNDPA), the UNDP, the

Inter-American Development Bank, and numerous NGOs. There are cases of success in these endeavors.[75] But on the whole, global priorities are skewed away from these types of activities. As the World Bank noted,[76]

> These programs are still not delivered to scale. It is much harder for countries to get international assistance to support development of their police forces and judiciaries than their militaries. . . . UN police capacity, doctrinal development, and training have increased, but are not fully linked to justice capacities. While some bilateral agencies provide specialized assistance for security and justice reform, their capacities are relatively new and underdeveloped in comparison to other areas.

Adopting a basic goods approach is one means of reemphasizing the importance of reconfiguring global priorities toward making human security services much more available. The standard national security perspective, the economic growth perspective, and even the capabilities approach underemphasize the importance of human security services, and this has led to misplaced priorities. In the opinion of the World Bank, the successful provision of human security services is actually tied to the simultaneous focus on human security services, justice services, and employment.

In the case of urban areas mentioned earlier, there is evidence of both increased concentrations of violence and the increased demand for human security services. The increases in urban violence are often associated with gangs as in the case in some Central American and Southern African countries. If in the face of increased urban violence, demands for human security are not met, local governance can be undermined.[77] With local governance undermined, urban economic and social development are undermined as well. Issues that need to be addressed include criminal networks, gangs, and the urban proliferation of firearms.[78]

More broadly, there is a set of ideas for the better provision of human security services. Drawn from a variety of sources, this set includes the following:[79]

- Ongoing risk assessment and early warning systems.
- Increased resources for diplomatic efforts and conflict mediation.
- Increased international support for capacity building in policing and justice services.
- Expansion of community-based jobs programs to reduce the incentives for political violence and to build the infrastructure that can help to provide other basic goods and services.
- Better preparation of peacekeeping forces so that these can be more effective and to avoid ongoing limitations and even outright failures.

- Efforts to reduce the volatility of aid flows to fragile and failed states.
- Efforts to address illicit trade and other criminal activities that fund armed groups, including illicit financial transactions.
- For urban violence, enhanced community policing, urban disarmament campaigns, and violence-reducing urban planning.

In cases where violence is already entrenched, such as civil wars, a number of other steps need to be taken:[80]

- Negotiate a halt to both attacks on civilians and the use of explosive weapons in areas with large civilian populations, preferably early in the violence cycle rather than at the end as is often the case.
- Negotiate a halt to all attacks on hospitals and schools.
- Eliminate the use of child soldiers.
- Allow for the free movement of humanitarian aid such as in the form of safe corridors.
- Allow for the provision of humanitarian and emergency health services.
- Allow for the free passage of displaced persons to safer areas without the threat of attack.

In some cases of conflict-based violence, the provision of security services falls, at least for a while, to official, United Nations peacekeeping operations (blue helmets). As part of R2P, there is a focus in these operations on the protection of civilians (PoC). Since the inception of these operations, there has been approximately seventy such missions. PoC considerations began in 1999 but crystallized in 2010 with a three-tier approach: conflict resolution, protection from violence, and further humanitarian and legal protection.[81] It is unfortunate that the record for these peacekeeping operations is mixed. However, there is also evidence that, when done properly with sufficient military and police resources, they can indeed be successful.[82]

One difficult issue that usually arises when violence has been entrenched is the continued availability and use of arms. This problem reflects past supply of arms but also the continued *demand* for them. The possession of arms is often concentrated socially or geographically. As one set of researchers noted,[83]

The use of arms that occurs in contexts of warfare, crime, and collective violence is often highly concentrated among specific demographic groups and in specific places: the direct perpetrators and victims of armed violence are generally young males. Perpetrators often include combatants, ex-combatants, and their dependents, but in the aftermath of an armed conflict, they also include mercenaries, paramilitary or militia groups, criminal and predatory gangs, and others who may not have been directly involved in the earlier conflict-associated violence.

Truth be told, the global development policy community has not figured out how to effectively address this problem.[84] So it is unlikely that I will be able to fully address it here. Some emerging elements include bottom-up and evidence-based approaches, voluntary weapons collection, changing urban design elements, addressing at-risk groups with specific interventions, leveraging local community organizations, and alternative livelihood policies for youth.[85]

One problematic approach that has been turned to in some desperate circumstances is the delegation of security services to private, nongovernmental groups. This, for example, has been pursued in Iraq and Afghanistan due to extreme human security failures. Previous chapters have embraced such private, bottom-of-the-pyramid approaches to other basic goods and services. And as noted above, the World Bank endorsed both "state" and "nonstate" provision of security services. However, caution is warranted in the case of privately provided security services because of uneven effectiveness and, more important, unforeseen political consequences.[86] Privatizing human security is, generally speaking, not the way forward.

It is worth emphasizing here that all of these steps are simply measures to ensure the most basic of human rights (physical safety). In the heat of conflict, the measures seem almost exotic, but that is merely due to the distorting lens of the conflict itself. All that is being called for here is a fundamental floor beyond which violations of rights will not fall, the "no small hope" of this book's title.

Summary

Human security is the last basic good and service considered in this book. But in a very real sense, the entire book has been about human security in all of its aspects. The reason for this is that both the human security and basic goods approaches are focused on human needs. The human security concept emphasizes freedom from want and freedom from fear. Previous chapters have been focused mostly on freedom from want, but in this chapter I have focused on freedom from fear.

Human security in the form of freedom from fear is the most basic of human rights and composes the more traditional realm of these rights. However, these basic rights are violated on a significant scale with half a million deaths annually and approximately 1.5 billion people being affected as citizens of fragile and conflict-affected countries. Changing this unfortunate situation involves accepting a R2P, the creation of humanitarian spaces, and a consequent rethinking of military operations. It also involves the understanding of the causes of conflict, including the role of drug and arms trade.

The costs of human insecurity are varied but include standard detrimental impacts on growth and development and postconflict reconstruction costs. But the costs even reach to the individual physiological and psychological levels in the form of the invisible wounds of multigenerational toxic stress.

The provision of security services includes local policing, national military, justice systems, and corrections systems. Extreme situations require outside intervention by the United Nations peacekeeping forces. Continued risk assessment, capacity building, diplomatic and humanitarian interventions, and negotiated "halts" to conflict-related activities are parts of the required responses. Unlike other basic goods and services, private solutions risk the rise of politicized militias. There is probably no substitute for public provision systems.

Notes

1. See Kaldor, Martin, and Selchow (2007). Freedom from fear and freedom from want are two of United States President Franklin Roosevelt's "four freedoms" from his 1941 State of the Union Address (https://fdrlibrary.org/four-freedoms). In recent form, the human security concept originated in United Nations Development Program (1994). The statement from that *Human Development Report* was, "The concept of security has for too long been interpreted narrowly: as security of territory from external aggression, or as protection of national interests in foreign policy or as global security from the threat of nuclear holocaust. . . . Forgotten were the legitimate concerns of ordinary people who sought security in their daily lives" (p. 22).
2. Kaldor, Martin, and Selchow (2007), p. 278.
3. See, for example, Paris (2001) and Inglehart and Norris (2012). Paris (2001) traced the history of the concept and suggested that it is characterized by "cultivated ambiguity" that diminished its effectiveness.
4. The role of violence in social orders was explicitly addressed by North, Wallis, and Weingast (2009). These authors stated, "All societies face the problem of violence. . . . No society solves the problem of violence by eliminating violence; at best, it can be contained and managed" (p. 13). They also stated, "How societies solve the ubiquitous threat of violence shapes and constrains the forms that human interaction can take, including the form of political and economic systems" (p. xi).
5. See *The Economist* (2016d).
6. Geneva Declaration on Armed Violence and Development (2011, 2015).
7. Muggah and Krause (2009), note 26.
8. World Bank (2011c).
9. Geneva Declaration on Armed Violence and Development (2015), p. 125.
10. Both quotes are from World Bank (2011c), p. 1.
11. World Bank (2011c), p. 5.
12. See, for example, *The Economist* (2007).
13. See Shue (1996).
14. Shue (1996), pp. 21–22.
15. See http://www.un.org/en/universal-declaration-human-rights/ and United Nations General Assembly (1948).
16. United Nations General Assembly (1966a).
17. United Nations General Assembly (1989).

18. See United Nations General Assembly (2005).

19. Benedek (2008), p. 10.

20. For example, Welsh (2016) stated that "state sovereignty should not be conceived solely in terms of undisputed control over territory, but rather should be linked to a state's capacity to protect and provide for its population" (p. 77).

21. http://www.genevadeclaration.org/fileadmin/docs/GD-Declaration-091020-EN.pdf.

22. Shue (1996), p. 18 and Braybrooke (1987), p. 131.

23. Welsh (2016), p. 78.

24. Cohen (2004), p. 191 and Ignatieff (2001), p. 173. Despite his support for "no small hope," Cohen saw the minimalist agenda in human rights (in particular bodily security) as too narrow.

25. Shue (1996), p. 15.

26. Welsh (2016) noted, "In spite of the cries of 'never again' following the genocides in Rwanda and Srebrenica, the early decades of the twenty-first century have continued to be marked by atrocity crimes. In far too many crises, vulnerable populations suffer from forms of violence that challenge our common humanity. In 2014–2015, acts that could constitute genocide, war crimes, ethnic cleansing, and crimes against humanity took place in the Central African Republic, the Democratic Republic of the Congo, Iraq, Libya, Nigeria, South Sudan, Sudan, Syria, and Yemen, among other regions" (p. 75).

27. See United Nations General Assembly (2005) in particular Articles 138 and 139.

28. Welsh (2016) provided a list of the peaceful means pursued to date: "mediation between warring parties to reduce or end violence; negotiation over specific protection issues, such as humanitarian access; monitoring and observer missions to report on serious violations of international humanitarian and human rights law, assess specific sources of threat, and deter the commission of atrocity crimes; fact-finding missions to establish impartially whether atrocity crimes have occurred; and public advocacy on protection by key United Nations officials and representatives of regional and other international organizations" (p. 82).

29. See also the International Coalition for the Responsibility to Protect at http://responsibilitytoprotect.org.

30. Kaldor, Martin, and Selchow (2007), p. 280.

31. Kaldor, Martin, and Selchow (2007), p. 283. The World Bank (2011c) gave further examples of this difference: "If security forces are set targets based on the number of rebel combatants killed or captured or criminals arrested, they may rely primarily on coercive approaches, with no incentive to build the longer-term trust with communities that will prevent violence from recurring. Targets based on citizen security (freedom of movement and so on), in contrast, create longer-term incentives for the role of the security forces in underpinning national unity and effective state-society relations" (p. 19).

32. On a personal note, I teach a class on development policy. I once had a student in that class who had served in civilian-military relations in both Iraq and Afghanistan. He told me: "If I had taken this class before serving in these countries, I would have done everything differently. I owe those people an apology!" Significant military operations take place with little thought about what comes after, and this wastes a significant amount of resources, including lives.

33. Kaldor, Martin, and Selchow (2007) stated, "In most counter-insurgency operations, victory is very difficult to achieve and can only be reached, if at all, through widespread destruction and repression. . . . Human security principles explicitly recognize the impossibility of swift outright victory and aim instead to establish safe zones where political solutions can be sought or where civilian instruments can help to provide the conditions for political processes. Techniques such as the establishment of safe havens, humanitarian corridors or no-fly zones are typical of a human security approach" (p. 284).

34. For more on this case, see Welsh (2016).

35. Again, see Welsh (2016).

36. See the British government investigation in Chilcot (2016).

37. See, for example Etzioni (2017).

38. For the case of civil wars, for example, see Buhaug and Gleditsch (2008). The clustering in these cases reflects ethnic ties that span national borders.
39. See Frost and Nowak (2014). These authors noted that "while urban areas are not necessarily more violent or less safe than rural areas, their size concentrates perpetrators and victims of violence" (p. 1).
40. Frost and Nowak (2014), p. 3.
41. See, for example, Zartman (2005) and references therein.
42. This ongoing insight had its roots in the work of Davies (1962).
43. Zartman (2005), p. 263. See also Rubenstein (2001).
44. For a famous dissent to the role of grievance in conflict, see Collier and Hoeffler (2004).
45. Some of these issues were explored by Sen (2006). Zartman (2005) stated, "Identity is involved in all conflicts, albeit in many different forms. In the current era, it frequently takes the form of ethnic identity" (p. 267).
46. Zartman (2005) stated, "The rebellion's troops and followers are mobilized and motivated by a sense of deprivation and discrimination, expressed through appeals to identity as targeted populations, not by get-rich-quick schemes based on lootable resources" (p. 276).
47. Zartman (2005) stated, "The more prolonged the struggle, the more resources have become strained and the more the search for resources becomes important, even dominant" (p. 268).
48. Zartman (2005), p. 263.
49. See Fukuyama (2005).
50. Muggah and Krause (2009), p. 142.
51. Muggah and Krause (2009).
52. Arias (2017), p. 115.
53. Arias (2017), p. 115.
54. For empirical evidence of this, see Van Dijk, J. (2007). On the issue of corruption, Arias (2017) stated, "The drug trade can also have serious implications for state corruption. Around the world, there is significant evidence of the drug trade infiltrating deep into state structures and corrupting the leaders not just of security forces but also of governments" (p. 125).
55. Keefer, Loayza, and Soares (2010).
56. Arias (2017), p. 126.
57. This point was made, among others, by Reinert (2004).
58. See Shelley (2017). This author stated, "Illicit trade is more than the sale of counterfeit purses, sneakers and of pirated videos both in the real and virtual world. Trade in illegal goods can be a key facilitator for many of the most destabilizing phenomena in the world— the perpetuation of deadly conflicts, the proliferation of arms and weapons of mass destruction, and the propagation of environmental degradation" (p. 100).
59. United Nations Office for Disarmament Affairs (2013), p. 2.
60. Theohary (2016).
61. See Valenti et al. (2014).
62. What follows was drawn from Leff and LeBrun (2014).
63. It is interesting that Sudanese-manufactured arms and ammunition also have been found in Côte d'Ivoire, the Democratic Republic of the Congo, Libya, Somalia, and Syria. See Leff and LeBrun (2014).
64. Cowell (2014).
65. See World Bank (2011c) and reference therein.
66. See World Bank (2011c), pp. 5–6, and references therein.
67. See, for example, Daley (2006).
68. See, for example, Ngaruko and Nkurunziza (2002).
69. This box was drawn from Almosawa and Youssef (2017); Burki (2016); *The Economist* (2017a); *The Guardian* (2012); Haidera et al. (2011); and Weis (2015).
70. Muggah and Krause (2009) noted that "ex-combatants from irregular armed forces often kept their weapons, or surrendered old or non-function ones, with the result that large

numbers of military-style weapons entered into society, with potentially negative consequences" (p. 138).

71. See, for example, Save the Children (2017) and Shonkoff et al. (2012).
72. World Bank (2011c), p. 11.
73. World Bank (2011c), p. 13.
74. World Bank (2011c), p. 19.
75. The World Bank (2011c) noted that "UN, regional, and NGO-sponsored mediation has
    played a significant role in a range of cases" (p. 23).
76. The World Bank (2011c), pp. 23 and 25. In addition, the World Bank showed that the more
    fragile is a country (and the greater the threats to human security), the greater is the vol-
    atility of its aid flows, and in some cases, fragile countries are subject to "stop-and-go" aid
    flows. This itself exacerbates fragility.
77. See Frost and Nowak (2014).
78. "The easy accessibility of firearms—a recognized risk factor for violence— helps shape the
    dynamics of armed violence in cities around the globe. Together with the presence of or-
    ganized crime and illicit markets, it affects both the level and the scope of armed violence"
    (Frost and Nowak, 2014, p. 4).
79. Sources include Frost and Nowak (2014); World Bank, (2011c); and Zartman (2005).
80. See, for example, Save the Children (2017).
81. See, for example, Williams (2013).
82. See, for example, Hultman, Kathman, and Shannon (2013). These authors suggested that
    the impacts of properly resourced UN peacekeeping operations can be "substantial" and
    even "dramatic."
83. Muggah and Krause (2009), p. 140.
84. Muggah and Krause (2009) noted that "donors and development agencies still lack the
    language, tools, and experience to deal with the changing landscapes of armed violence"
    (p. 144).
85. See Muggah and Krause (2009).
86. See, for example, Bayley (2011).

PART III

NO SMALL HOPE

‖ 12 ‖

No Small Hope

This book began with the simple but surprisingly controversial observation that human beings have *needs*. It recognized that the failure to meet these needs can have serious implications for human well-being, including ill health and death, as well as diminished abilities to participate effectively in societies. The argument went further to assert that needs imply *rights* to minimal levels of basic goods and services. The notion of *basic goods as basic rights* is one example of minimalist ethics, described by ethicist Sissela Bok as a "stepwise, limited, and admittedly imperfect minimalist [approach] to social change."[1] The social change called for by the basic goods approach involves a new focus on and policy steps toward the *universal provision* of basic goods and services. This policy goal claims precedence over other alternatives, including national security, economic growth, and the more recent emphasis on capabilities expansion.

In the realm of political philosophy, there are some notable examples of the recognition of basic needs such as David Braybrooke's *Meeting Needs*.[2] However, there is rather little to be found in these works on how to actually *accomplish* the task of meeting needs. There are also highly aspirational works focused on the very ends of human flourishing, namely the capabilities approach as expressed in Martha Nussbaum's *Creating Capabilities*.[3] But again, the steps forward are not well described beyond calls for constitutional guarantees and the off-hand mention of basic goods provision with accompanying, unhelpful cautions against "commodity fetishism." Political philosophy is beyond my expertise, but the book itself lies between the needs and capabilities notions: needs are satisfied by basic goods, and capabilities are developed by providing basic goods. Unlike other contributions, this book has tried to spell out *how* to provide basic goods and services.

In the realm of economics, human needs are commonly considered as just another sort of preference, and the advocacy of basic goods provision as a policy goal is therefore generally seen as a form of paternalism. To the extent that basic goods and services are recognized in economics (see the Appendix), they can be addressed through (unconditional) income transfers. Increases in income transfers are predicated on economic growth, which brings the focus to the reforms necessary to make this growth more likely. This book respectfully disagrees with the standard, economic view. It contends that growth and basic goods provision are mutually reinforcing, and that basic goods provision can be a *prerequisite* for growth. Such an observation is not often made by prominent economists, but it is commonly found in the financial press. Political philosophy and the concerns of business people are connected in this way.

Most efforts at global policymaking actually come down to various conceptions of national security. On the very outskirts of these near-daily deliberations, but also within the United Nations system, there is an ongoing discussion of the relationship between notions of national security and *human security*. Human security is conceived of as freedom from fear and freedom from want, and the basic goods approach is very much compatible with the human security concept. Indeed, the two approaches are mutually reinforcing, and together they provide a new way of thinking about security more appropriate to addressing "nontraditional threats" in the long run.[4] Pursuing this line of thought brings us back to the call by economists Shareen Hertel and Lanse Minkler for "a different kind of freedom and a new kind of security" to move to center stage.[5]

A simple representation of this book's view is presented in Figure 12.1. The figure begins with growth but recognizes that growth supports both basic goods provision and nonbasic goods provision, and that these two types of consumption are fundamentally different. Nonbasic goods provision fulfills *wants*, while basic goods provision fulfills *needs*. Needs fulfillment more directly contributes to capabilities expansion than wants fulfilment. It is through this process that the basic goods provision/needs fulfilment/capabilities expansion nexus helps to support growth processes in what is potentially a virtuous circle. The basic goods vision is to support such virtuous circles in all countries of the world.

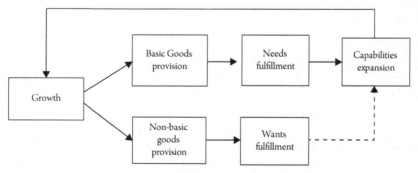

Figure 12.1 A framework of basic needs, basic goods, capabilities, and growth.

Rational Pessimism

Not everyone will feel comfortable with the concerns embodied in the basic goods approach. One potential criticism is that the book is simply *too pessimistic*. For example, in his book *The Rational Optimist*, Matt Ridley argued that the activities of the market system and innovation during the 21st century will allow "even the poorest people of the world to afford to *meet their desires as well as their needs*" (emphasis added).[6] Likewise, technology optimists Peter Diamandis and Steven Kotler argued that "abundance for all" will largely be realized by 2035.[7] Those who disagree with such predictions exhibit not just pessimism but "moaning pessimism."[8] Diamandis and Kotler cataloged the alleged cognitive biases behind moaning pessimism. These include loss aversion, being "divorced from reality," employing the "illusion of validity," coping with "limited mental resources," and therefore relying on heuristics that result in "severe and systematic errors," negativity bias, confirmation bias, overstimulated amygdala, and anchoring. The end result is that our brains are designed to "conspire to keep us pessimistic."[9]

Is this book simply a result of cognitive biases? I would like to suggest that this is *not* the case. The book draws on a wealth of evidence in the form of quantitative data and an extensive set of scientific research journal articles. Comparing sources with the Diamandis and Kotler volume, for example, shows that there is no relative lack of careful reasoning here. Indeed, there seems to be little evidence that "abundance for all" will be achieved by 2035. Although the outcomes may not turn out to be catastrophic, they will also be far from what has been advertised by the technology optimists who display their own potential cognitive biases, being somewhat captured by the "gee whiz" nature of technological evolution. The tentative conclusions of this book are probably not too far off the mark.[10]

What this book embraces is a sort of *rational pessimism*. It does not deny that technological advances can make extraordinary contributions to our lives, including basic goods provision. But there are observed limits even to technological change and diffusion, as well as some worrisome trends. With more refugees and number of individuals under threat of starvation since World War II, it might be best to be cautious and vigilant. Microsoft founder Bill Gates expressed this approach in his review of *The Rational Optimist* as follows: "What is wrong with worrying about and guarding against threats that might become real, large problems?"[11] This book suggests that there are some real, large problems in the present (e.g., the 2.4 billion individuals do not have access to clean and safe toilets) and potentially in the future (e.g., the impact of climate change and conflict on agricultural productivity).[12] This is the rational pessimist point of view.[13]

From Sustainable Development Goals to Basic Development Goals

If basic goods provision is really so important, why has it not received more attention from the development policy community? In fact, the basic goods and services covered in Chapters 4 to 11 each have their own development policy subcommunity and have received significant attention within these subcommunities. What has been missing is an integrating framework across these various subcommunities. This book has tried to supply such an integrating framework in the form of the basic goods approach. The hope is that this framework will help support conversations and collaborations among the relevant subcommunities as well as an overall policy perspective.

Despite this hope, the development policy community as a whole has forsaken minimalist frameworks in favor of super-aspirational goals in the form of the sustainable development goals (SDGs) now enshrined within the UN system. These goals have attracted some prominent defenders in the development policy community, including Jeffrey Sachs.[14] They also have attracted some prominent critics, including Bill Easterly.[15] This book falls into the latter group, and does so for two reasons. First, the SDGs, with their seventeen goals and an astonishing 169 targets, are simply *too broad* in scope to be effective. Second, many of the targets themselves are *too vague*. Consider for example, Target 12.8: "By 2030, ensure that people everywhere have the relevant information and awareness for sustainable development and lifestyles in harmony with nature." Or consider Target 16.6: "Develop effective, accountable and transparent institutions at all levels." How could we even know if we have met these targets if were possible to do so?

There are some SDG targets that *are* related to basic goods provision. There is a concern with poverty in Goal 1, but this too gets very vague. For example, in Target 1.3, we have, "Implement nationally appropriate social protection systems and measures for all, including floors, and by 2030 achieve substantial coverage of the poor and the vulnerable." It is not clear what this really means. Target 1.4 calls for "access to basic services," but which services it does not say. Goal 2 is on food security, and Target 2.1 is much more to the point: "By 2030, end hunger and ensure access by all people, in particular the poor and people in vulnerable situations, including infants, to safe, nutritious and sufficient food all year round." But Target 2.4 calls for: "By 2030, ensure sustainable food production systems and implement resilient agricultural practices that increase productivity and production, that help maintain ecosystems, that strengthen capacity for adaptation to climate change, extreme weather, drought, flooding and other disasters and that progressively improve land and soil quality." It is clear from Chapter 4 that the basic goods approach thinks this is a good idea, but it is not a target, it is an aspirational goal. Such confusion makes policy formation more difficult.

Goal 3 is on health, and this is a good thing, but there are again too many targets, including "promote mental health and wellbeing" (one part of Target 3.7) and "universal health coverage" (one part of Target 3.7), neither of which can be assured at all, no less by 2030. As this book has stated many times, it is better to focus on determinants rather than outcomes. Clean water and sanitation are two such determinants, and these are indeed considered in Goal 6. Target 6.1 is "By 2030, achieve universal and equitable access to safe and affordable drinking water for all," and Target 6.2 is "By 2030, achieve access to adequate and equitable sanitation and hygiene for all and end open defecation, paying special attention to the needs of women and girls and those in vulnerable situations." It would have been better to stop there to focus attention, but many more targets were added on to Goal 6. This is a pattern across all seventeen goals.

Suppose that we took determinants seriously. What would a more practical reconstitution of the SDGs in terms of basic goods and services provision look like? This is done in Table 12.1 as a set of BDGs that preserve the order and wording but not the actual numbering of the SDGs. Rather than 169 targets, there are only ten. This may seem to be under-ambitious, but reducing the targets down to ten dramatically focuses attention relative to the existing SDGs, makes forward progress more possible, and accountability more likely. And even if the BDGS were expanded to twelve or fourteen targets, this would be a fraction of the current 169 targets.

The conclusion here is that the SDGs should be *dramatically reduced* to a set of BDGs or the equivalent, set out in the form of basic goods and services, the things that would actually help meet the stated goals of the UN system. As documented in the chapters of this book, the resulting targets would map very closely to the existing subsistence rights language of UN system. As an added bonus, substituting some form of BDGs for SGDs would free the UN of the extensive ridicule it has suffered from its embrace of the SDGs. The BDGs are simply a better way forward.

Moral Minimalism and Open Access Orders

This book has drawn on a narrow aspect of political philosophy in the form of moral minimalism. Somewhat speculatively, there also may be implications of the basic goods approach for other aspects of political philosophy. Let us consider one example. In their book *Violence and Social Orders*, Douglass North, John Wallis, and Barry Weingast addressed the role of what they called *open access orders* in shaping modern political (and socioeconomic) evolution. These authors defined open access orders as being characterized by:[16]

Table 12.1 **Basic Development Goals (BDGs)**

BDG	Target
Goal 1: Food security	Target 1.1: Ensure access by all people to safe, nutritious, and sufficient food
Goal 2: Health	Target 2.1: End preventable deaths of newborns and children under five years of age Target 2.2: End the epidemics of AIDS, tuberculosis, and malaria
Goal 3: Education	Target 3.1: Ensure that all children complete free, equitable, and quality primary and secondary education Target 3.2: Ensure that all children have access to quality preprimary education
Goal 4: Water and sanitation	Target 4.1: Achieve universal access to safe and affordable drinking water for all Target 4.2: Achieve universal access to adequate sanitation and hygiene for all and end open defecation
Goal 5: Energy	Target 5.1: Ensure universal access to affordable and reliable energy services
Goal 6: Housing	Target 6.1: Ensure universal access adequate, safe, and affordable housing
Goal 7: Human security	Target 7.1: Significantly reduce all forms of violence and related death rates

- Political and economic development.
- Less negative economic growth.
- Vibrant civil societies.
- Large but more decentralized government.
- Social equity, the rule of law, and secure property rights.

As it turns out, there is a provisioning aspect to open access orders. Although North, Wallis, and Weingast did not employ explicit notions of basic needs or basic goods, they got quite close. Consider the following:[17]

> Citizens in open access orders share belief systems that emphasize equality, sharing, and universal inclusion. To sustain these beliefs, all open access orders have institutions and policies that share the gains of and reduce the individual risks from market participation, including universal education, a range of social insurance programs, and widespread infrastructure and public goods.

They also noted that "These programs are not mere transfers of income with deadweight losses, but are public goods that generate positive economic returns."[18] This is not a claim to basic goods as rights within a system of moral minimalism as made in this book. But it is very much compatible with such a claim and system. Further, these authors argued that the initial transition from limited to open access orders involves the transformation of elite privileges into elite rights. Subsequently, elite rights are extended to rights for the citizenry. One of these rights can be basic subsistence rights. Such rights support human capital broadly conceived, and these authors noted that "when public goods enhance human capital, the ability to provide impersonal policies allows open access orders to respond to citizens in ways that complement markets rather than undermine them. In this way, open access orders sustain democracy as a positive-sum game."[19]

As can be seen, basic goods provision is, at a minimum, compatible with and potentially supportive of open-access-based democracy. Although it is beyond the scope of this book to delve into these important political economy issues, the potential linkages are noteworthy and call for further exploration. That said, we must also recognize that basic goods provision can take place in political systems that fall short of open access. Although some authoritarian systems can profoundly fail to provide basic goods (e.g., North Korea, Venezuela, Zimbabwe) others certainly succeed (e.g., China; Vietnam). The contrast between the two might shed further understanding on the issue of open access regimes.

The Fierce Urgency of Now Is Feasible

In its focus on meeting basic human needs, this book is in full agreement with a famous statement of Martin Luther King, Jr. that "We are confronted with the fierce urgency of now. In this unfolding conundrum of life and history, there is such a thing as being too late."[20] With regard to basic goods provision, the world is perpetually too late, year after year and decade after decade. The result of being too late shows up in the unnecessary deaths of millions of infants and children each year, further millions of deaths of adults, and dramatically attenuated lives. Accumulated across decades, we are witnessing hundreds of millions of lost and compromised lives. In the words of development economist Charles Kenny, "We don't know if a dollar spent on a second flat-screen TV has any impact on the well-being of a child in America. But we do know—at least so some degree—the likely impact of a dollar spent on an insecticide-treated bed net on the health of a child in Kenya. Whatever the uncertainties regarding the most efficient policies and approaches to improve the quality of life for the most disadvantaged in the world, they are not so large as to diminish the imperative to act."[21]

Is it possible to address the "fierce urgency of now?" Is the universal provision of basic goods and services feasible or have those who are deprived of basic goods condemned to be so deprived? This book contends that the universal provision of basic goods and services is indeed *feasible*. The feasibility is evident using some conservative, back-of-the-envelope estimates. These estimates begin with recognizing the existence of recurring expenditures made in other areas, namely persistent and misguided subsidies, that could and should be diverted to the universal provision of basic goods.

Estimates of direct fossil fuel consumption subsidies range as high as US$500 billion annually.[22] Direct agricultural subsidies of a handful of high-income countries are approximately US$150 billion annually,[23] and fishery subsidies are approximately US$35 billion.[24] Add in US$30 billion spent by low- and middle-income countries on weapons imports,[25] and we already have over US$700 billion annually. Let us reduce this to US$700 billion to be conservative. Directing these resources to the BDGs in Table 12.1 would do much to alleviate human suffering and promote capabilities expansion.

The use of the US$700 billion to finance basic goods provision is represented in a very rough, illustrative manner in Table 12.2. For each of our basic goods, approximate required expenditures are listed. In each case, the estimates are rounded up or taken at the upper end of estimated ranges from their sources. What Table 12.2 shows in an approximate way is that there are indeed global resources to be directed to basic goods provision. Note that most of the subsidies included in the US$700 billion should be substantially reduced anyway to remove distortions from the markets they affect. But reducing and redirecting these subsidies would actually make substantial progress toward the universal provision of the *full range* of basic goods and services considered in this book. The fierce urgency of now and the no small hope of this book's title are within our grasp. We no longer need to be perpetually too late.

There is an argument that, to the extent that basic goods expenditures fall into foreign aid flows, that they will be simply ineffective.[26] Although results vary somewhat, this does not seem to be the general case. There is evidence that foreign aid can be effective in providing water and sanitation, health and education, for example.[27] Rather than simply assume ineffectiveness, we need to examine foreign aid for each type of basic good and service and begin to assess the evidence for different types of countries (e.g., income level or region). Our priors with regard to foreign aid processes should not be yet another excuse to be too late.

Table 12.2 **Back-of-the-Envelope Costs of Meeting Some Types of Basic Goods Provision**

Basic Goods Type or Subsidies to Be Redirected	Approximate Cost	Sources and Comments
Subsidies to be redirected	US$700 billion	A sum of direct fossil fuel consumption subsidies, direct agricultural subsidies, fishing subsidies, and weapons imports of low- and middle-income countries (see text and endnotes for further documentation)
Food	US$100 billion	This takes the estimates of FAO (2009) and adds US$20 billion. Note that this is US$50 billion less than the average direct agricultural subsidies of rich countries.
Water and sanitation	US$40 billion	This takes the estimates of Hutton and Varughese (2016) and adds US$10 billion. Their range of estimates is from US$14 to US$47 billion, so this is very much toward the high end of the range.
Health: Tuberculosis	US$10 billion	This is US$2 billion more than the estimate of WHO (2016).
Health: Malaria	US$10 billion	This is US$1 billion more than the estimate of WHO (2015).
Health: Infant and child mortality	US$30 billion	This is the very high end of of the estimates made by Stenberg et al. (2014).
Education	US$60 billion	This is US$4 billion more than the estimate of UNESCO (2013b).
Housing	US$300 billion	US$50 billion more than the estimated annual construction costs from McKinsey Global Institute (2014).
Electricity	US$60 billion	This is US$6 billion more than estimated by UNESCO (2013b).
Human security	US$40 billion	This is more than four times the current budget of UN peacekeeping operations.
Total cost	US$650 billion	
Remainder	US$50 billion	US$700 billion less US$650 billion.

Final Words

Human beings have needs, and these needs are addressed through the provision of basic goods and services. The global development community would more effectively address their stated goals by focusing on determinants, elevating basic goods and services in their deliberations in the form of a set of BDGs in place of the current SDGs. This agenda is a form of rational pessimism or reasonable vigilance in the face of some worrisome global trends. It is not a form of "moaning pessimism." Increased provision of basic goods and services might also play a role in maintaining open access orders, contributing to political development. Most important, the basic goods agenda is broadly feasible as is evident from back-of-the-envelope calculations. Embracing moral minimalism is therefore both just and possible. The fact that the *no small hope* of this book is both just and possible makes it imperative.

Notes

1. Bok (2002), p. 59.
2. Braybrooke (1987).
3. Nussbaum (2011).
4. For example, although arguments on the issue are still ongoing, the intelligence community is now aware that lack of water security has potentially serious national security spillovers (Kallis and Zografos, 2014).
5. Hertel and Minkler (2007), p. 1.
6. See Ridley (2010), p. 352.
7. In their words: "An end to most of what ails us by 2035" (Diamandis and Kotler, 2012, p. 25).
8. Interview with Matt Ridley in Diamandis and Kotler (2012), p. 38.
9. Diamandis and Kotler (2012), p. 31.
10. See, for example, *The Economist* (2017f).
11. Gates (2010).
12. I have noted the potential relationship between water scarcity and conflict at various points in this book. See also Schleussner et al. (2016).
13. Again, see *The Economist* (2017f).
14. Sachs (2012).
15. Easterly (2015), as well as *The Economist* (2015b).
16. North, Wallis, and Weingast (2009), p. 11.
17. North, Wallis, and Weingast (2009), p. 111.
18. North, Wallis, and Weingast (2009), p. 143.
19. North, Wallis, and Weingast (2009), p. 266.
20. King (1986), pp. 632–633.
21. Kenny (2011), p. 182.
22. *The Economist* (2014f) and http://www.worldenergyoutlook.org/resources/energysubsidies/. Total energy subsidies of all kinds are actually in the *trillions* of U.S. dollars. See Coady et al. (2015) and Sovacool (2017). I am only including the direct consumption subsidies here.
23. Peterson (2009).
24. Sumaila et al. (2016).
25. See Theohary (2016).

26. The research on foreign aid and its effectiveness is vast. See, for example, Chapter 5 of Goldin and Reinert (2012) and Baliamoune-Lutz (2017) for reviews. Baliamoune-Lutz stated that "foreign aid and its effectiveness is one of the most controversial topics in development economics, international development and international political economy" (p. 373).

27. On water and sanitation, see Gopalan and Rajan (2016). On health, see Mishra and Newhouse (2009). On education, see Dreher, Nunnenkamp, and Thiele (2008).

SOME ECONOMICS OF BASIC GOODS

Economists have done a remarkable job of making basic needs and, therefore, basic goods invisible and unnecessary. As the moral philosopher David
Braybrooke noted, "the most abundant and persistent source of charges against
the concept of needs are economists."[1] The notions of basic needs and basic
goods are largely *absent* from standard economic theory, only making an appearance in the subfield of development economics.[2] This invisibility of basic needs
and basic goods reflects the fact that notions of need are not *necessary* for the
development and application of modern economic (particularly microeconomic)
theory.[3] However, the fact that they are not *theoretically necessary* does not imply
that they are *irrelevant* from a practical, policy point of view or from the point
of view of economics ethics. The purpose of this appendix is to briefly explore
these issues.

Utility of Consumption

Economists have a *subjective* notion of well-being based on the concept of *utility*
derived from consumption. There is a longstanding and ongoing discussion of
what is actually meant by utility. For example, economist John Broome described
it as "usefulness" and suggested that it be deployed simply as a mathematical
representation of preferences that can be inferred from individuals' or households' choices.[4] This is the received wisdom of modern economics. More recent
discussions have suggested that utility may actually be measurable through neu-
ropsychological means.[5] These issues have not been fully resolved.

This subjective approach does have an important merit in that it requires individuals to *actually desire* something before value is conferred to it. Technically
speaking, this is the requirement that there be a "pro-attitude" toward the
valued object.[6] The pro-attitude requirement is a bulkhead against acute

paternalism. But there is nevertheless a problem inherent in the subjective valuation approach. This is the jump made by economists (with uncanny automaticity) from the notion of utility-of-consumption to *well-being* itself. This jump is not necessarily appropriate.[7]

This problem with the jump from utility-of-consumption to well-being is known in economic ethics as "nonprudential desire."[8] The philosopher James Patrick Griffin put the issue most succinctly when he said that "the trouble is that one's desires spread themselves so widely over the world that their objects extend far outside the bound of what, with any plausibility, one could take as touching one's well-being."[9] For example, we desire cigarettes and heroin as well as carrots and kale. One tempting way around the issue of nonprudential desire is to appeal to tautology: what we desire to consume contributes to well-being simply because we desire it. But if we relax this tautology, it simply cannot be the case that what we desire *always* contributes to well-being.[10] As noted by economists Daniel Hausman and Michael McPherson, "it is questionable whether preference satisfaction is an adequate conception of individual well-being."[11]

Economists have tried a number of routes to escape from the nonprudential desire problem.[12] The attempts range from the unconvincing to the comical. Appeals have been made to "mental states of intrinsic worth." Contrasts have been made between "manifest" preferences and "true" preferences, between "rational" preferences and "irrational" preferences, between "social" preferences and "antisocial" preferences, between ordinary preferences and those supervised by an imaginary "ideal advisor." It is indeed strange to assert that we cannot ever determine what *needs* may be but can somehow perceive invisible "true, rational, and social" preferences arrived at with the assistance of a conjured-up guardian angel.[13] It is difficult to conclude that such attempts to replace nonprudential desire with informed desire have succeeded. Reviewing the informed desire project, the philosopher James Patrick Griffin exclaimed: "Is it even intelligible"?[14] We are simply not going to escape the problem of nonprudential desire by assuming that we can observe the unobservable.

The problem of nonprudential desire is even more significant in the presence of a phenomenon known as *adaptive preferences*. Economists have a habit of conceiving of preferences as "exogenous," but the advertising industry knows better and spends vast sums to influence preferences. More important, individuals subject to severe deprivations may simply lose hope and attempt to adapt to or rationalize these deprivations. This can result in deprivations (particularly in basic goods) deforming preferences as individuals adapt to them.[15] This problem works the other way as well. Deprived individuals with previously deformed preferences can be slow to adapt to newly available health technologies.

The only way to adequately deal with the nonprudential desire problem is directly, by using an objective set of criteria to evaluate preferences. This approach follows that of Griffin, who made the following suggestion:[16]

What makes us desire the things we desire, when informed, is something about them—their feature or properties. But why bother then with informed desire, when we can go directly to what it is about objects that shape informed desires in the first place? If what really matters are certain sorts of reason for action, to be found outside desires in qualities of their objects, why not explain well-being directly in terms of them?

There is potentially a number of ways of doing this, and this book has taken up only one, namely restricting our vision to goods that address basic human needs. The basic goods approach therefore rests on an objectivist foundation. However, in so doing, it makes the likelihood that the included goods would indeed pass a "pro-attitude" test extremely likely. In nearly every case, objective basic needs are addressed by basic goods characterized by pro-attitudes on the part of human welfare subjects. This is a result of the fact that, as emphasized by Griffin, any adequate subjectivist approach will necessarily be found at a very close distance to objectivist accounts. Further, as noted by Hausman and McPherson, objectivist approaches "link up more naturally to the normative terms in which policy is debated."[17]

Basic Needs and Basic Goods

As discussed in this book Adam Smith had a notion of "necessaries" as part of his economic thought, and Alfred Marshall had a similar notion. Marshall made a distinction between "necessaries" or "things required to meet wants which must be satisfied," and "comforts or luxuries" or "things that meet wants of a less urgent character."[18] Thus, Marshall recognized a distinction between *needs* and *wants*. Marshall's student and later colleague Arthur Pigou recognized this distinction and specified needs in terms of a minimum standard. He stated that "the minimum standard . . . must be conceived, not as a subjective minimum of satisfaction, but as an *objective minimum of conditions*. . . . Thus the minimum includes some defined quantity and quality of house accommodation, of medical care, of education, of food, of leisure, of the apparatus of sanitary convenience and safety where work is carried on, and so on (emphasis added)."[19] It is striking how similar this call from a Cambridge economist of nearly a century ago is with the spirit of the basic goods approach advocated in this book.

After Marshall and Pigou, the distinction between wants and needs was, for the most part, lost, only to be revisited now and then. The Romanian economist Nicholas Georgescu-Roegen noted that needs (along with wants and uses) are prior to any well thought out conception of utility and that these needs had a potentially ordinal quality to them.[20] Similar distinctions (without the math) were made by Canadian-Colombian economist Lauchlin Currie.[21] Philosopher David Braybrooke paid attention to the way that economists folded needs into preferences and took issue with that approach, stating among other things that "People will not have any opportunity to have further preferences heeded if the needs that their biological functioning and survival imply go unmet."[22]

Sir Richard Stone's description of household demand via a "linear expenditure system" (LES) made a distinction between basic consumption (or subsistence requirements) and other expenditures, thereby allowing income elasticities of demand to vary from unity. One interpretation of basic consumption in the LES is in terms of basic goods. In a noted book on consumer behavior, Angus Deaton and John Muellbauer used the Smithian concept of "necessities" as being those goods for which the income elasticity of demand is less than unity and budget shares fall with income level.[23] And consumer economist Richard Blundell[24] provided evidence of the less than unity character of basic needs income elasticities and the fact that these elasticities decline with income levels. More recent, Baxter and Moosa provided an explicit list of basic needs characteristics from an economic perspective. They characterized basic needs (and therefore basic goods consumption) as follows:[25]

- *Universal*: they are common to all consumers.
- *Hierarchical*: they take precedence over nonbasic goods consumption.
- *Satiable*: the consumption of basic goods can be satisfied, with expenditures consequently reaching a maximum.
- *Measurable*: it is possible to measure requirements of basic goods.
- *Irreducible*: there is a minimum threshold for basic goods consumption below which life becomes precarious.
- *Continuing*: the needs to be fulfilled, and hence the expenditures on basic goods to support these needs, continue over time.
- *Stable*: basic goods consumption is relatively more stable than consumption of nonbasic goods.
- *Additive*: expenditures on basic goods are roughly proportional to populations.
- *Absolute*: basic goods consumption has an absolute rather than relative character.

Based on an econometric analysis, Baxter and Moosa demonstrated that: Basic goods consumption is characterized by income elasticities of demand that are less than unity; these income elasticities of demand decline with income; and that, from a number of different points of view, basic goods expenditures are more stable than other types of expenditures. Their overall conclusion was that "basic needs expenditures should be distinguished from other expenditures on non-durable items. This distinction should be made on the theoretical level as well as in . . . model building."[26]

When economists consider the idea of basic goods that reflect basic needs, they often ask: How can we identify them? We have a number of answers to this question. First, basic goods expenditures of households are more stable than other types of expenditures. Second, basic goods have estimated income elasticities of demand that are less than unity. Third, these income elasticities of demand decrease with levels of household income and expenditure. Fourth, basic goods have estimated price elasticities of demand that tend to be low in absolute value. Given the dramatic expansion in the empirical estimation of household demand over the last century, it is indeed possible to identify basic goods and services from an economic (econometric) point of view.[27]

Notes

1. Braybrooke (1987), p. 9.
2. In the context of health services and need, Filmer, Hammer, and Pritchett (2000) noted that "Economists tend to shy away from discussions of 'need' because it is not directly observable and is an emotionally charged term. But if an individual 'needs' something, she or he is likely to forgo other consumption in order to satisfy that need. If income falls or prices rise, consumption of such a good will be protected, and adjustment will be greater with regard to other uses of money and time" (p. 214). For the record, modern economics is built on the unobservable concept of "utility," and need is largely (if not completely) observable. Also, it is not clear why the concept of need is more emotionally charged than other concepts in economics such as poverty and income distribution that are routinely analyzed in the field.
3. See Georgescu-Roegen (1954) and Seeley (1992). Georgescu-Roegen stated that "Preferences . . . are all we need for a rational theory of demand" (p. 509).
4. See Broome (1991).
5. For a review, see Fumagalli (2013). This author makes a useful distinction among *decision utility, experienced utility* and *neural utility*.
6. On pro-attitudes, see Sumner (1995).
7. Modern consumer theory in economics rests on the work of Sir John Hicks. It is with some irony then that it was Hicks himself (1969) that questioned the jump from utility to *welfare*. This is not a question with regard to the use of utility maximization as a handy way of capturing consumer *choice*. It is only a question of utility-of-consumption as a proxy of *well-being*.
8. For example, W. Stanley Jevons (1965, originally 1905) claimed that "objects intended for immoral or criminal purposes . . . also have utility; the fact that they are desired by certain persons, and are accordingly manufactured, sold, and bought, establishes the fact." And "even that which is hurtful to a person may by ignorance be desired, purchased and used; it has then utility" (p. 12).
9. Griffin (1986), p. 17.
10. This logical problem was pointed out by Hurka (1999).
11. Hausman and McPherson (1993), p. 689. These authors note that preferences can be "based on false beliefs," "idiosyncratic," "based on highly-contestable beliefs," and "antisocial" (pp. 690–691).
12. These attempts at escape go back at least as far as Harrod (1936).
13. See Moore (1903); Harsani (1977); and Railton (1986). Here is a sample from Railton: "an individual's good consists in what he would *want himself to want*, or to pursue, were he to contemplate his present situation from a standpoint *fully and vividly informed* about

himself and his circumstances, and *entirely free of cognitive error* or lapsed of instrumental rationality" (p. 16). In other words, if we were not actually ourselves. As a consequence of such inadequacies, Sobel (1997) suggested that "the job of finding a convincing method of separating out the well-being-determining subset of our preferences from the other motivational factors remains a crucial but neglected component of a satisfactory subjectivist account of well-being" (p. 505). Braybrooke (1987) also noted that rational preferences are not necessarily prudential (p. 203).

14. Griffin (1986), p. 16.
15. For evidence of this, see Halleröd (2006).
16. Griffin (1986), p. 17.
17. Hausman and McPherson (1993), p. 692.
18. See Parsons (1931) for a three-part structure of wants (the first including needs), as well as Endres (1991). Endres noted that "Marshall's discussion of various categories of 'necessaries' was suggestive of a physiologically and sociologically determined structure of wants" (p. 335) and that "Marshall definitely had something like a structured needs hierarchy in mind" (p. 336).
19. See Pigou (1932), p. 759. Pigou also stated that "there is a general agreement among practical philanthropists that *some* minimum standard of conditions ought to be set up at a level high enough to make impossible the occurrence to anybody of extreme want; and that whatever transference of resources from relatively rich to relatively poor persons is necessary to secure this must be made, without reference to possible injurious consequences upon the magnitude of the dividend" (p. 760).
20. See Georgescu-Roegen (1954) who stated that "we find that before anyone speaks of utility, of value or of how the individual behaves, one mentions needs, wants, uses, etc. These latter concepts are, it is true, far from being precisely defined, but so is utility or satisfaction, if we care to look into the matter . . . The reality that determines the individual's behavior is not formed by utility . . . but by his wants, or his needs. Even that economic literature which considers utility theory so undisputable and so established that it dispenses with any discussion of wants or needs as entirely superfluous, cannot offer an independent presentation of utility" (p. 512).
21. See Currie (1975) who noted that "most of our wants or desires are created, as contrasted with our needs that remain unchanged" (p. 56).
22. Braybrooke (1987), p. 199.
23. Deaton and Muellbauer (1980).
24. Blundell (1988).
25. Baxter and Moosa (1996).
26. Baxter and Moosa (1996), p. 98. The role of basic goods in household demand has even entered into financial modeling. This appears due to the need of modelers to understand equity premiums over government debt. See, for example, Aït-Sahalia, Parker, and Yogo (2004).
27. See also Goldstein (1985) on the way that the satisfaction of basic needs via basic goods consumption follows an asymptotic curve, as well as Muñoz Conde (2011) who explicitly adopts the basic goods approach in an econometric investigation of basic goods in Colombia.

BIBLIOGRAPHY

Abadzi, H. (2009) "Instructional Time Loss in Developing Countries: Concepts, Measurement, and Implications," *World Bank Research Observer*, 24:2, 267–290.

Adelman, I. (2001) "Fallacies in Development Theory and Their Implications for Policy," in G.M. Meier and J.E. Stiglitz (eds.), *Frontiers of Development Economics: The Future in Perspective.* Oxford University Press, 103–134.

Adelman, S.W., D.O. Gilligan, and K. Lehrer (2008) "How Effective are Food for Education Programs? A Critical Assessment of the Evidence from Developing Countries," *Food Policy Review* 9, International Food Policy Research Institute.

Ahmed, A.U, A.R. Quisumbing, and J.F. Hoddinott (2007) *Relative Efficacy of Food and Cash Transfers in Approving Food Security and Livelihoods of the Ultra-Poor in Bangladesh.* International Food Policy Research Institute.

Ahuja, A., M. Kremer, and A.P. Zwane (2010) "Providing Safe Water: Evidence from Randomized Trials," *Annual Review of Resource Economics*, 2, 237–256.

Aït-Sahalia, Y., J.A. Parker, and M. Yogo (2004) "Luxury Goods and the Equity Premium," *Journal of Finance*, 59:6, 2959–3004.

Albisa, C., B. Scott, and K. Tissington (2013) "Demolishing Housing Rights in the Name of Market Fundamentalism: The Dynamics of Displacement in the United States, India, and South Africa," in L. Minkler (ed.), *The State of Economic and Social Human Rights: A Global Overview.* Cambridge University Press, 86–116.

Almosawa, S. and N. Youssef (2017, July 7) "Cholera Spreads as War and Poverty Batter Yemen," *The New York Times.*

Alstone, P., D. Gershenson, and D.M. Kammen (2015) "Decentralized Energy Systems for Clean Energy Access," *Nature Climate Change*, 5:4, 305–314.

Alvarez, A.A.A. (2007) "Threshold Considerations in Fair Allocation of Health Resources: Justice Beyond Scarcity," *Bioethics*, 21:8, 426–438.

Amnesty International (2009) *Kenya: The Unseen Majority: Nairobi's Two Million Slum Dwellers.*

Andrabi, T., J. Das, A.I. Khwaja, T. Vishwanath, and T. Zajonc (2007) *Pakistan Learning and Educational Achievements in Punjab Schools (LEAPS): Insights to Inform the Education Policy Debate.* World Bank.

Anseeuw, W., L.A. Wily, L. Cotula, and M. Taylor (2011) *Land Rights and the Rush for Land.* International Land Coalition.

Araral, E. (2009) "The Failure of Water Utilities Privatization: Synthesis of Evidence, Analysis and Implications," *Policy & Society*, 27:3, 221–228.

Arias, D.E. (2017) "Drug Trade and Human Security," in K.A. Reinert (ed.), *Handbook of Globalisation and Development.* Edward Elgar, 115–128.

Arneson, R.J. (1999) "Human Flourishing Versus Desire Satisfaction," *Social Philosophy and Policy*, 16:1, 113–142.

Arnold, B.F. and J.M Colford (2007) "Treating Water with Chlorine at Point-of-Use to Improve Water Quality and Reduce Child Diarrhea in Developing Countries: A Systematic Review and Meta-Analysis," *American Journal of Tropical Medicine and Hygiene*, 76:2, 354–364.

Arnott, R. (1995) "Time for Revisionism on Rent Control," *Journal of Economic Perspectives*, 9:1, 99–120.

Arvai, J. and K. Post (2012) "Risk Management in a Developing Country Context: Improving Decisions About Point-of-Use Water Treatment Among the Rural Poor in Africa," *Risk Analysis*, 32:1, 67–80.

Atta, R., T. Boutraa, and A. Akhkha (2011) "Smart Irrigation System for Wheat in Saudi Arabia Using Wireless Sensors Network Technology," *International Journal of Water Resources and Arid Environments*, 1:6, 478–482.

Attanasio, O. and A. Mesnard (2006) "The Impact of a Conditional Cash Transfer Program on Consumption in Colombia," *Fiscal Studies*, 27:4, 421–442.

Auerswald, P. (2012) *The Coming Prosperity: How Entrepreneurs Are Transforming the Global Economy*. Oxford University Press.

Ayee, J. and R. Crook (2006) "Urban Service Partnerships, 'Street-Level Bureaucrats' and Environmental Sanitation in Kumasi and Accra, Ghana: Coping with Organizational Change in the Public Bureaucracy," *Development Policy Review*, 24:1, 51–73.

Baird, S., C. McIntosh, and B. Özler (2011) "Cash or Condition? Evidence from a Cash Transfer Experiment," *Quarterly Journal of Economics*, 126:4, 1709–1753.

Baker, L., P. Newell, and J. Phillips (2014) "The Political Economy of Energy Transitions: The Case of South Africa," *New Political Economy*, 19:6, 791–818.

Baliamoune-Lutz , M. (2017) "Foreign Aid Effectiveness," in K.A. Reinert (ed.), *Handbook of Globalisation and Development*. Edward Elgar, 373–388.

Banerjee, A.J., S. Cole, E. Duflo, and L. Linden (2007) "Remedying Education: Evidence from Two Randomized Experiments in India," *Quarterly Journal of Economics*, 122:3, 1235–1264.

Banerjee, A.J. and E. Duflo (2006) "Addressing Absence," *Journal of Economic Perspectives*, 20:1, 117–132.

Banerjee, A.J. and E. Duflo (2011) *Poor Economics: A Radical Rethinking of the Way to Fight Global Poverty*. Public Affairs.

Bansal, S. (2014, August 21) "Innovation within Reach," *The New York Times*.

Barnett, M. (2011) *Empire of Humanity: A History of Humanitarianism*. Cornell University Press.

Barrera, A. (2007) "Economic Rights in the Knowledge Economy: An Instrumental Justification," in S. Hertel and L. Minkler (eds.), *Economic Rights: Conceptual, Measurement, and Policy Issues*. Cambridge University Press, 76–93.

Barrett, A.M. (2011) "Education Quality for Social Justice," *International Journal of Educational Development*, 31:1, 1–2.

Barrett, C.B. (2013) "Food or Consequences: Food Security and Its Implications for Global Sociopolitical Stability," in C.B. Barrett (ed.), *Food Security and Sociopolitical Security*. Oxford University Press, 1–34.

Barro, RJ. (2013) "Health and Economic Growth," *Annals of Economics and Finance*, 14:2, 329–366.

Barry, E. (2016) "Desperate for Slumber in Delhi, Homeless Encounter a 'Sleep Mafia,'" *The New York Times*, January 18.

Barry, J.M. (2005) *The Great Influenza*. Penguin.

Baxter, J.L. and I.A. Moosa (1996) "The Consumption Function: A Basic Needs Hypothesis," *Journal of Economic Behavior and Organization*, 31:1, 85–100.

Bayley, D.H. (2011) "The Morphing of Peacekeeping: Competing Approaches to Public Safety," *International Peacekeeping*, 18:1, 52–63.

Beath, A.L., I. Goldin, and K.A. Reinert (2009) "International Migration," in in K.A. Reinert, R.S. Rajan, A.J. Glass and L.S. Davis (eds.), *The Princeton Encyclopedia of the World Economy*. Princeton University Press, 764–770.

Beck, A. (2014) "Drought, Dams, and Survival: Linking Water to Conflict and Cooperation in Syria's Civil War," *International Affairs Forum*, 5:1, 11–22.

Benedek, W. (2008) "Human Security and Human Rights Interaction," *International Social Science Journal*, 59:S1, 7–17.

Bhagwati, J. (2013, July 23) "Why Amartya Sen Is Wrong," *Live Mint*.

Bhagwati, J. and A. Panagariya (2013) *Why Growth Matters: How Economic Growth in India Reduced Poverty and the Lessons for Other Developing Countries*. Public Affairs.

Bhaskaram, P. (2002) "Micronutrient Malnutrition, Infection, and Immunity: An Overview," *Nutrition Reviews*, 60:S5, 40–45.

Bhutta, Z.A. et al. (2013) "Evidence-Based Interventions for Improvement in Maternal and Child Nutrition: What Can Be Done and At What Cost?" *Lancet*, 382:9890, 452–477.

Black, R.E. et al. (2013) "Maternal and Child Undernutrition and Overweight in Low-Income and Middle-Income Countries," *Lancet*, 382:9890, 427–451.

Blackburn, S. (2001) *Being Good*. Oxford University Press.

Blimpo, M.P. and D.K. Evans (2011) "School-Based Management and Educational Outcomes: Lessons from a Randomized Field Experiment," Unpublished Paper, World Bank.

Bloom, D.E. (2011) "7 Billion and Counting," *Science*, 333:6042, 562–569.

Blundell, R. (1988) "Consumer Behavior: Theory and Empirical Evidence," *Economic Journal*, 98:389, 16–65.

Boelee, E., M. Yohannes, J.-N. Poda, M. McCartney, P. Cecchi, S. Kibret, F. Hagos, and H. Laamrani (2013) "Options for Water Storage and Rainwater Harvesting to Improve Health and Resilience against Climate Change in Africa," *Regional Environmental Change*, 13:3, 509–519.

Bok, S. (2002) *Common Values*. University of Missouri Press.

Boo, K. (2012) *Behind the Beautiful Forevers: Life, Death, and Hope in a Mumbai Undercity*. Random House.

Bouis, H.E., C. Holtz, B. McClafferty, J.V. Meenakshi, and W.H. Pfeiffer (2011) "Biofortification: A New Tool to Reduce Micronutrient Malnutrition," *Food and Nutrition Bulletin*, 31:S1, S31–S40.

Bourdon, J., M. Frölich, and K. Michaelowa (2010) "Teacher Shortages, Teacher Contracts and Their Effects on Education in Africa," *Journal of the Royal Statistical Society Series A*, 173:1, 93–116.

Bourguignon, F. (2003) "The Growth Elasticity of Poverty Reduction: Explaining Heterogeneity across Countries and Time Periods," in T.S. Eicher and S.J. Turnovsky (eds.), *Inequality and Growth: Theory and Policy Implications*. MIT Press, 3–26.

Bradbrook, A.J. and J.G. Gardham (2006) "Placing the Access to Energy Services in a Human Rights Framework," *Human Rights Quarterly*, 28:2, 389–415.

Braimah, I. and O. Amponsah (2012) "Causes and Effects of Frequent and Unannounced Electricity Blackouts on the Operations of Micro and Small Scale Industries in Kumasi," *Journal of Sustainable Development*, 5:2, 17–36.

Brass, J.N., S. Carley, L.M. MacLean, and E. Baldwin (2012) "Power for Development: A Review of Distributed Generation Projects in the Developing World," *Annual Review of Environment and Resources*, 37, 107–136.

Braybrooke, D. (1987) *Meeting Needs*. Princeton University Press.

Braybrooke, D. (2005) "Where Does the Moral Force of the Concept of Needs Reside and When?" *Royal Institute of Philosophy Supplement*, 57, 209–228.

Brazilian, M., I. Onyeji, M. Liebreich, I. MacGill, J. Chase, J. Shah, D. Gielen, D. Arent, D. Landfear, and S. Zhengrong (2013) "Reconsidering the Economics of Photovoltaic Power," *Renewable Energy*, 53, 329–338.

Brazilian, M., H. Rogner, M. Howells, S. Hermann, D. Arent, D. Gielen, P. Steduto, A. Mueller, P. Komor, R.S.J. Tol, and K.K. Yumkella (2011) "Considering the Energy, Water and Food Nexus: Towards an Integrated Modelling Approach," *Energy Policy*, 39:12, 7896–7906.

Bridge to India (2014) *Beehives or Elephants: How Should India Drive Its Solar Transformation?* Bridge to India.

Broome, J. (1991) "Utility," *Philosophy and Economics*, 7:1, 1–12.

Bruns, B., D. Filmer, and H.A. Patrinos (2011) *Making Schools Work: New Evidence on Accountability Reforms*. World Bank.

Buchanan, A.E. (1984) "The Right to a Decent Minimum of Health Care," *Philosophy and Public Affairs*, 13:1, 55–78.

Buckley, R.M. and J. Kalarickal (2005) "Housing Policy in Developing Countries: Conjectures and Refutations," *World Bank Research Observer*, 20:2, 233–257.

Buckley, R.M. and J. Kalarickal (2006) *Thirty Years of World Bank Shelter Lending: What Have We Learned?* World Bank.

Buhaug, H. and K.S. Gleditsch (2008) "Contagion or Confusion? Why Conflicts Cluster in Space," *International Studies Quarterly*, 52:2, 215–233.

Bukhari, S.K.S. et al. (2010) "Essential Medicines Management During Emergencies in Pakistan," *Eastern Mediterranean Health Journal*, 16:S, S106–S113.

Bundy, D., C. Burbano, M. Grosh, A. Gelli, M. Jukes, and L. Drake (2009) *Rethinking School Feeding: Social Safety Nets, Child Development, and the Education Sector*. World Bank.

Burki, T. (2016) "Yemen's Neglected Health and Humanitarian Crisis," *Lancet*, 387:10020, 734–735.

Burney, J., L. Woltering, M. Burke, R. Naylor, and D. Pasternak (2010) "Solar-Powered Drip Irrigation Enhances Food Security' in in the Sudano-Sahel," *Proceedings of the National Academy of Sciences*, 107:5, 1848–1853.

Busch-Geertsema, V., D. Culhane, and S. Fitzpatrick (2015) "A Global Framework to Understanding and Measuring Homelessness." Institute for Global Homelessness.

Buys, P., U. Deichmann, C. Meisner, T.T. That, and D. Wheeler (2007) "County Stakes in Climate Change Negotiations: Two Dimensions of Vulnerability," World Bank Policy Research Working Paper 4300.

Cain, A. (2007) "Housing Microfinance in Post-Conflict Angola: Overcoming Socioeconomic Exclusion through Land Tenure and Access to Credit," *Environment and Urbanization*, 19(2), 361–390.

Cairncross, S. et al. (2010) "Water, Sanitation and Hygiene for the Prevention of Diarrhoea," *International Journal of Epidemiology*, 39:S1, 193–205.

Canagarajah, S. and X. Ye (2001) "Public Health and Education Spending in Ghana 1992-1998: Issues of Equity and Efficiency," World Bank Policy Research Working Paper 2579, World Bank.

Cardwell, D. and C. Krauss (2017, January 14) "A Big Test for Batteries," *The New York Times*.

Casabonne, U. and C. Kenny (2012) "The Best Things in Life are (Nearly) Free: Technology, Knowledge, and Global Health," *World Development*, 40:1, 21–35.

Chapman, A.R. (2007) "The Status of Efforts to Monitor Economic, Social, and Cultural Rights," in S. Hertel and L. Minkler (eds.), *Economic Rights: Conceptual, Measurement, and Policy Issues*. Cambridge University Press, 143–164.

Chaudhury, N., J. Hammer, M. Kremer, K. Muralidharan, and F.H. Rogers (2006) "Missing in Action: Teacher and Health Worker Absence in Developing Countries," *Journal of Economic Perspectives*, 20:1, 91–116.

Chilcot, J. (2016) *The Report of the Iraq Inquiry*. http://www.iraqinquiry.org.uk.

Chun, N. (2014) "Increasing Access to Water Services: A Cost-Recoverable Pricing Model," *International Journal of Water Resources Development*, 30:4, 662–679.

Clark, P. (2012, August 9) "Environment: The End of the Line," *Financial Times*.

Clark, P. (2013, September 22) "IPCC Head Warns on Melting Himalayan Glaciers," *Financial Times*.

Coady, D., I. Parry, L. Sears, and B. Shang (2015) "How Large Are Global Energy Subsidies?" International Monetary Fund Working Paper WP/15/105.

Coffey, D. (2015) "Pregnancy Body Mass and Weight Gain in India and Sub-Saharan Africa," *Proceedings of the National Academy of Sciences*, 112:11, 3302–3307.

Cohen, D. and M. Soto (2007) "Growth and Human Capital: Good Data, Good Results," *Journal of Economic Growth*, 12:1, 51–76.

Cohen, J. (2004) "Minimalism about Human Rights? The Most We Can Hope For?" *Journal of Political Philosophy*, 12:2, 190–213.

Cole, S.A. and A.N. Fernando (2012) "The Value of Advice: Evidence from Mobile Phone-Based Agricultural Extension," Harvard Business School Working Paper, No. 13–047.

Collier, P. and A. Hoeffler (2004) "Greed and Grievance in Civil War," *Oxford Economic Papers*, 56:4, 563–595.

Commission on Growth and Development (2008) *The Growth Report: Strategies for Sustained Growth and Inclusive Development*. World Bank.

Contreras, D., P. Sepúlveda, and S. Bustos (2010) "When Schools Are the Ones that Choose: The Effects of Screening in Chile," *Social Science Quarterly*, 91:5, 1349–1368.

Copp, D. (1992) "The Right to an Adequate Standard of Living: Justice, Autonomy, and the Basic Needs," *Social Philosophy and Policy*, 9:1, 231–261.

Cord, L.J. (2007) "Overview," in T. Besley and L.J. Cord (eds.), *Delivering on the Promise of Pro-Poor Growth: Insights and Lessons from Country Exprirences*. World Bank, 1–27.

Corning, P.A. (2000) "Biological Adaptation in Human Societies: A 'Basic Needs' Approach," *Journal of Bioeconomics*, 2:1, 41–86.

Costanza, R. et al. (2007) "Quality of Life: An Approach Integrating Opportunities, Human Needs, and Subjective Wellbeing," *Ecological Economics*, 61:2–3, 267–276.

Cotula, L. (2012) "The International Political Economy of the Global Land Rush: A Critical Appraisal of Trends, Scale, Geography and Drivers," *Journal of Peasant Studies*, 39:3–4, 649–680.

Cowell, A. (2014, January 30) "Atonement for the Inventor of the AK-47," *The New York Times*.

Coyle, D. (2014) *GDP: A Brief But Affectionate History*. Princeton University Press.

Crocker, D.A. (2008) *The Ethics of Global Development: Agency, Capability, and Deliberative Democracy*. Cambridge University Press.

Currie, L. (1975) "Wants, Needs, Well-Being and Economic Growth," *Journal of Economic Studies*, 2:1, 47–59.

Cutler, D.M. and G. Miller (2005) "The Role of Public Health Improvements in Health Advances: The Twentieth-Century United States," *Demography*, 42:1, 1–22.

Daley, P. (2006) "Ethnicity and Political Violence in Africa: The Challenge to the Burundi State," *Political Geography*, 25:6, 657–679.

Davies, J.C. (1962) "Toward a Theory of Revolution," *American Sociological Review*, 27:1, 5–19.

Davis, D.E. (2004) *Discipline and Development: Middle Classes and Prosperity in East Asia and Latin America*. Cambridge University Press.

Dean, H. (2007) "Social Policy and Human Rights: Re-Thinking the Engagement," *Social Policy and Society*, 7:1, 1–12.

Dean, H. (2009) "Critiquing Capabilities: The Distractions of a Beguiling Concept," *Critical Social Policy*, 29:2, 261–273.

Dean, H. (2010) *Understanding Human Need: Social Issues, Policy and Practice*. Polity Press.

Deaton, A. and J. Muellbauer (1980) *Economics and Consumer Behavior*. Cambridge University Press.

de Brauw, A. and J. Hoddinott (2011) "Must Conditional Cash Transfer Programs Be Conditional To Be Effective? The Impact of Conditioning Transfers on School Enrollment in Mexico," *Journal of Development Economics*, 96:2, 359–370.

de Châtel, F. (2014) "The Role of Drought and Climate Change in the Syrian Uprising: Untangling the Triggers of the Revolution," *Middle Eastern Studies*, 50:4, 521–535.

de Janvry, A., F. Finan, E. Sadoulet, and R. Vakis (2006) "Can Conditional Cash Transfer Programs Serve as Safety Nets in Keeping Children at School and from Working When Exposed to Shocks?" *Journal of Development Economics*, 79:2, 349–373.

De la Fuente, A. and R. Doménech (2006) "Human Capital in Growth Regressions: How Much Difference Does Data Quality Make?" *Journal of the European Economic Association*, 4:1, 1–36.

del Rocío Sáenz, M., J.L. Bermúdez, and M. Acosta (2010) "Universal Coverage in a Middle Income Country: Costa Rica," World Health Report Background Paper, No. 11, World Health Organization.

Dembour, M.-B. (2010) "What Are Human Rights? Four Schools of Thought," *Human Rights Quarterly*, 32:1, 1–20.

De Schutter, O. (2010) "Report Submitted by the Special Rapporteur on the Right to Food," Human Rights Council, United Nations General Assembly.

de Soto, H. (2000) *The Mystery of Capital*. Basic Books.

Devarajan, S. (2014) "Why Should Governments Spend on Sanitation?" http://blogs.worldbank.org/futuredevelopment/.

Devarajan, S. and R. Reinikka (2004) "Making Services Work for Poor People," *Journal of African Economies*, 13:S1, 142–166.

Diamandis, P.H. and S. Kotler (2012) *Abundance: The Future Is Better Than You Think*. Free Press.

Diaz, R.J. and R. Rosenberg (2008) "Spreading Dead Zones and Consequences for Marine Ecosystems," *Science*, 321:5891, 926–929.

Díaz-González, F., A. Sumper, O. Gomis-Bellmont, and R. Villafáfila-Robles (2012) "A Review of Energy Storage Technologies for Wind Power Applications," *Renewable and Sustainable Energy Reviews*, 16, 2154–2171.

Di Gropello, E. (2006) "A Comparative Analysis of School-Based Management in Central America," World Bank Working Paper No. 72.

Doctors without Borders (2011) "No Way In: The Biggest Refugee Camp in the World Is Full."

Dolan, C.S., C.R. Ryus, S. Dopson, P. Montgomery, and L. Scott (2014) "A Blind Spot in Girls' Education: Menarche and Its Web of Exclusion in Ghana," *Journal of International Development*, 26:5, 643–657.

Donachie, P. and J. Krahn (2007) "Report on Microbiological Tests Carried out on LifeSaver Systems," London School of Hygiene and Tropical Medicine.

Dovlo, D. (2004) "Using Mid-Level Cadres as Substitutes for Internationally Mobile Health Professionals in Africa: A Desk Review," *Human Resources for Health*, 2:7, 1–12.

Doyal, L. (2001) "The Moral Foundations of the Clinical Duties of Care: Needs, Duties and Human Rights," *Bioethics*, 15:5/6, 520–535.

Doyal, L. and I. Gough (1991) *A Theory of Need*. Guilford Press.

Doyle, A. (2016, September 6) "Global Coal Power Plans Fall in 2016, Led by China, India: Study," *Reuters*.

Drakopoulos, S.A. (1994) "Hierarchical Choice in Economics," *Journal of Economic Surveys*, 8:3, 133–153.

Dreher, A., P. Nunnenkamp, and R. Thiele (2008) "Does Aid for Education Educate Children? Evidence from Panel Data," *World Bank Economic Review*, 22:2, 291–314.

Drèze, J. and A. Sen (2013) *An Uncertain Glory: India and Its Contradictions*. Princeton University Press.

Duflo, E., P. Dupas, and M. Kremer (2015) "School Governance, Teacher Incentives, and Pupil-Teacher Ratios: Experimental Evidence from Kenyan Primary Schools," *Journal of Public Economics*, 123, 92–110.

Duflo, E., R. Hanna, and S.P. Ryan (2012) "Incentives Matter: Getting Teachers to Come to School," *American Economic Review*, 102:4, 1241–1278.

Easterly, W.R. (2001) *The Elusive Quest for Growth*. MIT Press.

Easterly, W.R. (2003) "The Political Economy of Growth without Development: A Case Study of Pakistan," in D. Rodrik (ed.), *In Search of Prosperity: Analytic Narratives on Economic Growth*. Princeton University Press, 439–472.

Easterly, W.R. (2009, October 12) "Human Rights are the Wrong Basis for Healthcare," *Financial Times*.

Easterly, W. (2015, September 28) "The SDGs Should Stand for Senseless, Dreamy, Garbled," *Foreign Policy*.

The Economist (2007, March 22) "Stand Up for Your Rights".

The Economist (2008, August 21) "Running Dry: Business and Water."

The Economist (2010, September 2) "Power to the People".

The Economist (2011a, February 26) "The 9 Billion-People Question: A Special Report on Feeding the World."

The Economist (2011b, March 26) "Hidden Hunger: Agriculture and Nutrition."

The Economist (2013a, January 5) "No Sweat: Air Conditioning."

The Economist (2013b, October 12) "Water: All Dried Up."

The Economist (2014a, February 22) "In Deep Water: Governing the High Seas."

The Economist (2014b, February 22) "How to Keep Stomachs Full: Food Security in the Gulf."

The Economist (2014c, March 8) "African Demography: The Dividend is Delayed."

The Economist (2014d, April 26) "Nor Any Drop to Drink: Water in Brazil."

The Economist (2014e, May 31) "Cool Development: Fridge Ownership."

The Economist (2014f, June 14) "Energy Subsidies: Scrap Them."

The Economist (2014g, October 4) "Indonesian Politics: The Empire Strikes Back."

The Economist (2014h, November 29) "Feast and Famine: Malnutrition, Nutrients and Obesity."

The Economist (2014i, December 20) "Empire of the Pig: Swine in China."

The Economist (2014j, December 20) "Reservoir Hogs: São Paulo's Water Crisis."

The Economist (2015a, February 21) "The Poverty Alert."

The Economist (2015b, March 28) "Development: The 169 Commandments."

The Economist (2015c, August 1) "The $1-a-Week School."

The Economist (2015d, August 1) "Low-Cost Private Schools."

The Economist (2015e, August 15) "The Environment: Mapping the Invisible Scourge."

The Economist (2015f, September 19) "The Sustainable Development Goals."

The Economist (2016a, January 9) "Power Hungry: Electricity in Africa."

The Economist (2016b, February 27) "Ending Energy Poverty: Power to the Powerless."

The Economist (2016c, March 12) "African Agriculture: A Green Revolution."

The Economist (2016d, September 3) "Hunger Games: Nigeria's Food Crisis."

The Economist (2016e, October 29) "Africa Unplugged: Off-Grid Solar Power."

The Economist (2017a, April 1) "Famine Stalks Africa and Yemen."

The Economist (2017b, August 12) "Briefing Batteries."

The Economist (2017c, August 26) "Health Care: The Right Treatment."

The Economist (2017d, September 2) "Protein-Rich Diets: Feed As Well As Food."

The Economist (2017e, September 2) "Public Housing in Ethiopia."

The Economist (2017f, September 16) "Generation Games: The Gates Report."

The Economist (2017g, October 14) "Land to the Tiller."

Ehrlich, P.R. (1968) *The Population Bomb: Population Control or Race to Oblivion*. Sierra Club and Ballantine Books.

Ekman, B., N.T. Liem, H.A. Duc, and H. Axelson (2008) "Health Insurance Reform in Vietnam: A Review of Recent Development and Future Challenges," *Health Policy and Planning*, 23:4, 252–263.

Ellsworth, P.T. (1950) *The International Economy: Its Structure and Operation*. Macmillan.

Endres, A.M. (1991) "Marshall's Analysis of Economising Behavior with Particular Reference to the Consumers," *European Economic Review*, 35:2–3, 333–341.

Erdbrink, T. (2014, January 30) "Its Great Lake Shriveled, Iran Confronts Crisis of Water Supply," *The New York Times*.

Eskeland, G.S. and D. Filmer (2007) "Autonomy, Participation and Learning: Findings from Argentine Schools, and Implications for Decentralization," *Education Economics*, 15:1, 103–127.

Etzioni, A. (2017, January 14) "Out with Regime Change," *The Economist*, p. 14.

Eyal, N. and S.A. Hurst (2008) "Physician Brain Drain: Can Nothing Be Done?" *Public Health Ethics*, 1:2, 180–192.

Ezz, M. and N. Arafat (2015, August 4) "The Water Crisis Taking Hold across Egypt," *Guardian*.

Falkenmark, M., J. Lundquist, and C. Widstrand (1989) "Macro-scale Water Scarcity Requires Micro-scale Approaches: Aspects of Vulnerability in Semi-arid Development," *Natural Resources Forum*, 13:4, 258–267.

Ferguson, R., W. Wilkinson, and R. Hill (2000) "Electricity Use and Economic Development," *Energy Policy*, 28:13, 923–934.

Ferraz, C., F. Finan, and D.B. Moreira (2012) "Corrupting Learning: Evidence from Missing Federal Education Funds in Brazil," *Journal of Public Economics*, 96:9–10, 712–726.

Fields, E. (2005) "Property Rights and Investment in Urban Slums," *Journal of the European Economic Association*, 3:2, 279–290.

Filmer, D., J.S. Hammer, and L.H. Pritchett (2000) "Weak Links in the Chain: A Diagnosis of Health Policy in Poor Countries," *World Bank Research Observer*, 15:2, 199–224.

Fisher, K., E.T. Mansur, and Q. Wang (2012) "Costly Blackouts? Measuring Productivity and Environmental of Electricity Shortages," NBER Working Paper 17741.

Fiszbein, A. and N. Schady (2009) *Conditional Cash Transfers: Reducing Present and Future Poverty*. World Bank.

Flammini, A., M. Puri, L. Pluschke, and O. Dubois (2014) *Walking the Nexus Talk: Assessing the Water-Energy-Food Nexus in the Context of the Sustainable Energy for All Initiative*. Food and Agriculture Organization.

Food and Agriculture Organization (2005) *The Right to Food: Voluntary Guidelines.*

Food and Agriculture Organization (2006) *World Agriculture towards 2030/2050.*

Food and Agriculture Organization (2008) *Water for the Rural Poor: Interventions for Improving Livelihoods in Sub-Saharan Africa.*

Food and Agricultural Organization (2009) *How to Feed the World in 2050.*

Food and Agriculture Organization (2011a) *Global Food Losses and Food Waste: Extent, Causes and Prevention.*

Food and Agriculture Organization (2011b) *Climate Change, Water and Food Security.*

Food and Agriculture Organization (2012a) *World Agriculture towards 2030/2050: The 2012 Revision.*

Food and Agriculture Organization (2012b) *The State of World Fisheries and Aquaculture.*

Food and Agriculture Organization (2013) *The State of Food Insecurity in the World 2013.*

Food and Agriculture Organization (2014) *The State of Food Insecurity in the World 2014.*

Food and Agriculture Organization (2015) *The State of Food Insecurity in the World 2015.*

Frimpong, J., D. Okoye, and R. Pongou (2016) "Economic Growth, Health Care Reform, and Child Nutrition in Ghana," *Journal of African Development*, 18:2, 41–60.

Frison, E.A., I.F. Smith, T. Johns, J. Cherfas, and P.B. Eyzagguire (2006) "Agricultural Diversity, Nutrition, and Health: Making a Difference to Hunger and Nutrition in the Developing World," *Food and Nutrition Bulletin*, 27:2, 167–179.

Frost, E. and M. Nowak (2014) "Inclusive Security, Inclusive Cities," Geneva Declaration on Armed Violence and Development Policy Paper 1.

Fuchs, M. (2012, September 6) "Qatar's Next Big Purchase: A Farming Sector," *Reuters.*

Fuchs, T. and L. Wößmann (2007) "What Accounts for International Differences in Student Performance? A Re-examination Using PISA Data," *Empirical Economics*, 32:2–3, 433–464.

Fukuyama, F. (2005) "Nation Building and the Failure of Institutional Memory," in F. Fukuyama (ed.), *Nation Building: Beyond Afghanistan and Iraq*. Johns Hopkins University Press, 1–16.

Fukuyama, F. (2009) "International Institutional Transfer," in K.A. Reinert, R.S. Rajan, A.J. Glass and L.S. Davis (eds.), *The Princeton Encyclopedia of the World Economy*. Princeton University Press, 669–673.

Fumagalli, R. (2013) "The Futile Search for True Utility," *Economics and Philosophy*, 29:3, 325–347.

Galiani, S., P. Gertler, and E. Schargrodsky (2005) "Water for Life: The Impact of Privatization of Water Services on Child Mortality," *Journal of Political Economy*, 113:1, 83–120.

Galiani, S., P. Gertler, and E. Schargrodsky (2008) "School Decentralization: Helping the Good Get Better, But Leaving the Poor Behind," *Journal of Public Economics*, 92:10–11, 2106–2120.

Galiani, S. and E. Schargrodsky (2010) "Property Rights for the Poor: Effects of Land Titling," *Journal of Public Economics*, 94:9, 700–729.

Gates, B. (2010, November 30) "The Poor Need Aid, Not Flawed Theories," https://gatesnotes.com.

Gelb, A. and C. Decker (2012) "Cash at Your Fingertips: Biometric Technology for Transfers in Resource-Rich Countries," *Review of Policy Research*, 29:1, 91–117.

Gemenne, F. (2015) "One Good Reason to Speak of 'Climate Refugees,'" *Forced Migration Review*, 49, 70–71.

Geneva Declaration on Armed Violence and Development (2011) *Global Burden of Armed Violence 2011.*

Geneva Declaration on Armed Violence and Development (2015) *Global Burden of Armed Violence 2015.*

Georgescu-Roegen, N. (1954) "Choice, Expectations, and Measurability," *Quarterly Journal of Economics*, 68:4, 503–534.

Gerland, P. et al. (2014) "World Population Stabilization Unlikely This Century," *Science*, 346:6206, 234–237.

Ghosh, J. (2010) "The Unnatural Coupling: Food and Global Finance," *Journal of Agrarian Change*, 10:1, 72–86.

Ghosh, S. (2002) "Electricity Consumption and Economic Growth in India," *Energy Policy*, 30:2, 125–129.

Ghuman, S. and C. Lloyd (2010) "Teacher Absence as a Factor in Gender Inequalities in Access to Primary Schooling in Rural Pakistan," *Comparative Education Review*, 54:4, 539–554.

Giansiracusa, A. (2010) "Coping with Scarcity: Saudi Arabia and Water," Stimson Center, December.

Gilbert, A. (2016) "Rental Housing: The International Experience," *Habitat International*, 54:3, 173–181.

Gleick, P.H. (1996) "Basic Water Requirements for Human Activities: Meeting Basic Needs," *Water International*, 21:2, 83–92.

Gleick, P.H. (1998) "The Human Right to Water," *Water Policy*, 1:5, 487–503.

Glewwe, P., N. Ilias, and M. Kremer (2010) "Teacher Incentives," *American Economic Journal: Applied Economics*, 2:3, 205–227.

Glewwe, P. and A.L. Kassouf (2012) "The Impact of the Bolsa Escola/Familia Conditional Cash Transfer Program on Enrollment, Dropout Rates and Grade Promotion in Brazil," *Journal of Development Economics*, 97:2, 505–517.

Glewwe, P., M. Kremer, and S. Moulin (2009) "Many Children Left Behind: Textbooks and Test Scores in Kenya," *American Economic Journal: Applied Economics*, 1:1, 112–135.

Glewwe, P., E. Maïga, and H. Zheng (2014) "The Contribution of Education to Economic Growth, with Special Attention and an Application to Sub-Saharan Africa," *World Development*, 59, 379–393.

Godfray, H.C.J. et al. (2010) "Food Security: The Challenge of Feeding 9 Billion People," *Science*, 327, 812–818.

Goldemberg, J., T.B. Johansson, A.K.N. Reddy, and R.H. Williams (1985) "Basic Needs and Much More with One Kilowatt Per Capita," *Ambio*, 14:4/5, 190–200.

Goldin, I. (2014) "Introduction," in I. Goldin (ed.), *Is the Planet Full?* Oxford University Press.

Goldin, I. and K.A. Reinert (2010) "Ideas, Development and Globalization," *Canadian Journal of Development Studies*, 29:3–4, 329–348.

Goldin, I. and K.A. Reinert (2012) *Globalization for Development: Meeting New Challenges*. Oxford University Press.

Goldin, I., K.A. Reinert, and J.H. Beverinotti (2012) "Policies for Globalization and Development: Four Examples," *Journal of International Commerce, Economics and Policy*, 3:1, 1–17.

Goldstein, J.S. (1985) "Basic Human Needs: The Plateau Curve," *World Development*, 13:5, 595–609.

Goldstone, J. (2002) "Population and Security: How Demographic Change Can Lead to Violent Conflict," *Journal of International Affairs*, 56:1, 3–21.

Goodhart, M. (2007) "'None So Poor That His Is Compelled to Sell Himself': Democracy, Subsistence, and Basic Income," in S. Hertel and L. Minkler (eds.), *Economic Rights: Conceptual, Measurement, and Policy Issues*. Cambridge University Press, 94–114.

Gopalan, S. and R. Rajan (2016) "Has Foreign Aid Been Effective in the Water Supply and Sanitation Sector? Evidence from Panel Data," *World Development*, 85, 84–104.

Gould, C. (2004) *Globalizing Democracy and Human Rights*. Cambridge University Press.

Grassini, P., K.M. Eskridge, and K.G. Cassman (2013) "Distinguishing between Yield Advances and Yield Plateaus in Historical Crop Production Trends," *Nature Communications*, 4:2918, 1–11.

Grey, D. and C.W. Sadoff (2007) "Sink or Swim? Water Security for Growth and Development," *Water Policy*, 9:6, 545–571.

Griffin, J. (1986) *Well-Being: Its Meaning, Measurement, and Moral Importance*. Clarendon Press.

The Guardian (2012, August 27) "Time Running Out for Solutions of Yemen's Water Crisis."

Guengant, J.-P. and J. May (2013) "African Demography," *Global Journal of Emerging Market Economies*, 5:3, 215–267.

Gupta, J., R. Ahlers, and L. Ahmed (2010) "The Human Right to Water: Moving Toward Consensus in a Fragmented World," *Review of European Community and International Environmental Law*, 19:3, 294–305.

Gwatkin, D.R., A. Wagstaff, and A.S. Yazbeck (2005) "What Did the Reaching the Poor Studies Find?" in D.R. Gwatkin, A. Wagstaff, and A.S. Yazbeck (eds.) *Reaching the Poor with Health, Nutrition, and Population Services: What Works, What Doesn't, and Why*. World Bank, 47–64.

Haddad, L. and P. Isenman (2014) "Which Aid Spending Categories Have the Greatest Untapped Potential to Support the Reduction of Undernutrition? Some Ideas on Moving Forward," *Food and Nutrition Bulletin*, 35:2, 266–276.

Hagos, F., G. Jayasinghe, S.B. Awulachew, M. Loulseged, and A.D. Yilma (2012) "Agricultural Water Management and Poverty in Ethiopia," *Agricultural Economics*, 43:S1, 99–111.

Haidera, M. et al. (2011) "Water Scarcity and Climate Change Adaption for Yemen's Vulnerable Communities," *Local Environment*, 16:5, 473–488.

Hall, R. and C.I. Jones (1999) "Why Do Some Countries Produce So Much More Output per Worker than Others?" *Quarterly Journal of Economics*, 114:1, 83–116.

Halleröd, B. (2006) "Sour Grapes: Relative Deprivation, Adaptive Preferences and the Measurement of Poverty," *Journal of Social Policy*, 35:3, 371–390.

Hampshire, S. (1989) *Innocence and Experience*. Cambridge University Press.

Handa, S. and B. Davis (2006) "The Experience of Conditional Cash Transfers in Latin America and the Caribbean," *Development Policy Review*, 24:5, 515–536.

Hanjra, M.A. and E.M. Qureshi (2010) "Global Water Crisis and Future Food Security in an Era of Climate Change," *Food Policy*, 35:5, 365–377.

Hanuschek, E.A. and L. Woessmann (2008) "The Role of Cognitive Skills in Economic Development," *Journal of Economic Literature*, 46:3, 607–668.

Hanuschek, E.A. and L. Woessmann (2012) "Schooling, Educational Achievement, and the Latin America Growth Puzzle," *Journal of Development Economics*, 99:2, 497–512.

Harrod, R.F. (1936) "Utilitarianism Revised," *Mind*, 45:178, 137–156.

Harsani, J.C. (1977) "Morality and the Theory of Rational Behavior," *Social Research*, 44:4, 623–656.

Hart, S. and C. Christensen (2002) "The Great Leap: Driving Innovation from the Base of the Pyramid," *Sloan Management Review*, 44:1, 51–56.

Hausman, D. M. and M.S. McPherson (1993) "Taking Ethics Seriously: Economics and Contemporary Moral Philosophy," *Journal of Economic Literature*, 31:2, 671–731.

Heckman, J.J. (2008), "Schools, Skills and Synapses," *Economic Inquiry*, 46:3, 289–324.

Heilbroner, R.L. (1953) *The Worldly Philosophers*. Simon and Shuster.

Heinrich, C.J. (2007) "Demand and Supply-Side Determinants of Conditional Cash Transfer Program Effectiveness," *World Development*, 35:1, 121–143.

Henderson, J.V., A. Storeygard, and D.N. Weil (2012) "Measuring Economic Growth from Outer Space," *American Economic Review*, 101:2, 994–1028.

Hendrix, C.S. and I. Salehyan (2012) "Climate Change, Rainfall, and Social Conflict in Africa," *Journal of Peace Research*, 49:1, 35–50.

Hertel, S. and L. Minkler (2007) "Economic Rights: The Terrain," in S. Hertel and L. Minkler (eds.), *Economic Rights: Conceptual, Measurement, and Policy Issues*. Cambridge University Press, 1–35.

Hicks, J.R. (1969) "Preface- and a Manifesto," in K.J. Arrow and T. Scitovsky (eds.), *Readings in Welfare Economics*. Irwin, 95–99.

Hoekstra, A.Y. and A.K. Chapagain (2007) "Water Footprints of Nations: Water Use by People as a Function of Their Consumption Pattern," *Water Resource Management*, 21:1, 35–48.

Hogerzeil, H.V. (2006) "Essential Medicines and Human Rights: What Can They Learn from Each Other?" *Bulletin of the World Health Organization*, 84:5, 371–375.

Huchzermeyer, M. (2008) "Slum Upgrading in Nairobi within the Housing and Basic Services Market: A Housing Rights Concern," *Journal of Asian and African Studies*, 43:1, 19–39.

Hultman, L., J. Kathman, and M. Shannon (2013) "United Nations Peacekeeping and Civilian Protection in Civil War," *American Journal of Political Science*, 57:4, 875–891.

Hume, D. (1752) "Of the Balance of Trade," in *Political Discourses*. Kinkaid and Donaldson.

Hurka, T. (1999) "The Three Faces of Human Flourishing," *Social Philosophy and Policy*, 16:1, 44–71.

Hutton, G. and M. Varughese (2016) *The Costs of Meeting the 2016 Sustainable Development Goal Targets on Drinking Water, Sanitation, and Hygiene*. World Bank.

Ignatieff, M. (2001) *Human Rights as Politics and Idolatry*. Princeton University Press.

Inglehart, R. and P. Norris (2012) "The Four Horsemen of the Apocalypse: Understanding Human Security," *Scandinavian Political Studies*, 35:1, 71–96.

Ingraham, C. (2014, April 23) "1.6 Million Americans Don't Have Indoor Plumbing," *Washington Post*.

Ingram, B.L. and F. Malamud-Roam (2013) *The West without Water: What Past Floods, Droughts, and Other Climatic Clues Tell Us about Tomorrow*. University of California Press.

Inter-Academy Council. (2004) *Realizing the Promise and Potential of African Agriculture*.

Inter-Governmental Panel on Climate Change. (2014) *Climate Change 2014: Impacts, Adaption, and Vulnerability*.

Internal Displacement Monitoring Centre. (2015) *Global Overview 2015*.

International Energy Agency. (2010) *Energy Poverty: How To Make Modern Energy Access Universal?*

International Energy Agency. (2017) *World Energy Outlook 2017*.

International Labor Office. (1976) *Employment, Growth and Basic Needs: A One-World Problem*.

Islam, M.R., S. Mekhilef, and R. Saidur (2013) "Progress and Recent Trends of Wind Energy Technology," *Renewable and Sustainable Energy Reviews*, 21, 456–468.

Jacobs, D.E., J. Wilson, S. L. Dixon, J. Smith, and A. Evens (2009) "The Relationship of Housing and Population Health: A 30-Year Retrospective Analysis," *Environmental Health Perspectives*, 117:4, 597–604.

Jasper, C., T.-T. Le, and J. Bartram (2012) "Water and Sanitation in Schools: A Systematic Review of the Health and Educational Outcomes," *International Journal of Environmental Research and Public Health*, 9:8, 2772–2787.

Jeffords, C. (2013) "Constitutional Environmental Human Rights: A Descriptive Analysis of 142 National Constitutions," in L. Minler (ed.), *The State of Economic and Social Rights: A Global Overview*. Cambridge University Press, 329–364.

Jeffords, C. (2016) "On the Temporal Effects of Static Constitutional Environmental Rights Provisions on Access to Improved Sanitation Facilities and Water Resources," *Journal of Human Rights and the Environment*, 7:1, 74–110.

Jeffords, C. and F. Shah (2013) "On the Natural and Economic Difficulties of Fulfilling the Human Right to Water within a Neoclassical Economics Framework," *Review of Social Economy*, 71:1, 65–92.

Jenkins, M.W. and B. Scott (2007) "Behavior Indicators of Household Decision-Making and Demand for Sanitation and Potential Gains from Social Marketing in Ghana," *Social Science and Medicine*, 64:12, 2427–2442.

Jevons, W.S. (1965, originally 1905) *The Principles of Economics*. August M. Kelley.

Jomaa, L.H., E. McDonnell, and C. Probart (2011) "School Feeding Programs in Developing Countries: Impact on Children's Health and Educational Outcomes," *Nutrition Reviews*, 69:2, 83–98.

Joshi, S. and M.S. Khan (2010) "Aided Self-Help: The Million Houses Program: Revisiting the Issues," *Habitat International*, 34(3), 306–314.

Kaldor, M., M. Martin, and S. Selchow (2007) "Human Security: A New Strategic Narrative for Europe," *International Affairs*, 83:2, 273–288.

Kallis, G. and C. Zografos (2014) "Hydro-Climatic Change, Conflict and Security," *Climatic Change*, 123:1, 69–82.

Kant, I. (1938, orig. 1865) *Fundamental Principles of the Metaphysics of Ethics*. Longmans, Appleton-Century.

Kar, K. and R. Chambers (2008) *Handbook on Community-Led Total Sanitation*. Institute of Development Studies.

Karekezi, S., J. Kimani, and O. Onguru (2008) "Energy Access among the Urban Poor in Kenya," *Energy for Sustainable Development*, 12:4, 38–48.

Katona, P. and J. Katona-Apte (2008) "The Interaction between Nutrition and Infection," *Clinical Infectious Diseases*, 46:10, 1582–1588.

Kay, C. (2002) "Why East Asia Overtook Latin America: Agrarian Reform, Industrialization and Development," *Third World Quarterly*, 23:6, 1073–1102.

Keefer, P., N. Loayza, and R.R. Soares (2010) "Drug Prohibition and Developing Countries: Uncertain Benefits, Certain Costs," in P. Keefer and N. Loayza (eds.), *Innocent Bystanders: Developing Countries and the War on Drugs*. World Bank, 9–59.

Kenna, P. (2005) *Housing Rights and Human Rights*. FEANTSA.

Kenna, P. (2008) "Globalization and Housing Rights," *Indiana Journal of Global Legal Studies*, 15:2, 397–469.

Kenning, T. (2015) "India Releases State Targets for 40 GW Rooftop Solar by 2022," *PV Tech*, July 2.

Kenny, C. (2011) *Getting Better: Why Global Development Is Succeeding–And How We Can Improve the World Even More*. Basic Books.

Khattri, N., C. Ling, and S. Jha (2012) "The Effects of School-Based Management in the Philippines: An Initial Assessment Using Administrative Data," *Journal of Development Effectiveness*, 4:2, 277–295.

King, M.L. (1986) "Where Do We Go from Here? Chaos or Community?" in J.M. Washington (ed.), *A Testament of Hope: The Essential Writings and Speeches of Martin Luther King, Jr.* Harper, 555–633.

Klasen, S. (2002) "Low Schooling for Girls, Slower Growth for All? Cross-Country Evidence on the Effect of Gender Inequality in Education on Economic Development," *World Bank Economic Review*, 16:3, 345–373.

Klasen, S. and F. Lamanna (2009) "The Impact of Gender Inequality in Education and Employment on Economic Growth: New Evidence for a Panel of Countries," *Feminist Economics*, 15:3, 91–132.

Kollar, E. and A. Buyx (2013) "Ethics and Policy of Medical Brain Drain: A Review," *Swiss Medical Weekly*, 143, 1–8.

Komarulzaman, A., J. Smits, and E. de Jong (2014) "Clean Water, Sanitation and Diarrhoea in Indonesia: Effects of Household and Community Factors," *NiCE*, Working Paper 14-105.

Kosek, M. et al. (2013) "Fecal Markers of Intestinal Inflammation and Permeability Associated with the Subsequent Acquisition of Linear Growth Deficits in Infants," *American Journal of Tropical Medicine and Hygiene*, 88:2, 390–396.

Kotler, P. and N.R. Lee (2009) *Up and Out of Poverty: The Social Marketing Solution*. Wharton School Publishing.

Kremer, M., J. Leino, E. Miguel, and A.P. Zwane (2011) "Spring Cleaning: Rural Water Impacts, Valuation, and Property Rights Institutions," *Quarterly Journal of Economics*, 126:1, 145–205.

Krueger, A.B. and M. Lindahl (2001) "Education for Growth: Why and For Whom?" *Journal of Economic Literature*, 39:4, 1101–1136.

Lee, E. (2010) "Saudi Arabia and Desalination," *Harvard International Review*. December.

Leff, J. and E. LeBrun (2014) "Following the Thread: Arms and Ammunition Tracing in Sudan and South Sudan," Geneva Small Arms Survey Working Paper 32.

Lelieveld, J., J.S. Evans, M. Fnais, G. Giannadaki, and A. Pozzer (2015) "The Contribution of Outdoor Air Pollution Sources to Premature Mortality on a Global Scale," *Nature*, 525:7569, 367–371.

Levine, J.P. and S.A.T. Rizvi (2011) *Poverty, Work and Freedom: Political Economy and the Moral Order*. Cambridge University Press.

Lin, A. et al. (2013) "Household Environmental Conditions are Associated with Enteropathy and Impaired Growth in Rural Bangladesh," *American Journal of Tropical Medicine and Hygiene*, 89:1, 130–137.

Lisk, F. (1977) "Conventional Development Strategies and Basic Needs Fulfillment: A Reassessment of Objectives and Policies," *International Labour Review*, 115:2, 175–191.

Ljungman, D., J.G. Meara, and Y. Lin (2017, July 5) "Suturing a Divided World: How Providing Access to Surgery Drives Global Prosperity," *The Conversation*.

Loevinsohn, B. and A. Harding (2005) "Buying Results? Contracting for Health Service Delivery in Developing Countries," *Lancet*, 366:9481, 676–681.

Lomelí, E.V. (2008) "Conditional Cash Transfers as Social Policy in Latin America," *Annual Review of Sociology*, 34, 475–499.

Londoño, J.-L. and J. Frenk (1997) "Structured Pluralism: Toward an Innovative Model for Health System Reform in Latin America," *Health Policy*, 41:1, 1–36.

Luby, S., M. Agboatwalla, D. Feikin, J. Painter, W. Billhimer, A. Altaf, and R. Hoekstra (2005) "Effect of Handwashing on Child Health: A Randomised Control Trial," *Lancet*, 366:9481, 225–233.

Maas, P. (2001, October 21) "Emraz Khan Is Having a Bad Day," *The New York Times Magazine*.

Maddison, A. (1991) *Dynamic Forces in Capitalist Development: A Long-Run Comparative View*. Oxford University Press.

Maluccio, J.A. et al. (2009) "The Impact of Improving Nutrition during Early Childhood on Education among Guatemalan Adults," *Economic Journal*, 119:537, 734–763.

Mankiw, N.G., D. Romer, and D. Weil (1992) "A Contribution to the Empirics of Economic Growth," *Quarterly Journal of Economics*, 107:2, 407–438.

Marshall, A. (1949) *Principles of Economics*. Macmillan.

Martino, J. (2014, April 2) "Advances in Wind Turbine Technology: Improving Efficiency and Reducing Cost,' *Renewable Energy World*.

Marx, B., T. Stoker, and T. Suri (2013) "The Economics of Slums in the Developing World," *Journal of Economic Perspectives*, 27:4, 187–210.

Maslow, A.H. (1943) "A Theory of Human Motivation," *Psychological Review*, 50:4, 370–396.

Masood, S. (2015, February 12) "Starved for Energy, Pakistan Braces for a Water Crisis," *The New York Times*.

Matthews, A. (2014) "Trade Rules, Food Security and the Multilateral Trade Negotiations," *European Journal of Agricultural Economics* 41:3, 511–535.

McCartney, M. and V. Smakhtin (2010) "Water Storage in an Era of Climate Change: Addressing the Challenge of Increasing Rainfall Variability," International Water Management Institute.

McKinsey Global Institute. (2014) *A Blueprint for Addressing the Global Housing Challenge: Executive Summary*.

McMahon, W.W. (1998) "Education and Growth in East Asia," *Economics of Education Review*, 17:2, 159–172.

Mehta, P.S. and B. Chatterjee (2011) *Growth and Poverty: The Great Debate*. CUTS International.

Meier, B.M., G.L. Kayser, U.Q. Amjad, and J. Bartram (2013) "Implementing an Evolving Human Right through Water and Sanitation Policy," *Water Policy*, 15:1, 116–133.

Miller, C.M., M. Tsoka, and K. Reichert (2011) "The Impact of Social Cash Transfer Scheme on Food Security in Malawi," *Food Policy*, 36:2, 230–238.

Minkler, L. (2013) "Introduction: Why Economic and Social Rights," in L. Minkler (ed.), *The State of Economic and Social Rights: A Global Overview*. Cambridge University Press, 1–18.

Mishra, P. and D. Newhouse (2009) "Does Health Aid Matter?" *Journal of Health Economics*, 28, 855–872.

Mishra, S.N. and N.K. Sharma (1982) "Participation and Development: A Theoretical Framework," *Indian Journal of Political Science*, 43:2, 54–66.

Moore, G.E. (1903) *Principia Ethica*. Cambridge University Press.

Morrisson, C. and F. Murtin (2009) "The Century of Education," *Journal of Human Capital*, 3:1, 1–42.

Muggah, R. and K. Krause (2009) "Closing the Gap between Peace Operations and Post-Conflict Insecurity: Towards a Violence Reduction Agenda," *International Peacekeeping*, 16:1, 136–150.

Mukasa, A.D., E. Mutambatsere, Y. Arvanitis, and T. Triki (2013) "Development of Wind Energy in Africa," African Development Bank Working Paper Number 170.

Mullan, F. and S. Frehywot (2007) "Non-Physician Clinicians in 27 Sub-Saharan African Countries," *Lancet*, 370, 2158–2163.

Mun, T. (1924, orig. 1664) "England's Treasure by Foreign Trade," in A.E. Monroe (ed.) *Early Economic Thought*. Harvard University Press.

Muñoz Conde, M. (2011) *Calidad de Vida Urbana y Capacidad de Pago de Los Hogares Bogatanos*, Universidad Nacional de Colombia.

Muralidharan, K. and V. Sundararaman (2013) "Contract Teachers: Experimental Evidence from India," National Bureau of Economic Research Working Paper 19440.

Murtin, F. (2013) "Improving Education Quality in South Africa," OECD Economics Department Working Paper No. 1056.

Mutisya, E. and M. Yarime (2011) "Understanding the Grassroots Dynamics of Slums in Nairobi: The Dilemma of Kibera Informal Settlements," *International Transaction Journal of Engineering, Management and Applied Sciences and Technology*, 2:2, 197–213.

Nally, D. (2015) "Governing Precarious Lives: Land Grabs, Geopolitics, and 'Food Security,'" *Geographical Journal*, 181:4, 340–349.

Nandi, S.K., M.N. Hoque, H.R. Ghosh, and S.K. Roy (2012) "Potential of Wind and Solar Electricity Generation in Bangladesh," *Journal of Renewable Energy*, ID 40761, 10 pages.

Narula, S.K. (2014, April 28) "The Year Climate Change Closed Everest," *The Atlantic*.

Nenova, T. (2010) *Expanding Housing Finance to the Underserved in South Asia: Market Review and Forward Agenda*. World Bank.

Neset, T.-S.S. and D. Cordell (2012) "Global Phosphorus Scarcity: Identifying Synergies for a Sustainable Future," *Journal of the Science of Food and Agriculture* 92:1, 2–6.

New America Foundation. (2010) *Public Opinion in Pakistan's Tribal Regions*.

The New York Times (2017, January 19) "Freezing to Death at Europe's Door."

Ngaruko, F. and F. Nkurunziza (2002) "Explaining Growth in Burundi: 1960-2000," Center for the Study of African Economies, Oxford University, Working Paper.

Nichols, M. (2017, March 17) "South Sudan Government to Blame for Famine, Still Buying Arms, UN Report," *Reuters*.

North, D.C., J.J. Wallis, and B.R. Weingast (2009) *Violence and Social Orders: A Conceptual Framework for Interpreting Recorded Human History*. Cambridge University Press.

Nussbaum, M.C. (1997) "Capabilities and Human Rights," *Fordham Law Review*, 66, 273–300.

Nussbaum, M.C. (2000) *Women and Development: A Capabilities Approach*. Cambridge University Press.

Nussbaum, M.C. (2011) *Creating Capabilities: The Human Development Approach*. Harvard University Press.

Obeng, G.Y. and H.-D. Evers (2010) "Impact of Public Solar PV Electrification on Rural Microenterprises: The Case of Ghana," *Energy for Sustainable Development*, 14:3, 223–231.

Odhiambo, N.M. (2009) "Energy Consumption and Economic Growth Nexus in Tanzania: An ARDL Bounds Testing Approach," *Energy Policy*, 37:2, 617–622.

O'Donnell, O. (2007) "Access to Healthcare in Developing Countries: Breaking Down Demand Side Barriers," *Cadernos de Saúde Pública*, 23:12, 2820–2834.

Office of the United Nations High Commissioner for Human Rights. (n.d.) *Factsheet 21 (Rev.): The Right to Housing*.

Olshansky, S.J. et al. (2014) "A Potential Decline in Life Expectancy in the United States in the 21st Century," *New England Journal of Medicine*, 352:11, 1138–1145.

Olson, M. (1996) "Distinguished Lecture on Economics in Government: Big Bills Left on the Sidewalk: Why Some Nations are Rich, and Others Poor," *Journal of Economic Perspectives*, 10:2, 3–24.

Ombuor, R. (2016) "Power at Any Cost in Kenya's Kibera Slum," *Voice of America News*. http://www.voanews.com/a/power-any-cost-kenya-kibera-slum/3395757.html.

Omran, A.R. (1971) "The Epidemiological Transition: A Theory of the Epidemiology of Population Change," *The Milbank Memorial Fund Quarterly*, 49:4, 509–538.

Organization for Economic Cooperation and Development (2013) *Multilateral Aid Report*. Development Assistance Committee.

Orwell, G. (2001, orig. 1937) *The Road to Wigan Pier*. Penguin Modern Classics.

Osiatyński, W. (2007) "Needs-Based Approach to Social and Economic Rights," in S. Hertel and L. Minkler (eds.), *Economic Rights: Conceptual, Measurement, and Policy Issues*. Cambridge University Press, 56–75.

Ostroff, J. (2016, December 2) "India Just Turned on the World's Biggest Solar Power Plant," *Huffington Post Canada*.

Paddy and Water Environment (2011), 9:1, 1–182.

Palit, D., D.K. Sarangi, and P.R. Krithica (2014) "Energising Rural India Using Distributed Generation: The Case of Solar Mini-Grids in Chhattisgarh State, India," in S.C. Bhattacharyya and D. Palit (eds.), *Mini-Grids for Rural Electrification of Developing Countries*. Springer, 313–342.

Pandey, P., S. Goyal, and V. Sundararaman (2009) "Community Participation in Public Schools: Impact of Information Campaigns in Three Indian States," *Education Economics*, 17:3, 355–375.

Parfitt, J., M. Barthel, and S. Macnaughton (2010) "Food Waste within Food Supply Chains: Quantification and Potential for Change to 2050," *Philosophical Transactions of the Royal Society B*, 365, 3065–3081.

Paris, R. (2001) "Human Security: Paradigm Shift or Hot Air," *International Security*, 26:2, 87–102.

Parsons, T. (1931) "Wants and Activities in Marshall," *Quarterly Journal of Economics*, 46:1, 101–140.

Patel, P. (2010, April 8) "Solar-Powered Desalination," *MIT Technology Review*.

Paterson, C., D. Mara, and T. Curtis (2007) "Pro-Poor Sanitation Technologies," *Geoforum*, 38:5, 901–907.

Patrinos, H.A. and G. Psacharopoulos (2011) "Education: Past, Present and Future Global Challenges," World Bank Policy Research Working Paper 5616.

Payne, G. (2001) "Lowering the Ladder: Regulatory Frameworks for Sustainable Development," *Development in Practice*, 11: 2/3, 308–318.

Payne, G., D.-L. Alain, and C. Rakodi (2009) "The Limits of Land Titling and Home Ownership," *Environment and Urbanization*, 21:2, 443–462.

Payne, G. and M. Majale (2004) *The Urban Housing Manual: Making Regulatory Frameworks Work for the Poor*. Earthscan.

Pechansky, R. and J.W. Thomas (1981) "The Concept of Access: Definition and Relationship to Consumer Satisfaction," *Medical Care*, 19:2, 127–140.

Peñate, B. and L. García-Rodríguez (2012) "Current Trends and Future Prospects in the Design of Seawater Reverse Osmosis Desalination," *Desalination*, 284, 1–8.

Peppercorn, I.G. and C. Taffin (2013) *Rental Housing: Lessons from International Experience and Policies for Emerging Markets*. World Bank.

Perehudoff, S.K., R.O. Laing, and H.V. Hogerzeil (2010) "Access to Essential Medicines in National Constitutions," *Bulletin of the World Health Organization*, 88:11, 800.

Peterson, E.W.F. (2009) *A Billion Dollars a Day: The Economics and Politics of Agricultural Subsidies*. Wiley-Blackwell.

Pigou, A.C. (1932) *The Economics of Welfare*. Macmillan.

Pio, A. (1994) "New Growth Theory and Old Development Problems," *Development Policy Review*, 12:3, 277–300.

Popkin, B.M. (1993) "Nutritional Patterns and Transitions," *Population and Development Review*, 19:1, 138–157.

Popkin, B.M., L.S. Adair, and S.W. Ng (2012) "The Global Nutrition Transition: The Pandemic of Obesity in Developing Countries," *Nutrition Reviews*, 70:1, 3–21.

Prahalad, C.K. and A. Hammond (2002) "Serving the World's Poor, Profitably," *Harvard Business Review*, September, 4-11.

Prahalad, C.K. and S.L. Hart (2002) "The Fortune at the Bottom of the Pyramid," *Strategy+Business*, 26:1, 54–67.

Prasad, N. (2006) "Privatization Results: Private Sector Participation in Water Services After 15 Years," *Development Policy Review*, 24:6, 669–692.

Preston, S. (1975) "The Changing Relationship between Mortality and Level of Economic Development," *Population Studies*, 29:2, 231–248.

Pretty, J. (2008) "Agricultural Sustainability: Concepts, Principles and Evidence," *Philosophical Transactions of the Royal Society B*, 363:1491, 447–465.

Pretty, J. et al. (2006) "Resource-Conserving Agriculture Increases Yields in Developing Countries," *Environmental Science and Technology*, 40:4, 1114–1119.

Pretty, J., C. Toulmin, and S. Williams (2011) "Sustainable Intensification in African Agriculture," *International Journal of Agricultural Sustainability*, 9:1, 5–24.

Pritchett, L. (2001) "Where Has All the Education Gone?" *World Bank Economic Review*, 15:3, 367–391.

Psacharopoulos, G. (1994) "Returns to Investment in Education: A Global Update," *World Development*, 22:9, 1325–1343.

Psacharopoulos, G. (2006) "The Value of Investment in Education: Theory, Evidence, and Policy," *Journal of Education Finance*, 32:2, 113–136.

Qu, X., P.J.J. Alvarez, and Q. Li (2013) "Applications of Nanotechnology in Water and Wastewater Treatment," *Water Research*, 47:12, 3931–3946.

Qureshi, M.E., M.A. Hanjra, and J. Ward (2013) "Impact of Water Scarcity in Australia on Global Food Security in an Era of Climate Change," *Food Policy*, 38, 136–145.

Rachman, G. (2012, March 26) "The West Has Lost Afghanistan," *Financial Times*.

Railton, P. (1986) "Facts and Values," *Philosophical Topics*, 14:2, 5–31.

Raleigh, C. (2010) "Political Marginalization, Climate Change, and Conflict in African Sahel States," *International Studies Review*, 12:1, 69–86.

Ranganathan, C.R., K. Palanisami, K.R. Kakumanu and A. Baulraj (2010) *Mainstreaming the Adaptations and Reducing the Vulnerability of the Poor Due to Climate Change*, Asian Development Bank Institute Working Paper No. 333, Asian Development Bank

Ram, R. (2013) "Income Elasticity of Poverty in Developing Countries: Updated Estimates from New Data," *Applied Economic Letters*, 20:6, 554–558.

Ramani, S.V., S. SadreGhazi, and G. Duysters (2012) "On the Diffusion of Toilets as Bottom of the Pyramid Innovation: Lessons from Sanitation Entrepreneurs," *Technological Forecasting and Social Change*, 79:4, 676–687.

Randolph, S, S. Fukuda-Parr, and T. Lawson-Remer (2010) "Economic and Social Rights Fulfilment Index: Country Scores and Rankings," *Journal of Human Rights*, 9:3, 230–261.

Randolph, S. and S. Hertel (2013) "The Right to Food: A Global Perspective," L. Minkler (ed.), *The State of Economic and Social Human Rights: A Global Perspective*. Cambridge University Press, 21–60.

Rao, N.D. and P. Baer (2012) "'Decent Living' Emissions: A Conceptual Framework," *Sustainability*, 4, 656–681.

Rao, N.D. and J. Min (forthcoming) "Decent Living Standards: Material Prerequisites for Human Wellbeing," *Social Indicators Research*.

Rawlings, L.B. and G.M. Rubio (2005) "Evaluating the Impacts of Conditional Cash Transfer Programs," *World Bank Research Observer*, 20:1, 29–55.

Ray, D. and N.B. Tarrow (1987) "Human Rights and Education: An Overview," in N.B. Tarrow (ed.), *Human Rights and Education*. Pergamon, 3–16.

Reinert, K.A. (1983) "Mathematical Programming Models for the Economic Design and Assessment of Wind Energy Conversion Systems," *Wind Engineering*, 7:1, 43–59.

Reinert, K.A. (2004) "Outcomes Assessment in Trade Policy Analysis: A Note on the Welfare Propositions of the 'Gains from Trade,'" *Journal of Economics Issues*, 38:4, 1067–1073.

Reinert, K.A. (2011) "No Small Hope: The Basic Goods Imperative," *Review of Social Economy*, 69:1, 55–76.

Reinert, K.A. (2014) "Water in Development Ethics: Basic Goods Considerations," *Global Water Forum*.

Reinert, K.A. (2015) "Food Security as Basic Goods Provision," *World Medical and Health Policy*, 7:3, 171–186.

Reinikka, R. and J. Svensson (2002) "Coping with Poor Public Capital," *Journal of Development Economics*, 69:1, 51–69.

Reinikka, R. and J. Svensson (2004) "Local Capture: Evidence from a Central Government Transfer Program in Uganda," *Quarterly Journal of Economics*, 119:2, 679–705.

Reinikka, R. and J. Svensson (2005) "Fighting Corruption to Improve Schooling: Evidence from a Newspaper Campaign in Uganda," *Journal of the European Economic Association*, 3:2/3, 259–267.

Reinikka, R. and J. Svensson (2011) "The Power of Information in Public Services: Evidence from Education in Uganda," *Journal of Public Economics*, 95:7–8, 956–966.

Ridley, M. (2010) *The Rational Optimist*. Harper.

Rimawi, B.H., M. Mirdamani, and J.F. John (2014) "Infections and Homelessness: Risks of Increased Infectious Diseases in Displaced Women," *World Medical and Health Policy*, 6:2, 118–132.

Rondinelli, D.A. (1990) "Housing the Urban Poor in Developing Countries: The Magnitude of Housing Deficiencies and the Failure of Conventional Strategies are World-Wide Problems," *American Journal of Economics and Sociology*, 49:2, 153–166.

Rodrik, D., A. Subramanian, and F. Trebbi (2004) "Institutions Rule: The Primacy of Institutions over Geography and Integration in Economic Development," *Journal of Economic Growth*, 9:2, 131–165.

Rodrik, D. (2007) *One Economics, Many Recipes: Globalization, Institutions and Economic Growth*. Princeton University Press.

Roma, E. and I. Pugh (2012) *Toilets for Health*. London School of Hygiene and Tropical Medicine.

Rubenstein, R. (2001) "Basic Human Needs: The Next Steps for Theory Development," *International Journal of Peace Studies*, 6:1, 51–59.

Sachs, J. (2012) "From Millennium Development Goals to Sustainable Development Goals," *Lancet*, 379:9832, 2206–2211.

Sa'Da, C.A. and S. Bianchi (2014) "Perspectives of Refugees in Dadaab on Returning to Somalia," *Forced Migration Review*, 45, 88–89.

Samar, H.A., S.R. Khandker, M. Azaduzzaman, and M. Yunus (2013) "The Benefits of Solar Home Systems: An Analysis from Bangladesh," World Bank Policy Research Paper 6724.

Santiso, J. (2007) *Latin America's Political Economy of the Possible*. MIT Press.

Sastry, R.K., A. Shrivastava, and N.H. Rao (2013) "Prospects of Nanotechnology for Enhancing Water and Nutrition Security," *Asian Biotechnology and Development Review*, 15:3, 7–35.

Save the Children. (2017) *Invisible Wounds: The Impact of Six Years of War on the Mental Health of Syria's Children*.

Schleussner, C.-F., D.F. Donges, R.V. Donner, and H.C. Schellnhuber (2016) "Armed-Conflict Risks Enhanced by Climate-Related Disasters in Ethnically-Fractionalized Countries," *Proceedings of the National Academy of Sciences*, 113:3, 9216–9221.

Schmidt, W.-P. and S. Cairncross (2009) "Household Water Treatment in Poor Populations: Is There Enough Evidence for Scaling Up Now?" *Environmental Science and Technology*, 43:4, 986–992.

Schultz, T.P. (2002) "Why Governments Should Invest More to Educate Girls," *World Development*, 30:2, 207–225.

Schultz, T.P. (2004) "School Subsidies for the Poor: Evaluating the Mexican Progressa Poverty Program," *Journal of Development Economics*, 74:1, 199–250.

Seeley, E. (1992) "Human Needs and Consumer Economics: The Implications of Maslow's Theory of Motivation for Consumer Expenditure Patterns," *Journal of Socio-Economics*, 21:4, 303–324.

Sellar, S. and B. Lingard (2014) "The OECD and the Expansion of PISA: New Global Models of Governance in Education," *British Educational Research Journal*, 40:6, 917–936.

Sen, A. (1981) *Poverty and Famines: An Essay on Entitlement and Deprivation*. Clarendon Press.

Sen, A. (1987) *The Standard of Living*. Cambridge University Press.

Sen, A. (1989) "Development as Capability Expansion," *Journal of Development Planning*, 19, 41–58.

Sen, A. (2006) *Identity and Violence: The Illusion of Destiny*. Norton.

Sen, A. (2013, July 20) "Amartya Sen Responds," *The Economist*.

Seuss, D. (1954) *Horton Hears a Who*. Random House.

Shelley, L. (2017) "Illicit Trade," in K.A. Reinert (ed.), *Handbook of Globalisation and Development*. Edward Elgar, 100–114.

Shonkoff, J.P. et al. (2012) "The Lifelong Effects of Early Childhood Adversity and Toxic Stress," *Pediatrics*, 121:1, 232–246.

Shue, H. (1996) *Basic Rights: Subsistence, Affluence, and U.S. Foreign Policy*. Princeton University Press.

Singh, K. (2015, April 23) "Education is a Basic Human Right—Which is Why Private Schools Must Be Resisted," *The Guardian*.

Smedshaug, C.A. (2010) *Feeding the World in the 21st Century: A Historical Analysis of Agriculture and Society*. Anthem Press.

Smith, A. (1937, orig. 1776) *The Wealth of Nations*. Modern Library.

Sobel, D. (1997) "On the Subjectivity of Welfare," *Ethics*, 107:3, 501–508.

Solow, R. (1956) "A Contribution to the Theory of Economic Growth," *Quarterly Journal of Economics*, 70:1, 65–94.

Sommer, M. (2010) "Putting Menstrual Hygiene Management on to the School Water and Sanitation Agenda," *Waterlines*, 29:4, 268–278.

Sorenson, S.B., C. Morssink, and P.A. Campos (2011) "Safe Access to Safe Water in Low Income Countries: Water Fetching in Current Times," *Social Science and Medicine*, 72:9, 1522–1526.

Sovacool, B.K. (2017) "Reviewing, Reforming, and Rethinking Global Energy Subsidies: Towards a Political Economy Research Agenda," *Ecological Economics*, 135, 150–163.

Spears, D. (2013) "The Nutritional Value of Toilets: How Much International Variation in Child Height Can Sanitation Explain," World Bank Policy Research Paper 6351.

Spears, D. and S. Lamba (2013) "Effects of Early-Life Exposure to Sanitation on Childhood Cognitive Skills: Evidence from India's Total Sanitation Campaign," World Bank Policy Research Working Paper 6659.

Spiegel, H.W. (1983) *The Growth of Economic Thought*. Duke University Press.

Stenberg, K. et al. (2014) "Advancing Social and Economic Development by Investing in Women's and Children's Health: A New Global Investment Framework," *Lancet*, 383:9924, 1333–1354.

Stewart, F. (1989) "Basic Needs Strategies, Human Rights and the Right to Development," *Human Rights Quarterly*, 11:3, 347–374.

Stiglitz, J.E. (1996) "Some Lessons from the East Asian Miracle," *World Bank Research Observer*, 11:2, 151–177.

Stone, R. (1954) "Linear Expenditure Systems and Demand Analysis: An Application to the Pattern of British Demand," *Economic Journal*, 64:255, 511–527.

Streeten, P. (1979) "Basic Needs: Premises and Promises," *Journal of Policy Modeling*, 1:1, 136–146.

Streeten, P. (1984) "Basic Needs: Some Unsettled Questions," *World Development*, 12:9, 973–978.

Streeten, P. and S.J. Burki (1978) "Basic Needs: Some Issues," *World Development*, 6:3, 411–421.

Sumaila, U.R., V. Lam, F. La Manach, W. Swartz, and D. Pauly (2016) "Global Fishery Subsidies: An Updated Estimate," *Marine Policy*, 69, 189–193.

Sumner, L.W. (1995) "The Subjectivity of Welfare," *Ethics*, 105:4, 764–790.

Suri, T., M.A. Boozer, G. Ranis, and F. Stewart (2010) "Paths to Success: The Relationship between Human Development and Economic Growth," *World Development*, 39:4, 506–522.

Sustainable Energy for All (2015) *Progress Towards Sustainable Energy*.

Swinburn, B.A. et al. (2011) "The Global Obesity Pandemic: Shaped by Global Drivers and Local Environments," *Lancet*, 378:9792, 804–814.

Szirmai, A. (2015) *Socio-Economic Development*. Cambridge University Press.

Tefere, T. et al. (2011) "The Metal Silo: An Effective Grain Storage Technology for Reducing Post-Harvest Insect and Pathogen Loss in Maize While Improving Smallholder Farmers' Food Security in Developing Countries," *Crop Protection*, 30:3, 240–245.

Tembon, M. and L. Fort (2008) *Girls' Education in the 21st Century*. World Bank.

Theohary, C.A. (2016) *Conventional Arms Transfers to Developing Nations. 2008–2015*, United States Congressional Research Service.

Thomson, H. and M. Petticrew (2007) "Housing and Health," *British Medical Journal*, 334:7591, 434–435.

Tikly, L. and A.M. Barrett (2011) "Social Justice, Capabilities and the Quality of Education in Low Income Countries," *International Journal of Educational Development*, 31:1, 3–14.

Tir, J. and D.M. Stinnett (2012) "Weathering Climate Change: Can Institutions Mitigate International Water Conflict," *Journal of Peace Research*, 49:1, 211–225.

Trémolet, S. (2013) "Sanitation Economics: Understanding How Sanitation Markets Can Fail and How They Can Improve," *Waterlines*, 32:4, 273–285.

Tscharntke, T. et al. (2012) "Global Food Security, Biodiversity Conservation and the Future of Agricultural Intensification," *Biological Conservation*, 151:1, 53–59.

Tukahirwa, J.T., A.P.J. Mol, and P. Oosterveer (2013) "Comparing Urban Sanitation and Solid Waste Management in East African Metropolises: The Role of Civil Society Organizations," *Cities*, 30, 204–211.

Tully, S. (2006) "The Right to Access Electricity," *Electricity Journal*, 19:3, 30–39.

Tumwine, Y., P. Kutyabami, R.A. Odoi, and J.K. Kalyango (2010) "Availability and Expiry of Essential Medicines During the 'Pull' and 'Push' Drug Acquisition Systems in a Rural Ugandan Hospital," *Tropical Journal of Pharmaceutical Research*, 9:6, 557–564.

Uduku, O. (2011) "School Building Design for School Feeding Programmes and Community Outreach: Insights from Ghana and South Africa," *International Journal of Educational Development*, 31:1, 59–66.

United Nations (2008) *The Millennium Development Goals Report*.

United Nations (2015a) *World Population Prospects: The 2015 Revision*.

United Nations (2015b) *The World's Women 2015*.

United Nations Children's Fund (2012) *Pneumonia and Diarrhoea: Tackling the Deadliest Diseases of the World's Poorest Children*.

United Nations Children's Fund (2013) *Committing to Child Survival: A Promise Renewed*.

United Nations Children's Fund (2015) *Committing to Child Survival: A Promise Renewed*.

United Nations Committee on Economic, Social and Cultural Rights (1991) *General Comment No. 4: The Right to Adequate Housing*.

United Nations Development Program (1990) *Human Development Report 1990*.

United Nations Development Program (1994) *Human Development Report 1994*.

United Nations Development Program (1995) *Human Development Report 1995*.

United Nations Development Program (2009) *The Energy Access Situation in Developing Countries*.

United Nations Economic and Social Council (2009) *General Comment 21: Right of Everyone to Take Part in Social Life*.

United Nations Education, Scientific and Cultural Organization (2013a) *Adult and Youth Illiteracy Factsheet*.

United Nations Education, Scientific and Cultural Organization (2013b) *Education for All Global Monitoring Report*.

United Nations Education, Scientific and Cultural Organization (2014) *Teaching and Learning: Achieving Quality for All*.

United Nations Educational, Scientific and Cultural Organization (2015) *Incheon Declaration and Framework for Action*.

United Nations Environmental Program (2009) *The Environmental Food Crisis: The Environment's Role in Averting Future Food Crises*.

United Nations General Assembly (1948) *Universal Declaration of Human Rights*.

United Nations General Assembly (1959) *Declaration of the Rights of the Child*.

United Nations General Assembly (1966a) *International Covenant on Civil and Political Rights*.

United Nations General Assembly (1966b) *International Covenant on Economic, Social and Cultural Rights*.

United Nations General Assembly (1989) *Convention of the Rights of the Child*.

United Nations General Assembly (2005) *2005 World Summit Outcome, September*.

United Nations General Assembly (2010) *General Assembly Resolution on Water and Sanitation*, A/RES/64/292.

United Nations High Commissioner for Human Rights (1991) *General Comment 4: The Right to Adequate Housing*

United Nations High Commissioner for Human Rights (1991) *General Comment 7: The Right to Adequate Housing*.

United Nations High Commissioner for Human Rights (1999) *General Comment 12: The Right to Adequate Food*.

United Nations High Commissioner for Human Rights (2000) *General Comment 14: The Right to the Highest Attainable Standard of Health*.

United Nations High Commissioner for Human Rights (2003) *General Comment 15: The Right to Water.*

United Nations High Commissioner for Refugees (2010) *Convention and Protocol Relating to the Status of Refugees.*

United Nations High Commissioner for Refugees (2011a) *Ensuring Access to Health Care: Operational Guidelines on Refugee Protection and Solutions in Urban Areas.*

United Nations High Commissioner for Refugees (2011b) *Ensuring Access to Education: Operational Guidelines on Refugee Protection and Solutions in Urban Areas.*

United Nations High Commissioner for Refugees (2014) *Global Report 2013.*

United Nations High Commissioner for Refugees (2015) *Global Report 2014.*

United Nations High Commissioner for Refugees (2016) *Global Report 2015.*

United Nations High Commissioner for Refugees (2017) *Global Report 2016.*

United Nations Human Rights Council (2010) *Human Rights and Access to Safe Drinking Water and Sanitation*, A/HRC/RES/15/9.

United Nations Human Rights Council (2014) *The Human Right to Safe Drinking Water and Sanitation*, A/HRC/RES/27/7.

United Nations Inter-Agency Groups for Child Mortality Estimation (2013) *Levels and Trends in Child Mortality.*

United Nations Inter-Agency Groups for Child Mortality Estimation (2015) *Levels and Trends in Child Mortality.*

United Nations Office for Disarmament Affairs (2013) *The Impact of Poorly Regulated Arms Transfers on the Work of the United Nations.*

UN-HABITAT (2011) *Losing Your Home: Assessing the Impact of Eviction.*

United States Center for Naval Analysis Military Advisory Board (2014) *National Security and the Accelerating Risks of Climate Change.*

United States Energy Information Agency. https://www.eia.gov/ and https://www.eia.gov/outlooks/ieo/pdf/electricity.pdf

Valenti, M., R. Mtonga, R. Gould, and M. Christ (2014) "The Arms Trade Treaty (ATT): A Public Health Imperative," *Journal of Public Health Policy*, 35:1, 14–25.

Vandeveer, D. (1986) *Paternalistic Intervention: The Moral Bounds of Benevolence.* Princeton University Press.

Van Dijk, J. (2007) "Mafia Markers: Assessing Organized Crime and Its Impact upon Societies," *Trends in Organized Crime*, 10:4, 39–56.

Van Vuuren, D.P., A.F. Bouwman, and A.H.W. Beusen (2010) "Phosphorus Demand for the 1970-2100 Period: A Scenario Analysis of Resource Depletion," *Global Environmental Change*, 20:3, 428–429.

Venkatachalam, L. (2015) "Informal Water Markets and Willingness to Pay for Water: A Case Study of the Urban Poor in Chennai City, India," *International Journal of Water Resources Development*, 31:1, 134–135.

Victora, C.G. et al. (2008) "Maternal and Child Undernutrition: Consequences for Adult Health and Human Capital," *Lancet*, 371:9609, 340–359.

Vledder, M., J. Friedman, M. Sjoblom, and P. Yadav (2015) "Enhancing Public Supply Chain Management in Zambia," Ross School Business Paper 1269, University of Michigan.

Wacziarg, G. and K.H. Welch (2008) "Trade Liberalization ad Growth: New Evidence," *World Bank Economic Review*, 22:2, 187–231.

Von Ketelhodt, A. and A. Wöcke (2008) "The Impact of Electricity Crises on the Consumption Behaviour of Small and Medium Enterprises," *Journal of Energy in Southern Africa*, 19:1, 4–12.

Waddington, H. and B. Snilstveit (2009) "Effectiveness and Sustainability of Water, Sanitation, and Hygiene Interventions in Combatting Diarrhoea," *Journal of Development Effectiveness*, 1:3, 295–335.

Walters, V. and J.C. Gaillard (2014) "Disaster Risks at the Margins: Homelessness, Vulnerability and Hazards," *Habitat International*, 44, 211–219.

Walzer, M. (1994) *Thick and Thin: Moral Argument at Home and Abroad.* Notre Dame University Press.

Water Aid (2013) *We Can't Wait: A Report on Sanitation and Hygiene for Women and Girls.*

Weaver, J.H., M.T. Rock, and K. Kusterer (1997) *Achieving Broad-Based Sustainable Development*. Kumarian Press.

Weil, D.N. (2007) "Accounting for the Effect of Health on Economic Growth," *Quarterly Journal of Economics*, 122:3, 1265–1306.

Weis, M.I. (2015) "A Perfect Storm: The Causes and Consequences of Severe Water Scarcity, Institutional Breakdown and Conflict in Yemen," *Water International*, 40:2, 251–272.

Welsh, J.M. (2016) "The Responsibility to Protect after Libya and Syria," *Dædalus*, 145:4, 75–87.

Werbach, A. (2011, November 29), "How a Classic Model of Social Commerce Can Teach the World How to Save," *The Guardian*.

Wheeler, T. and J. von Braun (2013) "Climate Change Impacts on Global Food Security," *Science*, 341, 508–513.

White, C. (2012) "Understanding Water Scarcity: Definition and Measurements," Global Water Forum Discussion Paper 1217.

White, W.R. (2005) "World Water Storage in Man-Made Reservoirs: A Review of Current Knowledge," Foundation for Water Research.

Wiesner, M. (2013) "Progress towards the Responsible Application of Nanotechnology for Water Treatment," *Water Research*, 47:12, 3865.

Williams, P.D. (2013) "Protection, Resilience and Empowerment: United Nations Peacekeeping and Violence against Civilians in Contemporary War Zones," *Politics*, 33:4, 287–298.

Wisser, D., S. Frolking, E.M. Douglas, B.M. Fekete, A.H. Schumann, and C.J. Vörösmarty (2010) "The Significance of Local Water Resources Captured in Small Reservoirs for Crop Production: A Global Scale Analysis," *Journal of Hydrology*, 384:3-4, 264–275.

Wößmann, L. (2004) "Specifying Human Capital," in D.A.R. George, L. Oxley, and K.I. Carlow (eds.), *Surveys in Economic Growth: Theory and Empirics*. Blackwell, 13–44.

Wolff, J. (2012) *The Human Right to Health*. Norton.

Wolff, L. and C. de Moura Castro (2003) "Education and Training: The Task Ahead," in P.-P. Kuczynski and J. Williamson (eds.), *After the Washington Consensus: Restarting Growth in Latin America*. Institute for International Economics, 181–212.

Woodhouse, M. (2004–2005) "Threshold, Reporting and Accountability for a Right to Water under International Law," *University of Denver Water Law Review*, 8, 171–199.

Woodruff, C. (2001) "Review of de Soto's *The Mystery of Capital*," *Journal of Economic Literature*, 39:4, 1215–1223.

World Bank (1993) *The East Asian Miracle*. Oxford University Press.

World Bank (2003) *World Development Report 2004: Making Services Work for Poor People*.

World Bank (2011a) *World Development Report 2012: Gender Equality and Development*.

World Bank (2011b) *Rising Global Interest in Farmland: Can It Yield Sustainable and Equitable Development?*

World Bank (2011c) *World Development Report 2011: Conflict, Security and Development*.

World Bank (2014) *Food Price Watch*.

World Bank (2015, August 17) "Bringing Electricity to Kenya's Slums: Hard Lessons Lead to Great Gains," World Bank News.

World Bank, World Development Indicators. databank.worldbank.org

World Health Organization (1978) *Alma-Ata Declaration*.

World Health Organization (2007) *Combatting Waterborne Disease at the Household Level*.

World Health Organization (2008) *Primary Health Care: Now More Than Ever*.

World Health Organization (2009) *Global Health Risks*.

World Health Organization (2012) *Global Costs and Benefits of Drinking-Water Supply and Sanitation Interventions to Reach the MDG Target and Universal Coverage*.

World Health Organization (2014) *Antimicrobial Resistance: Global Report on Surveillance*.

World Health Organization (2015) *Global Malaria Report 2015*.

World Health Organization (2016) *Global Tuberculosis Report 2016*.

World Health Organization and UNICEF (2013) *Progress on Sanitation and Drinking Water*.

World Health Organization and UNICEF (2014) *Progress on Drinking Water and Sanitation*.

World Health Organization and UNICEF (2015) *Progress on Sanitation and Drinking Water: Update and MDG Assessment*.

World Trade Organization (2018) *The WTO Agreements: The Marrakesh Agreement Establishing the World Trade Organization and Its Annexes*. Cambridge University Press.

Wyrwoll, P. (2012, July 30) "India's Groundwater Crisis," *Global Water Forum*.

Yap, K.S. (2016) "The Enabling Strategy and Its Discontent: Low-Income Housing Policies and Practices in Asia," *Habitat International*, 54:3, 166–172.

Yee, A. (2016, October 4) "In Rural Bangladesh, Solar Power Dents Poverty," *The New York Times*.

Zartman, I.W. (2005) "Need, Creed, and Greed in Intrastate Conflict," in C.J. Arnson and I.W. Zartman (eds.), *Rethinking the Economics of War: The Intersection of Need, Creed, and Greed*. Johns Hopkins University Press, 256–284.

Zhang, X.Q. and M. Ball (2016) "Housing the Planet: Evolution of Global Housing Policies," *Habitat International*, 54:3, 161–165.

Zihindula, G., A. Meyer-Weitz, and O. Akintola (2015) "Access to Health Care Services by Refugees in Southern Africa: A Review of the Literature," *Southern Africa Journal of Demography*, 16:1, 7–35.

Zwane, A.P. and M. Kremer (2007) "What Works in Fighting Diarrheal Disease in Developing Countries? A Critical Review," *World Bank Research Observer*, 22:1, 1–24.

INDEX

Note: Tables and figures are indicated by an italic *t* and *f* following the page number.

acceptability (of health services), 132
access
   to food, 62, 63, 63t
   to health services, 132
achievement possibility frontiers (APFs), 39
adaptive preferences, 238
administrative procedures, 177
affiliation (capability), 18
affordability (of health services), 132
Afghanistan, 143f, 147, 183f, 200, 218
Africa. *See also* East Africa; North Africa;
      sub-Saharan Africa; West Africa
   education services deficiencies in, 142, 147, 153
   electricity deprivation in, 189
   food deprivation in, 58t, 60, 61, 62
   Green Revolution in, 66–69
   human insecurity in, 216
   land grabs in, 71–72
   sanitation services deficiencies in, 103
   wind power in, 191–92
agricultural extension services, 69
agricultural investment, 60, 71–72
agriculture, 64–69, 87–88, 184, 232. *See also* land;
      yields, agricultural
   agroecology and, 65–66, 67, 68–69, 76, 78n44
   biotechnology and, 65–66
   Green Revolution, 60, 65, 66–69
   more "crop per drop," 87, 88, 96
   precision, 88
agroecology, 65–66, 67, 68–69, 76, 78n44
AgroSalud, 76
air conditioning, 181
AK-47, 211
Albisa, Cathy, 166
Aleppo, Syria, 61
Algeria, 143f, 151t
Alma-Ata Conference on Primary Health Care, 123

Alma-Ata Declaration on Primary Health
      Care, 7, 123
Alzheimer disease, 125, 126t
Amnesty International, 124
amoebic dysentery, 106t
AMR (antimicrobial resistance), 136
Angola, 103f, 128, 174, 175, 183f, 191
Anheuser-Busch, 88
animal rights, 7, 18, 19
antimicrobial resistance (AMR), 136
APFs (achievement possibility frontiers), 39
aquaculture, 69, 73
Argentina, 83, 152
Arias, Desmond, 208–9
arms
   possession of, 217–18
   spending on, 232
   trade in, 209–11
Arms Trade Treaty (ATT), 210
Article 11 (ICESCR), 37, 38, 62, 84, 108,
      165, 183–84
Article 12 (ICESCR), 37, 84, 108, 123
Article 13 (ICESCR), 38, 144
Article 13 (UDHR), 155
Article 14 (CEDAW), 183
Article 25 (UDHR), 37, 38, 62, 123, 165, 183
Article 26 (UDHR), 37, 38, 144
Ashut Engineers Limited, 70
Asia. *See also* Central Asia; East Asia; South Asia;
      Southeast Asia
   food deprivation in, 58t, 60, 68
   sanitation services deficiencies in, 103
   water scarcity in, 92
   water storage capacity in, 93f
   wind power in, 191
asthma, 164
ATT (Arms Trade Treaty), 210